RELATION OF THE DIRECTORS
TO THE WORK AND PUBLICATIONS
OF THE NATIONAL BUREAU OF ECONOMIC RESEARCH

1. The object of the National Bureau of Economic Research is to ascertain and to present to the public important economic facts and their interpretation in a scientific and impartial manner. The Board of Directors is charged with the responsibility of ensuring that the work of the National Bureau is carried on in strict conformity with this object.

2. To this end the Board of Directors shall appoint one or more Directors of Research.

3. The Director or Directors of Research shall submit to the members of the Board, or to its Executive Committee, for their formal adoption, all specific proposals concerning researches to be instituted.

4. No report shall be published until the Director or Directors of Research shall have submitted to the Board a summary drawing attention to the character of the data and their utilization in the report, the nature and treatment of the problems involved, the main conclusions and such other information as in their opinion would serve to determine the suitability of the report for publication in accordance with the principles of the National Bureau.

5. A copy of any manuscript proposed for publication shall also be submitted to each member of the Board. For each manuscript to be so submitted a special committee shall be appointed by the President, or at his designation by the Executive Director, consisting of three Directors selected as nearly as may be one from each general division of the Board. The names of the special manuscript committee shall be stated to each Director when the summary and report described in paragraph (4) are sent to him. It shall be the duty of each member of the committee to read the manuscript. If each member of the special committee signifies his approval within thirty days, the manuscript may be published. If each member of the special committee has not signified his approval within thirty days of the transmittal of the report and manuscript, the Director of Research shall then notify each member of the Board, requesting approval or disapproval of publication, and thirty additional days shall be granted for this purpose. The manuscript shall then not be published unless at least a majority of the entire Board and a two-thirds majority of those members of the Board who shall have voted on the proposal within the time fixed for the receipt of votes on the publication proposed shall have approved.

6. No manuscript may be published, though approved by each member of the special committee, until forty-five days have elapsed from the transmittal of the summary and report. The interval is allowed for the receipt of any memorandum of dissent or reservation, together with a brief statement of his reasons, that any member may wish to express; and such memorandum of dissent or reservation shall be published with the manuscript if he so desires. Publication does not, however, imply that each member of the Board has read the manuscript, or that either members of the Board in general, or of the special committee, have passed upon its validity in every detail.

7. A copy of this resolution shall, unless otherwise determined by the Board, be printed in each copy of every National Bureau book.

(Resolution adopted October 25, 1926 and revised
February 6, 1933 and February 24, 1941)

Publications of the

National Bureau of Economic Research, Inc.

Number 51

The Transportation Industries, 1889–1946: A Study of

Output, Employment, and Productivity

Other National Bureau reports in this series dealing with production, employment, and productivity in American industry are:

BOOKS

*The Output of Manufacturing Industries, 1899-1937 (1940) — Solomon Fabricant

*Employment in Manufacturing, 1899-1939: An Analysis of Its Relation to the Volume of Production (1942) — Solomon Fabricant

*American Agriculture, 1899-1939: A Study of Output, Employment and Productivity (1942) — Harold Barger and Hans H. Landsberg

*The Mining Industries, 1899-1939: A Study of Output, Employment and Productivity (1944) — Harold Barger and Sam H. Schurr

Output and Productivity in the Electric and Gas Utilities, 1899-1942 (1946) — J. M. Gould

Trends in Output and Employment (1947) — George J. Stigler

OCCASIONAL PAPERS

*Manufacturing Output, 1929-1937 (1940) — Solomon Fabricant

*The Relation between Factory Employment and Output since 1899 (1941) — Solomon Fabricant

*Productivity of Labor in Peace and War (1942) — Solomon Fabricant

Labor Savings in American Industry, 1899-1939 (1945) — Solomon Fabricant

Domestic Servants in the United States, 1900-1940 (1946) — George J. Stigler

The Rising Trend of Government Employment (1949) — Solomon Fabricant

Employment and Compensation in Education (1950) — George J. Stigler

* Out of print.

The Transportation Industries
1889-1946

A Study of Output

Employment, and Productivity

by Harold Barger

Columbia University

National Bureau of
Economic Research, Inc.

NEW YORK 1951

Preface

As its subtitle indicates, this book deals with the output of transportation services, with the draft upon the labor force required to produce this output, and with the changing relationship between traffic and employment. Like others issued by the National Bureau, the volume reviews a segment of the American economy and reports upon the progress that has been made in physical efficiency since the end of last century. Concerned with global magnitudes and long-range tendencies, it complements an earlier volume focused on cyclical fluctuations, Thor Hultgren's *American Transportation in Prosperity and Depression* (NBER, 1948).

My desire has been to play no favorites, yet in the outcome the attention given to different kinds of transportation varies greatly. To some readers the choice of topics for discussion may seem arbitrary. A few words of explanation are in place.

The three chapters in Part One profess to cover the entire field of commercial or for-hire transportation, excluding only the operations of the private passenger car and the privately owned truck. Yet data for taxicabs, local trucking, and contract air carriers are not included. Failure to cover these activities, which undoubtedly fall within the scope of the study, is due simply and solely to lack of data.

In Part Two, five industries are chosen for individual consideration. The principle of selection was to treat in the body of the text only those industries for which both output and employment indexes could be constructed, so that trends in productivity might be assessed. Because no employment indexes could be constructed for buslines or for motor trucking, these two industries do not figure in Part Two. However, motor trucking is discussed in Appendix F.

The five chapters dealing with individual industries in Part Two are of very unequal length. The scope of the discussion in each case was influenced partly by the complexity of the industry and partly by availability of data. Thus ample data and a rich technical literature prompted extended consideration of steam railroads, despite the fact that — structurally and technologically — they are relatively homogeneous. Electric railways, pipelines, and airlines are also — in their separate spheres — somewhat homogeneous; for each the data are sparse, though for the two latter now rapidly becoming more ample. For these three industries our standard measures of output, employment, and output per worker are presented; but lengthy discussion did not seem rewarding, and the chapters dealing with them are consequently brief. Waterways, on the other hand, offer the investigator a mass of material, much of it poorly organized. Moreover, waterways are in many respects far less homogeneous than the other agencies considered. These factors made for a somewhat fuller treatment of waterways.

Reference has freely been made to technological changes, wherever they seemed to illuminate trends in productivity. The neglect of technological change in water transportation is deliberate, and results from the partial character of our employment and productivity indexes in this field. Since it was impossible to measure shore employment before 1929, our index of output per worker on waterways does not reflect the advances in waterway terminals — one of the most interesting technological developments in waterway transportation. Moreover, vessel employment could not be distributed among individual waterways, whose technological characteristics differ widely. It would therefore have been quite impossible to relate technological changes to advances in productivity, as we were able to do, for instance, in the case of steam railroads.

The Appendices include basic series on output and employment for all industries considered, detailed discussion of certain points of methodology, and an analysis of the motor trucking industry which (for reasons mentioned above) was not treated in the text.

Author's Acknowledgments

My principal obligation is to my co-worker Jacob M. Gould, formerly of the National Bureau staff, now with the Econometric Institute. Mr. Gould undertook much of the basic research; he is the author of Appendix C; and he was responsible for initial drafts of the first half of Chapter 4, Chapter 7, and Appendix F. To Solomon Fabricant I owe a mounting debt for encouragement and helpful criticism, a debt that runs all the way back to the start of the project, now more than ten years ago. Particularly in its final stages, the work benefited greatly from discussions with Geoffrey H. Moore and Thor Hultgren.

For unpublished tabulations, information, or advice I have to thank: Edward F. Denison, Walther Lederer, Robert L. Sammons, Charles F. Schwartz, and Herbert A. Wilkinson, of the Bureau of Foreign and Domestic Commerce; Daniel Creamer, formerly of the Bureau of Foreign and Domestic Commerce, now with the National Bureau; Charles W. Caswell of the Interstate Commerce Commission; Henry L. Deimel, Jr. (now with the Department of State) and Admiral Emory S. Land, formerly of the Maritime Commission; Herbert A. Breakey, formerly of the Bureau of Mines, now with the Munitions Board; Herbert S. Fairbank, John T. Lynch, and Robert E. Royall, of the Public Roads Administration; Colonel R. G. Powell, formerly of the War Department; Eugene B. McCaul and the late Edmund J. Murphy, of the American Transit Association; Julius H. Parmelee of the Association of American Railroads; O. P. Pearson of the Automobile Manufacturers Association; Carl W. Stocks of *Bus Transportation;* and G. C. Buzby of the *Commercial Car Journal.*

The manuscript was read, in whole or in part, and useful comments were made by C. Canby Balderston, G. A. Elliott,

Oswald W. Knauth, and Frederick C. Mills, Directors of the
National Bureau; by J. Steele Gow of The Maurice and Laura
Falk Foundation; by Ernest W. Williams, Jr. of Columbia University; by H. S. Davis of the University of Pennsylvania; and
by Alden F. Bixby of the Railroad Retirement Board.

I have still further obligations. Irving H. Siegel, formerly of
the National Bureau and now with the Veterans Administration,
worked on the project in its early stages. H. Irving Forman drew
the charts with his customary skill. Roselyn Silverman checked
the manuscript in proof. Finally, Martha Anderson suggested
numerous textual improvements, and steered the book through
the press.

The study upon which this volume and the previously issued
reports are based was made possible by funds granted by The
Maurice and Laura Falk Foundation of Pittsburgh. The Falk
Foundation is not, however, the author, publisher or proprietor
of this publication, and is not to be understood as approving or
disapproving by virtue of its grant any of the statements made
or views expressed therein.

Contents

TEXT TABLES

TEXT TABLES

APPENDIX TABLES

APPENDIX TABLES

CHARTS

CHARTS

Summary

How much transportation service do we use? How much traffic moves and who carries it? How has transportation's place in the American economy altered since 1889? How have the roles of different agencies — railroads, waterways, and highways, not to speak of airways — varied with the passage of time? What can we say about trends in employment and productivity, in technological progress, and the return to human effort? The concern of this book is with such questions.

Sixty years ago commercial transportation produced about a twelfth of the national income; today it produces a fifteenth. In 1889 the transportation agencies employed about one worker in twenty-five; today about one worker in thirty is on the payroll of a commercial carrier. Transportation workers today are more than twice as numerous as in 1889, but percentagewise they constitute a smaller share of the labor force than formerly. The shrinkage is to be explained partly by a rapid expansion of output per worker, but also by the coming of the private automobile and motor truck. Garage and filling-station attendants, and drivers of privately owned trucks, are not counted as transportation workers. If they were included, transportation could probably claim a proportionate share of the labor force as large, or larger, than formerly. But here accurate measurement is impossible, and our main concern is with the industries producing and selling transportation.

Although the share of the transportation industries in the economy declined, traffic expanded vastly. To be sure, total passenger travel and the movement of freight grew much faster than the output of transportation service by commercial agencies. Today in the course of a year the average American travels perhaps twenty times as much as his grandparents did in 1889. The prime condition for such enhanced mobility was of course the coming of the private automobile. Traffic by commercial agencies is no longer a satisfactory measure of total passenger travel. Yet even travel by commercial carriers has increased faster than population.

In a proportionate sense, the impact of the privately owned truck has been less than that of the passenger automobile, and traffic on public carriers is still a better guide to total freight movement than to total passenger travel. Partly for this reason freight traffic on public transportation lines increased faster than passenger traffic. The movement of freight increased faster than commodity output also. In part this rapid growth in our use of commercial transportation facilities reflects a lengthening of the average passenger journey, and the average haul of a freight shipment, consequent upon the denser settlement of the west. Commutation distances, too, have increased as metropolitan areas have expanded.

Combined passenger and freight traffic of all commercial agencies (land, water, and air) grew five times during the half century between 1889 and 1939, and almost doubled once again between 1939 and 1946. But such aggregates conceal the varying fortunes of different agencies, and especially the marked shifts that have occurred from older to newer forms of carriage. Certainly one of the oldest branches — the coastwise shipping trade — is still as lusty as it ever was. And a relative newcomer — the electric railway — is already old: it rose to maturity, decayed, and almost disappeared within our period of study. Yet these are exceptions. For the most part the newer agencies have grown rapidly, and the older ones have expanded only slowly or have actually contracted. By and large the shift has been from rail to highway. Pipelines burgeoned and airlines were established. Where waterways could be adapted to bulk carriage, they expanded; but water transportation in the aggregate only just held its own.

We do not know enough about current and future patterns to assert that the traditional agencies have entirely lost their power of growth. Certainly the expansion of railroad and waterway traffic ended abruptly about 1920, and was not resumed until the outbreak of World War II. Already before World War I signs of change were at hand, for pipelines had branched out to meet the specialized needs of the oil industry. From about 1920, claiming much business that might have moved by rail, but also developing many new customers, highway traffic by truck and busline grew rapidly, and after 1930 airline traffic. To the highways the rail-

roads lost mainly short haul traffic, much of it highly profitable. The airlines claimed long-distance passengers and competed chiefly with the Pullman service. In the case of waterways, continued expansion of bulk freight movements on the Great Lakes, and of tanker shipments in the coastwise trade, was offset during the interwar period by the progressive loss of international traffic (both passenger and freight) to foreign-flag operators.

Many of these trends were sharply reversed, at least for the time being, as a result of World War II. Coastwise shipping was temporarily cut off by the threat of submarine action. Airline traffic, exceptionally, continued to expand despite shortages of equipment. A dearth of rubber and gasoline drove much highway traffic back to the railroads. The transportation industries as a group achieved a partial comeback against the competition of the private automobile and the privately owned truck. Within the group, a reversion to the older forms of carriage gave steam railroads, and waterways as a whole, alltime traffic peaks.

The draft made upon the labor force by the transportation industries reflects these changes. In 1889 fewer than a million persons were employed in producing transportation services, and four out of five of these worked on the nation's railroads. By 1920 total employment had risen to more than 2½ million, and the proportion of those who worked for the railroads had not greatly changed. In 1946 not quite 2½ million persons were employed in transportation, and only about half of them were railroad workers. Today highway transportation employs as many workers as did the railroads in 1889, and airline employment is now as large as was waterway at the beginning of our period.

Practically throughout the six decades traffic rose more rapidly than employment. As a result, per worker output of transportation service in 1939 was three times, in 1946 four times, the 1889 level. Over the half century 1889-1939 productivity in the transportation industries measured in this fashion increased at an average annual rate of 2.2 percent. For a major and well-established sector of the economy, this is a rather rapid increase. Over a like period the annual gain in output per worker in manufacturing was 1.8 percent; in agriculture, and also in mining (excluding oil and gas *wells), the annual increase was 1.6 percent. Because in many cases hours of work were cut, such figures understate the rise in output per manhour. They indicate genuine increases in the return from human effort in the industry concerned. Occasionally advances in productivity recorded for a single industry may be offset in the economy as a whole by increased consumption of fuel or materials, or greater use of equipment produced elsewhere. But such qualifications are usually minor. On the other hand observed increments in output per worker or output per manhour need not, and usually do not, denote greater efficiency of individuals working under comparable conditions. Predominantly they reflect changes in technology or increased capital per worker; occasionally a more generous bounty of nature.*

Among individual transportation industries the change in output per worker varied greatly. The newer industries showed the sharpest gains in productivity. Airline employment rose steeply, pipeline employment moderately, but in each case the growth of traffic was far more rapid than the growth in employment, so that output per worker shot up, multiplying three to four times within two decades. (For other new industries, buslines and trucking, we lack data.) The older industries, electric railways, steam railroads, and waterways, showed steady but much more moderate increases in output per worker. These results conform to Solomon Fabricant's earlier finding for manufacturing industries: among the young, large increases both in output and in productivity are common; among the more mature, the growth of output is retarded or ceases altogether, while productivity changes are quite moderate.

For railroads and for waterways we can measure not only the input of labor but also the volume of equipment in use. In the former case, the number of locomotives and cars increased and later declined, as did railroad employment. The railroads owned just about as many locomotives and cars in 1939 or 1946 as in 1903. But technology did not stand still. The tractive power of locomotives and the capacity of freight (if not of passenger) cars rose steadily: on the average, the capacity of equipment about doubled. (Passenger equipment became more comfortable, thus rendering better service, but this we leave out of account.) Roughly speaking, the same amount of labor is needed to operate a large piece of equipment as a small. The doubling of equipment capacity per worker therefore contributed to the rise in output per worker. Labor productivity so measured rose more than threefold, and output per manhour still faster. Thus the increase in the capacity of equipment is not in itself sufficient to explain the rise in labor productivity, although we can see that the former made a substantial contribution to the latter. To be sure, more powerful locomotives could pull heavier trains with a train crew scarcely larger than before; but there were many other ways of saving labor, as in train dispatching and the maintenance of way. In the case of waterways the boost given to labor productivity by more capacious equipment seems to have been confined to the coastwise tanker trade and to bulk carriage on the Great Lakes.

The indexes of output, employment, and output per worker which furnish these results are shown in the charts and tables. The indexes were computed from traffic data (mainly passenger-miles and ton-miles) and number of workers or manhours. The basic material is printed in the Appendices and, except for waterways, traffic and employment data are here collected from many different primary sources. In the case of waterway traffic, no previous measures were available; here the data for passenger-miles and ton-miles were compiled for this study, and are now offered for the first time.

Part One

The Transportation Industries as a Whole

Chapter 1

The Transportation Industries at the Outbreak of World War II

This study of the service rendered by our transportation facilities seeks to answer several related questions. How much traffic is carried and who carries it? Have the transportation industries grown faster or more slowly than other industries? Do we travel more or less, ship more or fewer goods, than our grandparents?

Other questions concern the shifting status of the various forms of transportation. How have their roles changed with the passage of time? How has the rise of the private automobile and the motor truck affected the use of older transportation agencies?

Still other matters include the draft made by transportation upon the labor force. How many persons are engaged in producing transportation? To what extent can labor savings be imputed to technological advance? Has output per worker increased more or less rapidly in transportation than in, say, manufacturing or agriculture?

To answer these questions we need measures of output and employment. In the case of steam railroads and electric railways much work has already been done;[1] the intention of the present study is to explore also areas that have been too much neglected — waterways, highways, airlines, and pipelines. Our desire has been both to construct as comprehensive indexes as possible for transportation as a whole, and also to establish a firm basis for comparisons between types of transportation. Because many new indexes of output and employment are offered, much space is necessarily devoted to technical details connected with the appraisal and use of data.

[1] See, for instance, Witt Bowden, 'Productivity, Hours, and Compensation of Railroad Labor', *Monthly Labor Review*, Dec. 1933; Edwin Frickey, *Production in the United States, 1860-1914* (Harvard University Press, 1947), Ch. V-VII.

By all odds the most striking feature of transportation history during the past half century has been the shift from older to newer agencies — especially from steam railroads to highway transportation. As a concomitant change, the production of transportation services by specialized producers, e.g., railroad companies, for sale to the public at large has given place to the production of such services by their immediate users, as when private automobiles carry their owners or trucks their owners' goods. This circumstance makes for a certain vagueness in the concept of transportation output if every kind of transportation is to be included; and a still greater vagueness in the concept of employment.[2] Undoubtedly for many purposes, for instance to appraise the shift from commercial to private traffic, we must concern ourselves with private as well as commercial transportation. Yet to construct indexes of private automobile travel, or to estimate employment in private trucking, is a manifest impossibility for lack of data. Hence the major statistical results are defective as a measure of total transportation.

In fact the transportation industries of this book — the industries whose aggregate output and employment we estimate — owe their definition largely to statistical accident. Roughly they comprise agencies engaged in furnishing service *for sale to others*. If a mining concern operates a private railroad, or a baking firm delivers crackers in its own vehicles, such transportation is regarded as part of the output of the primary industry — mining or baking. The large amounts of transportation produced by final consumers for their own immediate consumption, as in the operation of private passenger cars, we rate a household function falling outside the scope of industrial activity. Most transportation is sold at published (and often publicly regulated) common-carrier rates. However, considerable amounts of freight move over highways and waterways on a contract basis, and sometimes the transportation is performed by a wholly-owned subsidiary of the customer. It is a question, for

[2] The vagueness of output may be illustrated by asking whether the driver of a private automobile always furnishes himself, as well as his passengers, with transportation service. The vagueness of employment is shown by asking in what sense the driver of a private automobile is 'employed' in producing transportation; and whether or not garage mechanics (who roughly correspond to railroad shopmen) are engaged in producing transportation.

example, whether consistency would be better served by including the tanker-owning affiliates of the oil companies in the transportation or in the petroleum industry. In practically all such cases the boundary is drawn for the investigator by statistical limitations.[3]

The transportation industries are confined to enterprises actually producing transportation service. Businesses manufacturing transportation equipment or operating garages or filling stations are therefore excluded. However, when railroad companies, for instance, operate their own repair shops, their employment is included in the industry total. We regard the Railway Express Agency and the Pullman Company as engaged in providing transportation. On the other hand, warehousing and storage, frequently considered a transportation industry, must be excluded if only for lack of data. In addition to strictly domestic activities, waterway and airline traffic between the United States and noncontiguous territories, and American-flag traffic with foreign countries, are included.

To judge by the usual tests the transportation industries have occupied for some decades a relatively declining segment of the national economy. For instance, income originating in transportation as a percentage of total national income may be roughly estimated as follows:[4]

1889	1929	1939	1949
8.6	7.5	6.3	5.5

[3] The statistics for railroads, electric railways, and buslines follow our definition rather closely in that they measure transportation for sale. We try to derive figures for the trucking industry that segregate for-hire trucking, and so conform to the definition. Although interstate petroleum and gasoline pipelines are common carriers, many are owned directly or indirectly by the companies whose oil they carry. The statistics for oil pipelines cover all trunk-line activity and therefore go beyond our definition. For waterways also, data cover all reported freight movements and no segregation of commercial (common-carrier and contract) from private (or 'captive') traffic is possible. By contrast airline statistics are available only for common carriers; since they omit contract traffic, they are less inclusive than they should be to accord with the definition. Natural gas pipelines are not common carriers and practically all are owned by the companies whose gas they transport. They are not considered in this study.

[4] Figures for 1929, 1939, and 1949 are Department of Commerce estimates (Survey of Current Business, July 1947, Supplement, and July 1950). Extrapolation for 1889 uses R. F. Martin's data (National Income in the United States, 1799-1938, National Industrial Conference Board, 1939, Tables 1 and 16).

The percentage of the labor force engaged in transportation also declined over the period. For example, the employment figures in Table 11 below represent about 3.9 percent of the labor force in 1890 but only 3.1 percent in 1940.[5] To what extent does this decline reflect slower growth of transportation than of other products, or more rapid rise in output per worker in producing transportation? Or may it simply be attributed to the shift from commercial to noncommercial transportation — from the railroad to the private automobile and the privately owned truck?

To answer these questions we shall measure the output of transportation service from 1889 to 1946 of the industries which fall within the definition of commercial transportation, and shall evaluate roughly the amount of private transportation falling outside the definition. For the industries within the definition, we seek indexes of employment comparable with those of output, in order to assess the trend in output per worker.

Better figures are available for 1939 or 1940 than for any other recent years. For this reason the following introductory survey sketches the industries as they stood at the outbreak of World War II.

RELATIVE SIZE OF THE INDUSTRIES

In 1940 the transportation industries employed about 2 million, or slightly less than 5 percent of all persons at work. Railroads employ more than half of all transportation workers, while another one-fifth is engaged in trucking (Table 1). Neither street railways and buslines nor waterways employed as many as 10 percent of all transportation workers, while employment by pipelines and airlines was relatively negligible.

[5] For figures on the labor force, see Daniel Carson, 'Changes in the Industrial Composition of Manpower since the Civil War', *Studies in Income and Wealth, Volume Eleven* (NBER, 1949). The employment percentages quoted are smaller than the national income percentages just given. The reason is partly that employment in transportation is here compared with the total labor force (including persons out of work); and partly that the employment totals of Table 11 are incomplete in that they exclude the Pullman and Express companies, longshoremen, taxicabs, warehousing and storage, and services incidental to transportation. If proper adjustment could be made for these factors, the employment percentages would be closer to the national income percentages, and the former would still decline.

Table 1

THE TRANSPORTATION INDUSTRIES, 1939-1940[a]
Census Definition

	Employment, 1940 Population Census[b]		Income Originating, 1939, Department of Commerce[c]	
	(th.)	%	($ mil.)	%
Industries considered here	1,987	91.3	3,260	95.1
Railroads	1,135	52.1	2,091	61.0
Street railways and buslines	203	9.3	433	12.6
Trucking service	428	19.6	441	12.9
Petroleum and gasoline pipelines	18	0.8	43	1.3
Water transportation	181	8.3	218	6.4
Air transportation	23	1.1	34	1.0
Industries not considered here	190	8.7	169[d]	4.9[d]
Taxicab service	84	3.9	n.a.	n.a.
Warehousing and storage	61	2.8	n.a.	n.a.
Services incidental to transportation	29	1.3	n.a.	n.a.
Not specified	16	0.7	n.a.	n.a.
TOTAL TRANSPORTATION, CENSUS DEFINITION	2,178	100.0	3,429	100.0

n.a.: not available.
[a] Differences of classification impair the comparability of the two percentage distributions, and probably cause the income figures slightly to overstate the coverage of our treatment in this book. Thus the Department of Commerce includes taxicabs, and warehousing and storage (neither of which is treated here), with street railways and buslines, and trucking service, respectively. On the other hand it excludes stevedoring and the operation of piers and docks from water transportation, regarding them as 'services allied to transportation'.
[b] *Sixteenth Census, Population*, Vol. III, Part I, Table 74.
[c] *Survey of Current Business*, July 1947, National Income Supplement, Table 13.
[d] 'Services allied to transportation'.

Immediately before World War II income originating in the transportation industries exceeded $3 billion (Table 1). In 1939 it represented about 6 percent of national income. So judged, transportation was three times the size of mining, but only half as large as retail and wholesale distribution, or a quarter the size of manufacturing.

For warehousing and storage (whose status as a transportation industry is anyhow in doubt) and for taxicabs, scarcity of data precludes any further mention.[6] If these, and other unspecified services incidental to transportation, are excluded there remain the major transportation industries — steam railroads, electric railways, buslines, trucking, pipelines, waterways, and airlines — which in 1940 accounted for not quite 2 million workers, or roughly 91 percent of all transportation employment (Table 1). It is with these major branches of transportation that the book is concerned.[7]

THE MAJOR INDUSTRIES

Some leading statistics for these major industries for the year 1939 will now be reviewed (Table 2). Transportation consists in the movement of persons and property, respectively represented by passengers carried[8] and ton-miles of freight. The most significant way to combine the two kinds of traffic is by means of revenue data,[9] and accordingly passenger, freight, and total transportation revenues are also shown. For some agencies traffic and revenue statistics were readily available; for others they had to be estimated by methods described below.

Of the nearly $7 billion of transportation sold by the industries in 1939, $1.5 billion, or between a fourth and a fifth, was passenger and the remainder freight. From this we might conclude that the community consumes between three and four times as much freight as passenger transportation. And so far as services rendered commercially by the transportation industries are concerned, such a conclusion would be justified. Yet it is easy to demonstrate that, as

[6] For taxicabs some estimates are available for very recent years. The Cab Research Bureau, for example, puts taxicab passengers at slightly under a billion in 1941 (Automobile Manufacturers Association, *Automobile Facts and Figures*, 1944 ed., p. 27).
[7] We are in fact concerned with rather less than 91 percent (in terms of employment) of the entire field. Coverage of railroads and electric railways is believed to be substantially complete, but statistical ignorance prevents any adequate discussion of school, charter, and sight-seeing buses; local for-hire trucking; gathering (as distinct from trunk line) activity of pipeline companies; lightering, stevedoring, and similar port activities; and chartered air traffic.
[8] Passengers carried appear in Table 2 rather than passenger-miles because satisfactory estimates for the latter could not be derived for all industries in the table: see, however, Table 3.
[9] Although sanctified by custom, the use of unit revenues for weighting output indexes (as in Chapter 2) perhaps requires explicit justification. An attempt to rationalize the practice, with special reference to measurement of the output of public utilities, is made in Appendix A.

a measure of what we spend respectively for traveling and for shipping goods, the picture is grossly distorted. For if our stand-point is travel and freight movement in general, account must be taken of the minor industries not considered here; and especially of the large amounts of transportation produced outside the trans-

Table 2

THE TRANSPORTATION INDUSTRIES,
LEADING STATISTICS, 1939[a]

	Passenger Transportation		Freight Transportation		Total Transportation Revenue	
	Revenue passengers carried (mil.)	Passenger revenue ($ mil.)	Revenue ton-miles (bil.)	Freight revenue ($ mil.)	($ mil.)	%
Railways	7,412	905	336	3,317	4,222	63.9
Steam railroads	454	418	335	3,297	3,715	56.2
Electric railways, urban and interurban	6,958	487	1	20	507	7.7
Highways	3,686	463	22	887	1,350	20.4
Buses, city and intercity	3,686	463	....	....	463	7.0
Intercity trucking, for-hire	....	....	22	887	887	13.4
Oil pipelines	....	....	49	188	188	2.8
Waterways	259	83	410	710	793	12.0
Airlines	2	40	[b]	20	60	0.9
TOTAL	11,359	1,491	817	5,122	6,613	100.0

[a] Sources of data or derivation of estimates will be found in individual Appendices.
[b] Less than 0.5.

portation industries. Local for-hire trucking, and the operation of trucks owned by those whose merchandise they deliver, might well add $2 billion to the freight total; and passenger revenues would have to be boosted perhaps $8 or $10 billion to include the imputed value of services of private passenger cars.[10] With revisions of this

[10] Private intercity trucking accounted for slightly more ton-miles than for-hire in 1939 (Table 4). In addition to about 1 million trucks engaged in intercity operations, about 3.5 million were in local service or on farms (Appendix Table F-1). Therefore $2 billion, or twice the revenues from for-hire intercity trucking, would appear to be a conservative imputation for the value of the remainder. As for private passenger cars, if the 500 billion passenger-miles mentioned in Table 3 is valued at the average revenue per passenger-mile for all steam railroads (1.84 cents) the product is about $9 billion.

Table 3

PASSENGER TRAFFIC, 1939[a]

	Revenue Passengers Carried (mil.)	Revenue Passenger-miles (bil.)	Average Journey[d] (miles)	Passenger Revenue[d] ($ mil.)	Revenue per Passenger ($)	Revenue per Passenger-mile (cents)	% Distribution, Passenger Revenue
The transportation industries							
Steam railroads	454	22.7	50	418	0.92	1.84	28.0
Electric railways[b]	6,958	n.a.	n.a.	487	0.07	n.a.	32.7
Interurban	114	n.a.	n.a.	15	0.13	n.a.	1.0
Urban	6,844	n.a.	n.a.	472	0.07	n.a.	31.7
Buslines	3,686	n.a.	n.a.	463	0.13	n.a.	31.1
Intercity	313	9.6	31	245	0.78	2.6	16.4
City	3,373	n.a.	n.a.	218	0.06	n.a.	14.6
Waterways[c]	259	n.a.	n.a.	83	n.a.	n.a.	5.6
Coastwise	17.7	n.a.	n.a.	4.7	0.27	n.a.	0.3
Intercoastal	0.009	0.050	5,900	1.6	182	3.1	0.1
Great Lakes (domestic only)	5.35	1.5	n.a.	9.6	1.8	n.a.	0.6
Inland	12.7		n.a.	8.5	0.67	n.a.	0.6
Noncontiguous	0.131	0.218	1,660	10[e]	n.a.	n.a.	0.7
International, American-flag vessels	0.384	0.927	2,410	41.8	109	4.51	2.8
Ferries	223	n.a.	n.a.	7	0.03	n.a.	0.5
Airlines	1.83	0.755	413	39.8	22	5.3	2.7
Domestic	1.70	0.683	401	34.8	20	5.10	2.3
International	0.129	0.072	557	5.0	39	6.9	0.3
TOTAL	11,359	....	....	1,491	....	....	100.0
Comparative figures for other agencies							
Automobile travel	n.a.	500[f]	n.a.	....	....	....	....
Waterways — international, foreign-flag vessels	0.745	2.314	3,110	93.9	126	4.06	....

order, the national consumption (in value terms) of passenger would exceed that of freight transportation.

For total transportation revenue, the distribution between industries in Table 2 is not unlike those in Table 1. In 1939 railroads accounted for over half, and if electric railways are included nearly two-thirds, of the $7 billion total. Remaining revenues were divided among intercity trucking, waterways, buses, oil pipelines, and airlines, in that order.

PASSENGER TRAFFIC

Trucks and pipelines transport no passengers. For the other industries a more detailed analysis of passenger traffic for 1939 is given in Table 3. More or less reliable records are available for the

---

Notes to Table 3
n.a.: not available.
[a] Except as otherwise noted, sources of data and derivation of estimates are given in the Appendices.
[b] Includes trolleybuses.
[c] Coastwise covers traffic along the Atlantic and Gulf coasts, and along the Pacific coast. Intercoastal means from the Atlantic and Gulf coasts to the Pacific coast and vice versa. Great Lakes domestic traffic moves between some U. S. port on the Lakes and some other U. S. port. Inland means traffic on rivers, canals, and lakes other than the Great Lakes. Noncontiguous covers movement between the Continental United States and Puerto Rico, Alaska, Hawaii, Guam and Samoa. International traffic includes all movement between U. S. and foreign ports, whether ocean-borne or Lakewise, together with ocean cruises. For sources of data, see notes to Table 30.
[d] Revenue data for all electric railways from American Transit Association, 'Transit Fact Book' (annual); for interurban lines from ICC, 'Statistics of Electric Railways' (annual); and for urban lines by difference. For buslines, National Association of Motor Bus Operators, *Bus Facts* (annual). For waterways see Table 30 and Chapter 7. For domestic airlines, Civil Aeronautics Administration, *Statistical Handbook of Civil Aviation*, 1948 issue. For international airlines, revenue per passenger-mile earned by Pan American Airways was used.
[e] Assumes revenue per passenger-mile same as for American-flag vessels in international trade.
[f] Surveys have indicated annual mileage per passenger car is in the region of 8,000 *(Automobile Facts*, 1941 ed., p. 57) ; in 1939 about 26 million passenger cars were registered. Average loading is thought to fall between two and three persons. See also estimate by H. E. Hale (495 billion passenger-miles) in *Petroleum Facts and Figures, 1947,* American Petroleum Institute, p. 153. Again, the Interstate Commerce Commission puts total *intercity* highway traffic (including buses) at 246 billion passenger-miles in 1939 (*55th Annual Report*, 1941, p. 9), or say 236 billion for private passenger cars; this might imply a somewhat lower total than 500 billion for all private automobile passenger-miles.

number of passengers carried, and we can make estimates to fill
the gaps in passenger revenue, so that these columns are complete.
However, the first set of figures — number of passengers — gives
equal weight to a New York City subway commuter and a transcontinental traveler; consequently it lacks homogeneity. The distribution of passenger revenue more accurately reflects the amount
of transportation service supplied. Of the total, steam railroads,
electric railways, and buses each show just under a third, the small
remainder being divided unequally between waterways and airlines. The average revenue per passenger differs, of course, very
greatly among the several industries, and confirms the irrelevance
of the passenger count.

The much more interesting figures for passenger-miles are officially available only for steam railroads and airlines. For intercity
buses and for several types of waterway, estimates are shown whose
construction is described later in the volume. Satisfactory figures
for passenger-miles — or of their correlative, average length of
journey — could unfortunately not be derived for the remaining
types of transportation. The agencies for which we do not have
data are all more or less local in character, and obviously would
bulk much smaller judged by passenger-miles than judged by the
number of their passengers. For the industries where estimates are
shown we may say that — in terms of passenger-miles — intercity
buses carried nearly half as much traffic as steam railroads, and
that (as might be expected) waterways and airlines were negligible in comparison. As a study of the unit cost to the passenger
of different types of travel, the column showing computed revenue
per passenger-mile is worth attention: in 1939 the figures ranged
from under 2 cents for railroads to 7 cents for American-flag airlines between the United States and foreign countries.[11]

As already explained, the intention is to confine the scope of this
book to the industries listed. In passing, however, some further
comparisons are illuminating. The moment we allow for automobile travel, it becomes obvious that in passenger-mile terms the
output of the transportation industries represents a relatively small

[11] The dispersion has narrowed somewhat since 1939, partly through a decline
in international airline fares, and partly through a rise in railroad fares.

fraction of total transportation service, as the following calculation will show. The partial estimates in Table 3 amount to 36 billion passenger-miles. The two principal gaps in the table are urban electric railways and city buses which together carry about 10 billion passengers. The average journey for such local transportation can scarcely exceed 10 miles. If, then, we add 100 billion passenger-miles to the 36 billion just mentioned, total travel on the facilities of the transportation industries would still be only a quarter of the 500 billion passenger-miles inserted at the foot of Table 3 to represent automobile travel.

Another comparison may be made between international waterway traffic in the American and foreign industries respectively. Traffic in American-flag vessels between United States and foreign ports, or on cruises from United States ports, totaled just under a billion passenger-miles in 1939, but similar travel in foreign-flag vessels came to over two billion.[12] Of total waterborne passenger traffic between the United States and foreign countries, somewhat less than a third was carried in American-flag vessels in 1939. Average revenue per passenger-mile was somewhat lower for foreign than for United States vessels.

FREIGHT TRAFFIC

Buses and urban electric railways do not transport significant amounts of freight. For all industries except these, freight traffic for 1939 is surveyed in Table 4.[13] The data here are more comprehensive than those for passenger traffic in Table 3, for we have been able to approximate a complete distribution, not only of revenue and shipments, but also of ton-miles. Ton-mile data come from official sources except for waterways, where original

[12] Note that the distinction is based upon the flag of the vessel, not upon the domicile or citizenship of its owners: in the case of passenger traffic the latter criterion would probably yield almost the same result. Note also that the distinction between American and foreign is not founded on the residence or citizenship of the passengers: the figures show the output of overseas transportation by the American industry, not the use made of such transportation by Americans. Figures that would enable a classification of passenger-miles by the nationality of the traveler do not appear to exist.

[13] Besides buslines and urban electric railways, Table 4 omits noncontiguous and international air traffic, the freight component of which is small and unrecorded.

estimates compiled at the National Bureau are now offered (see Appendix H). Revenue figures are somewhat less reliable, depending in some instances (e.g., trucking) upon sophisticated guesswork.

In terms of revenue and freight shipped, steam railroads were still in 1939 the most important freight-carrying agency. When measured in ton-miles, however, waterways accounted for just half the total, compared with but two-fifths for steam railroads. Yet owing to the cheapness of water transportation, the share of waterways in revenue was only about 14 percent — less than a quarter of railroad revenues. The share in revenue of for-hire inter-city trucking is somewhat uncertain, although undoubtedly it greatly exceeds trucking's share in ton-miles. The contributions of oil pipelines to the total are quite modest; and the shares of interurban electric railways and domestic airlines relatively insignificant — as might be expected.

Of course the distribution of ton-miles among agencies gives in a sense an exaggerated prominence to water transportation, for waterways often represent 'the longest way round'. The circuitous character of waterway (and even to some extent of rail) movements is reflected in the accompanying random comparisons of air, rail and water distances.

DISTANCES BETWEEN SELECTED POINTS[a]
(statute miles)

	By air	By rail	By water
Duluth and Cleveland	630	910	830
Chicago and Buffalo	470	530	860
St. Louis and New Orleans	610	700	1,080
New York and New Orleans	1,180	1,380	1,980
New York and San Francisco	2,580	3,400	6,100

[a] For air, great-circle distances between airports (U. S. Civil Aeronautics Board). Rail distances from the *Official Guide*. Waterway distances from the *World Almanac* and map measurements.

For the same reason the figures for revenue per ton-mile (Table 4) give at best but a rough indication of the relative cost to shippers of moving freight by different transportation agencies. The revenue quotients, that is to say, are calculated from the

Table 4 FREIGHT TRAFFIC, 1939[a]

	Revenue Freight Shipped (mil. s.t.)	Revenue Ton-miles (bil.)	Average Haul (miles)	Freight Revenue[d] ($ mil.)	Revenue per Ton-mile (cents)	% Distribution Ton-miles	% Distribution Revenue
The transportation industries							
Steam railroads	955	335	351	3,297	0.983	41.0	64.4
Electric railways, interurban[b]	n.a.	0.7	n.a.	20	3	0.1	0.4
Intercity trucking, commercial	n.a.	22	n.a.	887	4	2.7	17.3
Oil pipelines	187	49.3	264	188	0.38	6.0	3.7
Waterways[c]	622	410	660	710	0.17	50.2	13.9
Coastwise	141	174	1,230	225	0.13	21.3	4.4
Intercoastal	8.37	51.9	6,200	82	0.157	6.4	1.6
Great Lakes (domestic only)	113	69.0	609	74	0.107	8.4	1.4
Inland	329	19.9	61	82	0.4	2.4	1.6
Noncontiguous	6.13	15.7	2,560	80	0.5	1.9	1.6
International, American-flag vessels	23.0	79.5	3,460	167	0.200	9.7	3.3
Airlines, domestic	n.a.	0.0119	n.a.	20.4	172	°	0.4
TOTAL	...	817	...	5,122		100.0	100.0
Comparative figures for other agencies							
Intercity trucking, private	n.a.	27	n.a.	...	...	...	...
Water transportation — international, foreign-flag vessels	80.7	360	4,460	575	0.160	...	...

n.a.: not available.

[a] Except as noted, sources of data and derivation of estimates are given in the Appendices.

[b] Revenue of interurban railroads is believed to have been of the order of 3 cents per ton-mile; whence the number of ton-miles is obtained by division into total revenue.

[c] The various waterways are defined in note c to Table 3. For sources of data, see notes to Table 30.

[d] For interurban electric railways from ICC, 'Statistics of Electric Railways' (annual). For commercial intercity trucking, revenue is derived from revenue per ton-mile; the latter is the average for carriers reporting to the ICC ('Statistics of class I Motor Carriers', annual). For pipelines, data come in the same manner from carriers reporting to the ICC ('Statistics of Oil Pipe Line Companies', annual). For waterways, see Table 30 and Chapter 7. For airlines, see Civil Aeronautics Administration, *Statistical Handbook of Civil Aviation*, 1948 issue.

° Less than 0.05.

ton-mile totals shown, and the latter measure the actual distance covered, not the distance as the crow flies. In judging the reported revenue per ton-mile we should remember also that the dispersion is sometimes to be explained by differences in the kind of freight moved. For instance, coastwise and Great Lakes traffic moves more cheaply than other forms of waterway freight because of the prevalence of bulk shipment in these two cases — of petroleum in the former and of iron ore in the latter. Also, a partial explanation of the high revenue per ton-mile earned by trucks, and of the very high revenue associated with airline freight transportation, lies in the large amount of package freight they carry.[14]

Yet when these qualifications are made, the dispersion in revenue per ton-mile plainly reflects an analogous dispersion (which we cannot determine statistically) in the charges for carrying identical commodities between identical pairs of points. Put otherwise, the dispersion actually shown in Table 4 reflects many factors besides differences in the roundaboutness of the route or the composition of the traffic. We may feel sure, for instance, that average per ton-mile revenue for waterways is a mere fraction of that for railroads partly because water transportation moves slowly; just as airlines can charge high rates because they furnish speedy movement. We should notice also that the incidence of cost of maintaining right of way, and of taxes and subsidies, differs sharply from one agency to another: these differences too must influence revenue per ton-mile.

As with passenger traffic, comparison can usefully be made with certain activities that lie outside the scope of this book. Thus the study of highway traffic leads naturally to estimates of freight carried in private intercity trucking, i.e., in vehicles owned by those whose commodities are transported, as well as in the commercial or for-hire intercity trucking industry. The 22 billion ton-

[14] Revenue per ton-mile for airlines and, say, steam railroads, are not strictly comparable. Thus mail and express — the chief classes of property transported by the airlines — are not included in the rail data. The inclusion of mail and express with railroad freight traffic would slightly raise revenue per ton-mile on the railroads, and to that extent diminish the disparity between the rail and airline figures.

miles for the for-hire trucking industry compares with 27 billion for private intercity trucking (see Appendix F). Since local trucking can to only a slight extent be upon a for-hire basis, and since farmers do their own trucking, it is a safe conclusion that in terms of ton-miles the trucking industry (i.e., for-hire or commercial trucking as considered in this book) represents far less than half total truck transportation.

Another comparison of the same order relates the part of total waterway freight between American and foreign ports that is carried by the American industry to the part carried by foreign-flag vessels. Of a total of 440 billion ton-miles, about 80 billion were performed in 1939 by the American industry and 360 billion by foreigners. Of total freight traffic between American and foreign ports, the share carried by American vessels in that year was about 18 percent, or distinctly less than the 29 percent reported as the domestic share of water-borne international passenger traffic (Table 3).

Chapter 2

Growth and Decline of Traffic since 1889

Combined passenger and freight traffic of all commercial agencies (land, water, and air) quintupled between 1889 and 1939, and almost doubled once again between 1939 and 1946. Between 1889 and 1920 freight traffic rose twice as fast as commodity output; since 1920 it has just kept pace with the latter. During the early years passenger traffic grew faster than population. To be sure, railroad accommodations in the late nineteenth century were less luxurious than today; yet our ancestors do not seem to have been as fond of traveling as we are. In 1889 the average American traveled 200 miles by commercial intercity agencies; in 1920 nearly 500 miles. Despite the widespread private ownership of automobiles and the modern highway system he still traveled 260 miles by rail, bus, air or water in 1939 — or 60 miles further than in 1889.

A recurrent theme of this book is the substitution of newer for older forms of transportation. Yet one of the oldest — coastwise shipping — is as lusty as it ever was, and in 1940 carried more traffic (mainly oil) than ever before in its history. Estimates given here for ton-miles in coastwise shipping and American-flag foreign commerce are apparently the first to be compiled. They lead to the remarkable result that recently ton-miles of waterborne freight traffic have roughly equaled all other types — rail, highway, pipeline, and air — combined.

WEIGHTED AND UNWEIGHTED INDEXES

It is argued here that the natural units for measuring transportation service are the passenger-mile and the freight ton-mile, and where possible these units are employed. Sometimes we are forced to fall back upon passengers carried or freight shipped as the unit of output, because of deficient data. The starting point of our study is fixed by the fact that the first satisfactory Census of Water Transportation relates to 1889, while the Interstate Commerce Commission began to collect railroad traffic statistics in the same year. However, coverage of the transportation industries on a continuous annual basis does not begin until 1920.

Simple summations of passenger-miles and of freight ton-miles yield unweighted indexes of traffic. Such indexes — for passenger and freight traffic, respectively — have a simple physical significance which makes their use attractive. If we wish to combine passenger and freight traffic, passenger-miles could readily be reduced to ton-miles, for passengers average about sixteen to the ton. The result would continue to possess a straightforward physical interpretation. Yet the economic significance of sixteen passenger-miles may obviously differ greatly from that of a ton-mile of freight. Consequently, an unweighted index that combined passenger and freight traffic in the fashion indicated would be of little interest.

In combining passenger and freight traffic we have chosen to weight passenger-miles (or passengers carried, where passenger-miles were not available) by revenue per passenger-mile (or per passenger) and ton-miles by revenue per ton-mile in 1939.[1] Railroad passenger revenue per ton-mile of passengers is perhaps thirty times freight revenue per freight ton-mile; thus passenger traffic is accorded far more importance than its ton-mileage would justify. The weighted indexes of output represent dollar totals measured in 1939 prices: i.e., we may speak of 1939 as the weight base. It has been convenient to choose 1939 as the comparison base also (i.e., the year when all series equal 100) in the summary tables partly because in that year all types of output are represented and none vanish, and partly because the outbreak of World War II seems a convenient reference point.

An obvious extension of the notion that sixteen passengers are not the economic equivalent of a ton of freight leads us to query the appropriateness of treating ton-miles and passengers-miles,

[1] However, the excellence of the data for steam railroads suggested the use of a slightly more sophisticated weighting scheme for that industry.

respectively, as homogeneous. Certainly the services of transporting a ton of oil in bulk and a ton of package freight over the same
distance sell for different prices; moreover they may involve the
use of different amounts of resources. The same thoughts apply
to coach and pullman, or first and second class ocean travel.

Table 5

INDEXES OF TRANSPORTATION OUTPUT, 1889-1946
Weighted Indexes[a]
1939 : 100

	All Transportation Agencies			Steam Railroads	Intercity Highways	Waterways
	Passenger	Freight	All traffic	All traffic[b]	All commercial traffic[c]	All traffic[d]
1889	25.5	16.5	18.5	27.1	....	16.7
1920	127	96	103	136.7	3	119
1921	115	72	81	103.9	5	90
1922	116	81	88	110.8	7	101
1923	122	96	102	131.0	9	107
1924	121	91	98	123.6	11	106
1925	120	97	102	129.9	14	104
1926	121	104	108	136.9	17	111
1927	119	102	106	131.5	20	113
1928	117	103	106	131.2	24	109.8
1929	118	108	110	133.7	30	114.5
1930	108	95	97	114.6	34	102.4
1931	94	79	82	92.5	36	84.6
1932	79	62	66	70.0	36	69.2
1933	76	68	70	73.6	39	79.1
1934	84	74	76	79.8	46	84.3
1935	87	77	79	83.7	52	87.8
1936	99	92	93	100.9	62	97.4
1937	103	101	101	108.1	76	111.1
1938	97	87	89	88.1	84	90.6
1939	100	100	100	100.0	100	100.0
1940	108	114	113	111.0	123	115.6
1946	248	176	192	192.9	176	196.9

[a] Construction of these indexes is discussed in individual chapters. Basic data
are printed in Appendices. Railroad data for 1889 refer to year ending June
30, 1890.
[b] See Table 17.
[c] Intercity buslines and for-hire trucking. This column combines indexes from
Table 7 (column 4) and Table 8 (column 3), using 1939 unit revenues (Tables
3 and 4) as weights.
[d] See Table 32.

Whether or not such differentiation is desirable, the necessary data exist to a very limited extent only. The weighted indexes for individual industries are in fact based upon a very limited breakdown of transportation services, which is perhaps the reason their behavior closely resembles that of the unweighted indexes. Thus passenger-miles in parlor and sleeping cars, in coaches at regular rates, and at commutation rates, were separately weighted; and weights were assigned in combining the traffic (passenger or freight) for different transportation agencies. Lack of data precluded the construction of more elaborately weighted output indexes.

PASSENGER AND FREIGHT TRAFFIC COMBINED

The most comprehensive measures of transportation service are weighted indexes of traffic for all transportation agencies taken together (Table 5 and Chart 1). For passenger and freight traffic combined, the index of transportation output increased sixfold between 1889 and 1920, and, despite some fairly sharp fluctuations, showed little net change between 1920 and 1939, then rose to a new peak during World War II. The behavior of freight traffic resembles that of the total; because of its large weight in the total, this accords with expectation. Passenger traffic, on the other hand, grew somewhat more slowly than freight traffic between 1889 and 1920, and experienced a net decline between 1920 and 1939, recovering again sharply between 1939 and 1946.

The contrast in behavior between passenger and freight traffic is illustrated from a different angle by the ratio of passenger to total traffic, measured in 1939 prices (Table 6). For all agencies taken together this ratio fell from 30 percent in 1889 to 27 percent in 1920, then declined irregularly to 22 percent in 1939.

It is possible that people's needs, direct and indirect, for freight transportation increased relatively to their ability or desire to travel. A much more likely explanation is that potential passengers shifted more rapidly to providing their own transportation by means of automobiles than did the owners of property to carrying that property in their own vehicles.

In Chart 2 traffic indexes are shown for the three principal

kinds of transportation — rail, water and highway. Steam railroads and waterways show generally similar movements in contrast with the meteoric rise of intercity highway traffic (buslines
and for-hire trucking).

Chart 1
ALL TRANSPORTATION AGENCIES:
PASSENGER, FREIGHT, AND COMBINED TRAFFIC
Weighted indexes

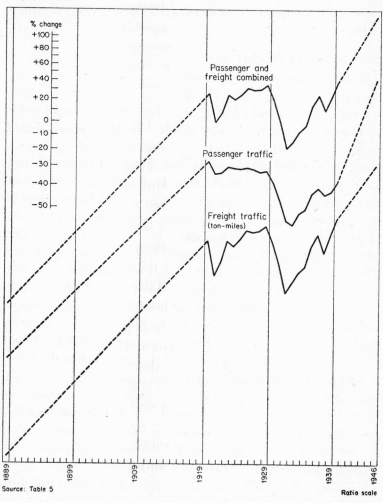

Source: Table 5

Ratio scale

Table 6

RATIOS OF PASSENGER TO COMBINED PASSENGER AND
FREIGHT TRAFFIC, 1889-1946[a]
Comparison made in 1939 Prices

	All Agencies	Steam Railroads	Intercity Highways[b]	Waterways
1889	0.30	0.21	....	0.16
1920	0.27	0.17	n.a.	0.08
1921	0.31	0.18	n.a.	0.14
1922	0.29	0.16	n.a.	0.09
1923	0.26	0.15	n.a.	0.08
1924	0.27	0.15	n.a.	0.09
1925	0.26	0.14	0.6	0.07
1926	0.25	0.13	0.6	0.06
1927	0.25	0.13	0.5	0.07
1928	0.24	0.12	0.5	0.08
1929	0.24	0.12	0.5	0.08
1930	0.24	0.11	0.4	0.09
1931	0.25	0.11	0.4	0.09
1932	0.26	0.11	0.4	0.09
1933	0.24	0.11	0.3	0.08
1934	0.24	0.11	0.3	0.08
1935	0.24	0.11	0.3	0.09
1936	0.23	0.11	0.3	0.09
1937	0.22	0.11	0.3	0.08
1938	0.24	0.12	0.2	0.08
1939	0.22	0.11	0.20	0.07
1940	0.21	0.11	0.21	0.06
1941	n.a.	0.10	0.22	n.a.
1942	n.a.	0.14	n.a.	n.a.
1943	n.a.	0.19	0.41	n.a.
1944	n.a.	0.20	0.39	n.a.
1945	n.a.	0.20	0.36	n.a.
1946	0.28	0.17	0.31	n.a.

n.a.: not available.
[a] For basic data, see Appendices.
[b] Intercity buslines and for-hire trucking.

PASSENGER TRAFFIC

Diverse movements are reported by passenger traffic. As might be
expected, the four agencies of long distance travel fall easily into
two groups. On the one hand railroad and waterway travel each
increased about four times between 1889 and 1920 and fell
roughly 50 percent between 1920 and 1939 (Chart 3). In the
other group the newcomers, intercity buslines and domestic air-

Chart 2
PASSENGER AND FREIGHT TRAFFIC COMBINED
Weighted indexes

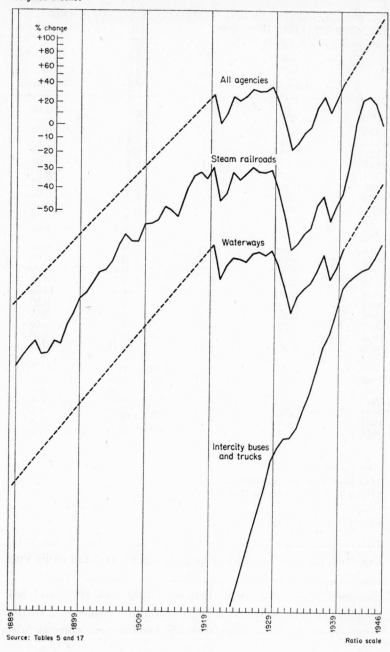

Source: Tables 5 and 17   Ratio scale

Chart 3
LONG DISTANCE AGENCIES: PASSENGER-MILE INDEXES

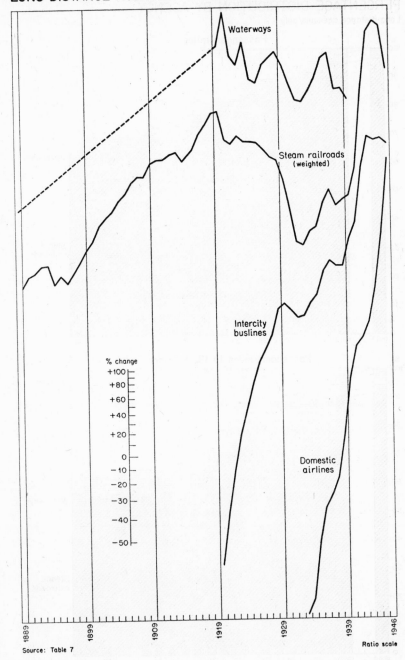

Waterways

Steam railroads
(weighted)

Intercity
buslines

% change
+100
+80
+60
+40
+20
0
−10
−20
−30
−40
−50

Domestic
airlines

1889   1899   1909   1919   1929   1939   1946

Ratio scale

Source: Table 7

Chart 4
PASSENGER TRAFFIC:
PERCENTAGE DISTRIBUTION BY AGENCY
Long distance agencies only

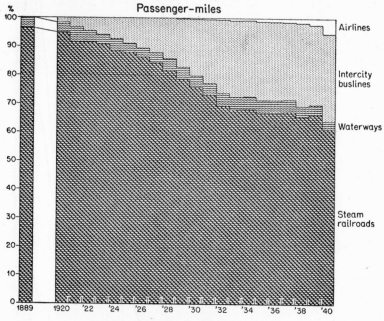

Passenger-miles

Airlines

Intercity buslines

Waterways

Steam railroads

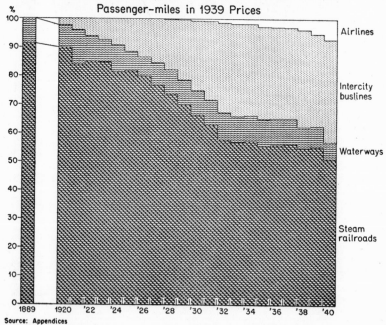

Passenger-miles in 1939 Prices

Airlines

Intercity buslines

Waterways

Steam railroads

Source: Appendices

Chart 5
LOCAL AGENCIES: INDEXES OF PASSENGERS CARRIED

Electric
railways

City buslines

% change
+100
+80
+60
+40
+20
0
−10
−20
−30
−40
−50

1889   1899   1909   1919   1929   1939   1946

Source: Table 7   Ratio scale

Table 7

INDEXES OF PASSENGER TRAFFIC, 1889-1946
1939 : 100

| | Steam Railroads | | Electric Railways | Intercity Buslines | City Buslines | Waterways | Airlines | Long Distance Agencies | Local Agencies | Total Passenger Transportation Weighted Index |
	Passenger-miles (1)	Weighted passenger-miles (2)	Passengers (3)	Passenger-miles (4)	Passengers (5)	Passenger-miles (6)	Passenger-miles (7)	Passenger-miles (1+4+6+7) (8)	Passengers (3+5) (9)	(2 through 7) (10)
1889	....	....	....	...	...	38 }	...	36	19.6	25.5
1890	53.0	50.4	29.1	...	...	...	...	...	46.1	...
1902	87.1	82.8	68.7	...	...	...	...	...	...	...
1907	123.5	117.3	106.9	...	...	...	...	...	72.0	...
1908	128.8	122.6	107.9	...	...	...	...	...	72.7	...
1909	128.7	122.5	115.0	...	...	...	...	...	77.5	...
1910	142.9	136.0	122.8	...	...	...	...	...	82.7	...
1911	146.7	139.6	129.7	...	...	...	...	...	87.4	...
1912	146.3	139.8	137.2	...	...	...	...	...	92.4	...
1913	152.7	146.2	143.5	...	...	...	...	...	96.7	...
1914	155.7	149.2	143.8	...	...	...	...	...	96.9	...
1915	143.0	138.1	142.3	...	...	...	...	...	95.8	...
1916	155.1	151.1	152.8	...	...	...	...	...	102.9	...
1917	176.6	172.7	162.5	...	...	...	...	...	110.4	...
1918	190.3	184.4	160.6	...	...	...	...	...	110.1	...
1919	206	204	168.4	...	...	...	...	...	116.3	...

Year										
1920	209	207	176.3	9	10	141	...	146	122.1	127
1921	166.0	164.2	165.6	14	13	188	...	120	115.7	115
1922	157.7	157.9	175.4	19	16	131	...	114	123.3	116
1923	168.6	169.9	179.3	25	19	122	...	123	127.0	122
1924	160.1	161.4	176.1	31	21	147	...	120	125.5	121
1925	159.2	161.3	173.8	36	24.0	108	...	120	124.9	120
1926	157.1	159.6	174.0	46	29.2	105	.1	121	126.7	121
1927	148.8	150.7	170.2	51	34.6	122	.3	117	126.0	119
1928	139.6	141.3	164.6	58	36.6	129.0	1.3	113	122.8	117
1929	137.2	138.2	162.4	71	40.3	135.4	4.9	116	122.6	118
1930	118.3	117.8	148.9	74	40.0	121.5	12.1	104	113.3	108
1931	96.6	94.3	132.0	70	39.3	104.4	14.0	88	101.8	94
1932	74.8	71.1	111.9	66	38.5	90.8	17.1	72	88.0	79
1933	72.1	69.2	104.8	67	39.2	90.0	23.2	70	83.4	76
1934	79.6	77.8	109.1	74	53.6	98.1	26.2	77	91.0	84
1935	81.5	80.3	107.6	80	61.8	109.3	42.0	81	92.6	87
1936	98.9	98.2	111.2	96	76.2	128.3	55.1	98	99.8	99
1937	108.7	108.7	106.9	104	81.1	133.6	61.6	107	98.5	103
1938	95.4	95.5	100.8	101	94.4	99.2	70.6	96	98.7	97
1939	100.0	100.0	100.0	100	100.0	100.0	100.0	100	100.0	100
1940	104.9	103.6	98.9	124	113.3	92	152.6	111	103.6	108
1941	129.5	129.5	102.0	142	134.7	...	205	134	112.7	124
1942	237	243	119.4	224	192.7	...	219	231	143.3	187
1943	387	390	148.7	286	219	...	249	352	171.6	256
1944	421	425	152.9	277	255	...	330	375	186.3	274
1945	404	409	152.9	281	235	...	505	368	179.6	272
1946	285	288	151.0	268	251	...	934	293	183.5	248

For notes, see next page

lines, have been growing rapidly since their appearance, and scarcely hesitated even during the Great Depression. The same tendencies are reflected in Chart 4, the upper panel of which shows for 1889 and for 1920-39 the distribution of total passenger-miles between the four long distance agencies, and the lower panel a similar distribution for passenger-miles weighted by 1939 revenue. The rising relative position of airlines and buses is plain. The smaller share of railroads in the lower panel is of course due to their relatively low revenue per passenger-mile (Table 3 above).

The two local passenger traffic agencies afford a similar contrast between the old and the new (Chart 5). The older form, electric railways, carried six times as many passengers in 1920 as in 1890, but between 1920 and 1939 travel was roughly halved. During World War II the traffic of other agencies rose to all-time records, but the number of electric railway passengers did not reach the peak of the early 1920's. Meanwhile the newer form of local transportation, city buslines, grew tenfold between 1920 and

Notes to Table 7

Col. (1)   Class I, II, and III railroads. From 1890 to 1915 data refer to years ending June 30. Adjusted for coverage in 1912 and prior years on basis of passenger revenue; coverage always exceeded 97 percent. See Appendix Table B-1.

Col. (2)   Same remarks as col. (1), except as follows. After 1911 data are based on class I railroads only, and passenger-miles are weighted by receipts per passenger-mile according to the following classification. 1911 to 1922: (a) commutation and coach, (b) parlor and sleeping car; 1922 and later years: (a) commutation, (b) coach, (c) parlor and sleeping car, (d) parlor and sleeping car passengers paying no railroad fare. See Table 17 and note a to that table.

Col. (3)   Urban and interurban; electrically operated divisions of steam railroads not included. Figure for 1890 refers to year ending June 30. Trolleybus, but not motorbus, operations of street railway companies are included. See Table 26.

Col. (4)   See Appendix Table E-1.

Col. (5)   Includes buses operated by street railway companies. See Appendix Table E-1.

Col. (6)   Intercoastal, noncontiguous, and American-flag international. Not available for 1941 and later years. See Table 33.

Col. (7)   Domestic and international. See Appendix Table I-1.

Cols. (8), (9) and (10)   In computing figures for 1889, data for railroads and electric railways for the year ending June 30, 1890, have been used. The relatives in cols. (8) and (9) represent simple aggregates of passenger-miles and passengers, respectively. In computing col. (10), 1939 revenues per passenger or per passenger-mile have been used as weights (see Table 3).

Chart 6
LONG DISTANCE AND LOCAL PASSENGER TRAFFIC:
INDEXES OF OUTPUT

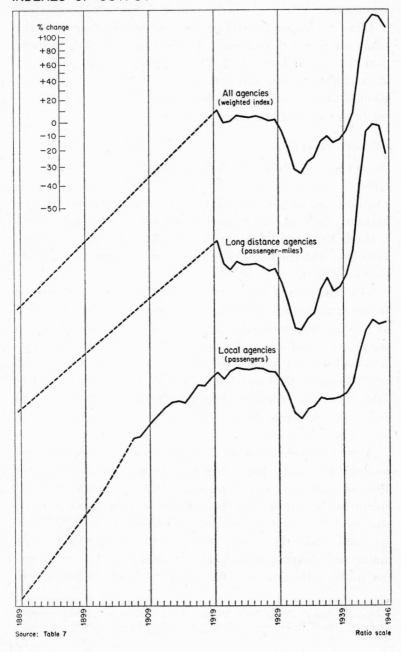

% change

All agencies
(weighted index)

Long distance agencies
(passenger-miles)

Local agencies
(passengers)

Source: Table 7

Ratio scale

1939, and has indeed since that time easily outpaced electric railway traffic.

Chart 6 compares travel on the four long distance agencies taken together with total traffic for the two forms of local transportation. From 1889 to 1920 local traffic grew six times, long distance three to four times. Between 1920 and 1939 the movement of the two series was similar, although local traffic was (as might be expected) the more stable.

FREIGHT TRAFFIC

As in Chart 3 (Passenger Traffic), a sharp contrast emerges in Chart 7 between the old and the new. Freight traffic carried by the older agencies (steam railroads and waterways) rises steeply between 1889 and 1920, and undergoes a small net decline between 1920 and 1939. On the other hand the newer agencies (pipelines and trucking) rise rapidly from a relatively insignificant level in the early 1920's.

The expansion of freight traffic, both railroad and waterway, before 1920 is steeper, and the subsequent decline more gradual (Chart 7), than with passenger traffic (Chart 3). The diminishing proportion of passenger to total traffic, already noted in Table 6, is evidently not confined to railroads. Again the rise in freight traffic between 1889 and 1920 is steeper for waterways (sevenfold) than for railroads (fivefold); and after 1920 railroad freight traffic tends downward, whereas waterways show no appreciable trend (Chart 7).[2]

A partial explanation of these differences in behavior may plausibly be found in the greater diversion to highways of railroad than of waterway, and of passenger than of freight traffic. It might be thought the fact that intercity highways also exhibit a sharply declining ratio of passengers to freight after 1924 (Table 6) conflicts with the assumption that more passenger than freight traffic was diverted to highways. But the diversion of passenger traffic at the expense of the agencies considered here was of

---

[2] Between 1920 and 1940 absence of trend in the waterway total conceals a decline in American-flag international and a corresponding expansion in domestic (especially coastwise) traffic (see Table 32 and Chart 21).

Chart 7
FREIGHT TRAFFIC: TON–MILE INDEXES

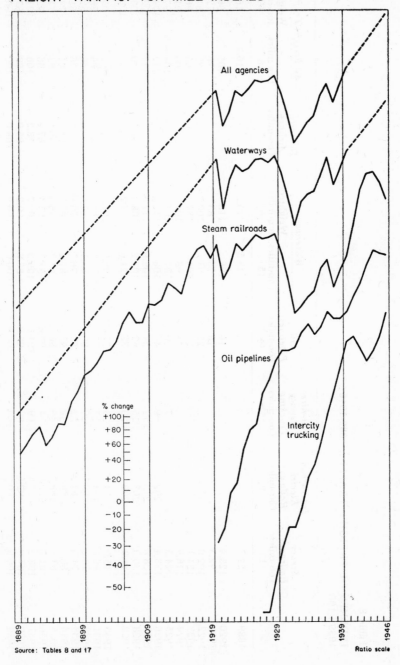

All agencies

Waterways

Steam railroads

Oil pipelines

Intercity
trucking

% change
+100
+ 80
+ 60
+ 40
+ 20
0
− 10
− 20
− 30
− 40
− 50

1889   1899   1909   1919   1929   1939   1946

Source: Tables 8 and 17

Ratio scale

Table 8

INDEXES OF FREIGHT TRAFFIC, 1889-1946

1939 : 100

	Steam Railroads Ton-miles (1)	Interurban Electric Railways Car-miles (2)	For-hire Intercity Trucking Ton-miles (3)	Oil Pipelines Ton-miles (4)	Waterways		Domestic Airlines Ton-miles (7)	All Freight Traffic	
					Ton-miles (5)	Weighted ton-miles (6)		Ton-miles (8)	Weighted ton-miles (9)
1889	22.7	...	...	....	13.5	15.2	...	16.2	16.5
1920	123.4	...	...	16	106	118	...	105	96
1921	92.3	...	...	18	73	83	...	76	72
1922	102.0	151	...	25	91	100	...	89	81
1923	124.1	...	...	27	104	107	...	105	96
1924	116.9	...	...	34	98	104	...	100	91
1925	124.5	...	7	40	101	104	...	104	97
1926	133.4	202	9	43	108	112	...	112	104
1927	128.8	213	12	54	109.0	112.8	...	111	102
1928	130.0	203	15	62	105.2	108.7	...	110	103
1929	134.2	208	20	72	111.6	113.2	...	116	108
1930	115.0	174.9	23	77	98.0	101.1	...	102	95
1931	92.8	144.7	27	77	79.9	83.5	...	84	79
1932	70.2	99.5	29	80	63.1	67.6	...	66	62
1933	74.7	87.2	32	89	76.7	78.6	...	76	68
1934	80.6	98.9	39	95	81.4	83.7	25	81	74
1935	84.6	108.7	45	86	83.2	86.4	46.2	83	77
1936	101.7	126.9	54	93.6	94.7	95.4	67.2	96	92
1937	108.2	122.3	69	104.8	109.9	109.7	78.2	108	101
1938	87.0	92.8	80	99.0	87.8	90.2	85.0	88	87
1939	100.0	100.0	100	100.0	100.0	100.0	100.0	100	100

Year	(1)	(2)	(3)	(4)	(5)	(6)	(7)	(8)	(9)
1940	111.9	105.9	122	105.7	115.9	117.5	120.1	114	114
1941	142.4	119.5	128	121.3	⋯	⋯	162.3	⋯	⋯
1942	191.1	123.9	⋯	132.5	⋯	⋯	292	⋯	⋯
1943	218	133.4	105	155.7	⋯	⋯	452	⋯	⋯
1944	221	141.1	112	174.3	⋯	⋯	602	⋯	⋯
1945	204	133.2	126	169.9	⋯	⋯	771	173	⋯
1946	177.4	113.1	152	167.5	171.6	200	632	⋯	176

Col. (1) Class I, II, and III railroads. For 1889 data refer to year ending June 30, 1890. Adjusted for coverage in 1910 and prior years on basis of freight revenue; coverage always exceeded 97 percent. See Table 17.

Col. (2) See Appendix Table D-2.

Col. (3) See Appendix Table F-4.

Col. (4) Trunk-line movement, crude and refined oils, interstate and intrastate. See Table 29.

Col. (5) See Appendix Table H-1.

Col. (6) See Table 33. Separate ton-mile totals for coastwise, intercoastal, Great Lakes, inland, noncontiguous, and American-flag international traffic, respectively, were weighted by estimated revenue per ton-mile in 1939 (Table 4).

Col. (7) Express, freight, and mail traffic. See Appendix Table I-1.

Col. (8) Series represents a simple ton-mile total for data underlying columns (1) through (5) and (7). For interurban electric railways a uniform carloading of 17.75 tons was assumed.

Col. (9) Columns (1) through (4), (6), and (7) weighted by respective 1939 revenues (Table 4).

Chart 8
FREIGHT TRAFFIC:
PERCENTAGE DISTRIBUTION BY AGENCY

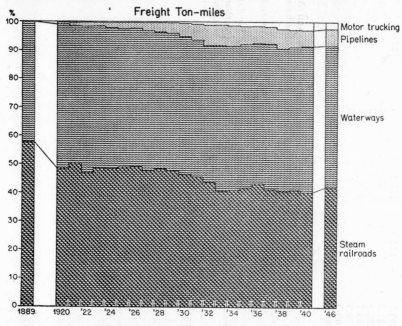

Freight Ton-miles

Motor trucking
Pipelines

Waterways

Steam railroads

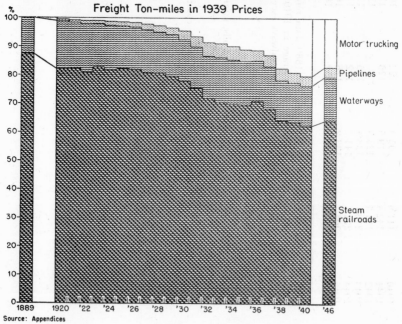

Freight Ton-miles in 1939 Prices

Motor trucking

Pipelines

Waterways

Steam railroads

Source: Appendices

course a diversion in favor of the private automobile rather than of the intercity bus, the only type of long-distance highway travel for which data are offered. Indeed the decline in the ratio of passenger to freight on intercity highways, i.e., the slower growth of bus travel than of trucking, can itself be viewed as evidence of the much greater expansion of private automobile travel than of private (i.e., not for-hire) trucking. As we saw in Chapter 1, private automobile travel measured in passenger-miles, had by 1929 reached a level many times that of all the agencies considered here taken together. Much of the new kind of travel would doubtless never have occurred had the private automobile failed to develop; yet a substantial part of such travel would doubtless have used existing agencies.

Through 1929 intercity trucking grew at about the same pace as buslines and pipelines (Charts 3 and 7). Like airline passenger travel, trucking's growth was scarcely slowed by the Great Depression; yet its rate of expansion cannot compare with that for airline passenger traffic. The more rapid and sustained rise in output for trucking (Chart 7) than for intercity buslines (Chart 3) explains the decline in the ratio of passenger to total highway traffic after 1924 (Table 6), upon which we have already commented.

The speedy rise of motor trucking and pipelines is also reflected in these agencies' increased share of total ton-miles and of ton-miles in constant prices (Chart 8). Here the much larger share of railroads and motor trucking in revenue than in ton-miles is apparent.

SOME FURTHER COMPARISONS

We have noted major trends in passenger and freight traffic. How do these movements compare with growth in other sectors of the economy? Table 9 reduces some physical measures of traffic to a per capita basis.

Per Capita Traffic

In 1889 electric railways were still in their infancy and mechanically operated buses had yet to be invented. The 33 trips per

person on street railways in that year grew to 118 in 1920 and
declined to 79 in 1939. One might think that the 118 trips a
year for every man, woman and child in the United States that
obtained 30 years ago represented saturation.[3] Certainly the subsequent decline in trips per capita is associated with the introduction of the private automobile for suburban and even city travel.
Yet in 1946 we consumed 136 local bus or streetcar trips apiece,
despite considerable automobile commuting by car pool and
otherwise (Table 9).

Passenger travel by railroads, intercity buses, airlines and waterways shows a similar pattern. On a per capita basis the annual
consumption of passenger-miles rose between 1889 and 1920,
then declined, to rise again to a fresh peak in 1946. The average
person (if not the typical individual) traveled 200 miles a year
at the opening of our period, nearly 500 in 1920, 260 in 1939,
and about 700 in 1946 — not counting travel by local agencies
or by private automobile. Freight traffic per capita also reached
peaks in 1920 and 1946. Of course figures for 1946 reflect the
aftermath of World War II, just as 1920 is influenced by World
War I; it is still too early to chart new peacetime traffic levels.

Perhaps the most striking feature of Table 9 is the surprisingly
small amount of travel and freight transportation in which the
nation chose — or could afford — to indulge at the opening of
our period. Admittedly the figures for 1890 do not measure transportation by animal power, any more than current figures take
account of privately owned automobiles or trucks not plying for
hire. Moreover our use of the 1889 Census of Waterways may
possibly have understated the ton-mile volume of canal and river
traffic at that date. Even when these qualifications have been
made, the contrast still astonishes.

In 1889 the railroad and canal networks were substantially

[3] A possibly more appropriate figure might use the population in cities over
50,000 as the denominator. Trips per head on this basis were: 1890, 170; 1920,
386; and 1940, 236. Trips per head of working population in such cities may
have been two or two and a half times bigger; perhaps 800 to 900 in 1920.
Such a figure would allow two trips every working day for the gainfully
employed and still leave a useful number of trips for the schoolboy and the
housewife. It would seem therefore that urban and suburban local transportation needs were pretty well satisfied by the electric railways of 1920.

Table 9

PER CAPITA USE OF TRANSPORTATION FACILITIES, 1889-1946

	1889[a]	1907	1920	1925	1929	1932	1939	1946
United States population (million)	61.8	87.0	106.5	115.8	121.8	124.8	130.9	139.9
Passenger traffic per capita								
Local transportation agencies — annual trips by bus and electric railway	33	86	118	111	104	73	79	136
Long distance transportation agencies								
Steam railroads — annual passenger-miles	195	322	445	312	256	136	174	463
All intercity (steam railroads, intercity buses, and domestic airlines) — annual passenger-miles	195	322	453	344	312	188	252	697
All intercity and overseas (steam railroads, intercity buses, domestic airlines, and waterways) — annual passenger-miles	202	n.a.	469	355	325	196	261	n.a.
Freight traffic per capita								
Steam railroads — annual ton-miles (thous.)	1.23	2.72	3.88	3.60	3.70	1.89	2.56	4.25
Total rail and highway — annual ton-miles (thous.)	1.23	2.72	3.91	3.63	3.76	1.96	2.75	4.50
All land traffic (rail, highway and pipelines) — annual ton-miles (thous.)	1.23	2.72	3.98	3.80	4.05	2.28	3.12	5.09
All land and water traffic — annual ton-miles (thous.)	2.14	n.a.	8.06	7.37	7.80	4.35	6.26	10.12

n.a.: not available.

[a] Based on data for steam railroads and electric railways for year ending June 30, 1890.

complete, yet per capita passenger travel was not significantly higher than in the depression year 1932, and was about three-quarters of its 1939 level. And in 1889 there were no private automobiles to help out! Allowance for automobile travel, on the lines indicated in Chapter 1, would reduce the average American's total travel in 1889 to as little as a fifth of his travel in 1939. The figures in Table 9 suggest a similar scantiness in the amount of freight transportation with which the nation got by sixty years ago. It is hard to interpret the statement that in 1939 the average person used, directly or indirectly, about 6,000 freight ton-miles. But it is easy enough to grasp the thought that the average American got along in 1889 with only a third this amount — and furthermore had none of the privately owned motor trucks that in 1939 are necessarily left out of our calculations. Of course there were horses, but they would hardly be used for the intercity or long-distance traffic here in question.

The rapid rise in transportation output between 1889 and 1920 does little to explain transportation's declining share of national income and employment reported in Chapter 1. On the other hand the much slower growth, or even decline, of output after 1920 is in line with the decline in transportation's relative share.

Freight Traffic and Commodity Output

The growth of traffic may be compared also with other measures of the physical expansion of the economy. Between 1889 and 1920 freight traffic (measured in ton-miles) increased more rapidly than manufacturing or mining and nearly four times as fast as agricultural output (Table 10). For the fifty-year comparison 1889-1939, freight traffic grew sixfold and commodity output in general fourfold.

It will be recalled that our freight traffic index is based upon ton-mileage totals. In fact, its rapid growth in part reflects a long-time lengthening of haul. For example, for *railroad* freight traffic — the principal component — average haul increased about 35 percent from 1890 to 1920 or 55 percent from 1890 to 1939 (Chapter 4). These figures undoubtedly overstate the lengthening of haul for freight transportation as a whole. They suggest, however, that on a basis of tons shipped (in place of ton-miles) the increase in freight traffic would be more moderate. Yet growth

Table 10

OUTPUT TRENDS IN TRANSPORTATION AND
OTHER INDUSTRIES, 1889-1946
1889-90 : 100

	1889-90[a]	1920	1929	1939	1946
All transportation agencies combined					
Passenger and freight traffic combined	100	560	600	540	1,040
Freight traffic					
Weighted ton-miles[b]	100	580	650	610	1,070
Unweighted ton-miles[b]	100	650	720	620	1,070
All transportation agencies, except noncontiguous and					
American-flag international waterways					
Freight traffic					
Weighted ton-miles[b]	100	540	640	610	1,030
Unweighted ton-miles[b]	100	500	680	640	930
Output of other industries					
Manufacturing[c]	100	350	520	530	870
Mining[d]	100	450	640	610	760
Agriculture[e]	100	160	180	200	260
Three commodity-producing industries combined[f]	100	260	360	370	560
Traffic/Output comparisons					
Ratio: Weighted ton-miles (excluding noncontiguous and international waterways) to total commodity output	100	210	180	170	180
Ratio: Unweighted ton-miles (excluding noncontiguous and international waterways) to total commodity output	100	190	190	170	170

[a] The principal component of traffic, that carried by railroads, relates to the year ending June 30, 1890.
[b] Weighted indexes of ton-miles combine ton-mile totals for individual agencies using respective revenues per ton-mile in 1939. Unweighted indexes represent simple ton-mile summations.
[c] Frickey and Persons agree that manufacturing output in 1889-90 was about 70 percent of its level in 1899; for comparing later years with 1899 we have Fabricant's index and (for 1946) the Federal Reserve Board index. See Frickey, *Production in the United States,* Table 6, p. 54; Warren M. Persons, *Forecasting Business Cycles* (Wiley, 1931), pp. 170-1; Solomon Fabricant, *Employment in Manufacturing, 1889-1939* (NBER, 1942), p. 331; *Federal Reserve Bulletin.*
[d] Using 1899 unit values, we may say that the combined output of iron ore, mercury, gold, silver, copper, lead, zinc, bituminous and anthracite coal, petroleum and phosphate rock increased about 65 percent between 1889-90 and 1899 (data from U. S. Geological Survey, *Mineral Resources of the United States*). Later years were compared with 1899 using the index in Harold Barger and Sam H. Schurr, *The Mining Industries* (NBER, 1944), Table 1, p. 14; and (in the case of 1946) the Federal Reserve Board index.
[e] For the first three comparisons, see Harold Barger and Hans H. Landsberg, *American Agriculture* (NBER, 1942), Table 39, p. 253. The last comparison is based upon U. S. Bureau of Agricultural Economics figures (see *Statistical Abstract of the United States*).
[f] The three preceding indexes were combined using 1929 value added in manufacturing ($30.1 billion), mine value of minerals ($4.1 billion) and value of net output of agriculture ($11.7 billion).

in freight traffic — however measured — would still appear to have exceeded the expansion of commodity output between 1889 and 1920 by a wide margin.

Comparison between freight traffic and commodity output is somewhat distorted by fluctuations in the share of the nation's water-borne foreign commerce carried in American-flag vessels. This share was much higher in 1920 and in 1946 than in other years. We have accordingly computed freight traffic indexes which exclude international (and, for technical reasons, also non-contiguous) waterways, and these indexes are compared with commodity output at the foot of Table 10.

Evidently such ton-mile indexes (weighted or unweighted) increased between 1889 and 1920 about twice as rapidly as commodity output. As just noted, this contrast is to be explained in minor degree only by the lengthening that occurred in average haul. We must suppose that it reflects also an increase in the fraction of all commodities transported by long-distance agencies (as distinct from local drayage) — or in the number of times each commodity was so transported. Certainly the average size of American factories grew during the period: perhaps central-ized manufacture, requiring long-distance transportation of raw materials and finished products, was gradually being substituted for production in local workshops dependent mainly upon dray-age.

After 1920 ton-mile indexes (excluding, as before, international and noncontiguous traffic) moved roughly in accordance with commodity output. The ratio of ton-miles to commodity output remained stable or tended slightly downward. Conflicting factors appear to have been at work during the interwar period. On the one hand some further lengthening of average haul may have occurred, and perhaps additional substitution of centralized for local manufacture. These influences would raise the ratio. On the other hand some traffic undoubtedly shifted from railroads or other commercial agencies to highway trucking in trucks owned by the shippers. Our indexes of freight traffic report waterway movements in 'captive' vessels, but not highway movements in privately owned trucks. Such a shift would therefore tend to depress the ratio. We may conclude that the parallelism between freight traffic (ton-miles) and production since 1920 is roughly what might be expected.

HOW DID TOTAL TRANSPORTATION BEHAVE?

From the story of this chapter may be gleaned some evidence of retardation in the growth of transportation service by the commercial agencies considered here. In 1946 neither passenger nor freight traffic approached the level suggested by projections of the rates of growth between 1889 and 1920 (Chart 1). Had passenger traffic continued to grow after 1920 as before, at an annual rate of 5.4 percent, its 1946 volume would have been twice as large as it actually was. Continuation of the corresponding pre-1920 growth rate for freight traffic (6.3 percent annually) would have yielded in 1946 three times the volume actually observed in that year; if international traffic is excluded, the rate of growth is 5.4 percent and the projected 1946 level slightly more than twice the actual.

To this evidence of slackening of growth it may be objected that 1920 was a peak year, its levels inflated by the aftermath of World War I. Traffic fell sharply in 1921 to the lowest level of the 1920's. If we base a calculation of growth rates on a comparison of 1921 (instead of 1920) with 1889, the upward trends are less steep, but in each case the projections still lie above the actual 1946 level.

With respect to passenger traffic more convincing evidence of retardation of growth is given by the per capita data in Table 9. Annual trips on local agencies more than tripled during thirty years before 1920, but scarcely rose between 1920 and 1946. Per capita passenger-miles by all intercity agencies in 1920 were more than twice the 1889 level, but they did not double again by 1946. In our comparison of freight traffic with commodity output (Table 10), we noticed a very decided slackening of growth: traffic increased twice as fast before 1920, but barely kept pace with commodity output thereafter.

Such retardation of growth reflects — at least in part — diver-

sion of traffic from commercial agencies to private automobiles
and privately owned trucks. The question arises whether diversion
can entirely account for the slackening we observe in the growth
of commercial transportation service. Would total transportation
— commercial and private — exhibit retardation of growth?

In view of the paucity of data we cannot expect a conclusive
answer to this question. Let us suppose the accompanying figures
apply. It is assumed that an automobile runs 8,000 miles a year

	1889	1920	1939	1946
Private automobiles				
Registrations (million)	....	8	26	28
Passenger-miles (billion)	....	150	500	500
Commercial transportation				
Passenger-miles (billion)	12	50	34	100
Total transportation				
Passenger-miles (billion)	12	200	534	600

with an average load of $2\frac{1}{2}$ persons (see note f to Table 3
above). If these figures are correct, annual growth rates for total
transportation were 10 percent for 1889-1920, 5 percent for
1920-39, and 2 percent for 1939-46; retardation is clearly established. If per capita figures are used, corresponding growth rates
are 8, 4, and $\frac{1}{2}$ percent respectively.

Yet we may vary the assumptions plausibly and reach an
opposite conclusion. In the first place we may prefer a lower
figure than 8,000 miles per year for the use of an automobile in
1920, in view of the character of the automobile and the condition of the highway system at that period. We may note that if
an average of only 4,000 miles per car is used for 1920, still with
$2\frac{1}{2}$ passengers, total travel drops from 200 to 125 billion passenger-miles, and the growth rate (without adjustment for population change) both before and after 1920 is 8 percent. Evidence
of retardation is then confined to the comparison 1939-46, and
can perhaps be explained away by the shortage of vehicles in the
latter year. In the second place we have considered only the
behavior of an (unweighted) ton-mile aggregate. Were we to
value automobile travel at cost of operation, a passenger-mile of
private travel would probably receive a smaller weight than a
passenger-mile of commercial transportation service. A weighted

index of total transportation service would therefore rise some-what less rapidly, and be somewhat more likely to show slacken-ing of growth, than an unweighted index. Of course the growth of aggregate passenger travel (commercial and private) must eventually slow down. The figures we have been able to assemble are insufficient to determine whether retardation had already begun during our period of study.

For freight traffic the question posed above is easier to answer. Intercity ton-miles in private trucks rose from a negligible amount in 1920 to about 27 billion in 1939 and 1946 (Appendix Table F-4). Still only 2 or 3 percent of all ton-miles recorded for com-mercial agencies, the addition of private intercity trucking could plainly not significantly alter the trends in freight traffic already reported by our indexes. There remains the matter of local truck-ing, for-hire and private. Local trucking succeeded animal dray-age in a continuous development. We are ignorant of the number of tons carried or ton-miles of service performed, and we do not know whether or how rapidly these have grown. Yet no traffic has been diverted here from an activity we can measure to one we cannot. And it seems inconceivable that major trends in long-distance freight traffic could be swamped by contrary trends in local transportation, could we add data for the latter. We must conclude that the retardation of growth observable in our indexes (Chart 1 and Table 10) would also characterize an index of total freight traffic, commercial and private, long-distance and local; and that such retardation is not to be explained in any appreciable degree by diversion to activities not covered by our indexes.

Chapter 3

Trends in Employment and Productivity

Employment in all commercial transportation agencies grew from under 1 million in 1889 to 2½ million during the 1920's, fell below 2 million in 1939, and rose again to over 2 million in 1946 (Table 11). The employment figures given here for 1939 differ rather sharply from the Occupation Census figures for 1940 in Table 1: conjectural reasons for these differences are mentioned in the notes to Table 11. The data for employment come from various sources and are intended to measure full-time equivalent workers, i.e., man-years. Their reliability is uneven, figures for highways and waterways being especially uncertain. However, the total reflects with fair accuracy the draft of these industries upon the labor force.

From the employment figures of Table 11, in conjunction with the output figures of Table 5, we can estimate changes in labor productivity. Accordingly the movement of output per employee is recorded in Table 12. It will be seen that over the fifty-year period productivity almost tripled. In the transportation industries the average rise in output per employee from 1889 to 1939 lay between 2.1 and 2.2 percent annually.[1] The average annual rate of increase appears to have been larger in transportation than in any other major industrial division — except mining, when mining is taken to include oil and gas wells (Table 13). For manufacturing and agriculture, and for mining other than oil and gas wells, productivity increased less rapidly than in transportation.

The relatively rapid rise in output per worker in the transportation industries as a whole invites comment from several distinct

[1] Between 1889 and 1946 output per worker quadrupled, rising 2.5 percent annually; but 1946 conditions were perhaps not representative.

Table 11

EMPLOYMENT IN THE TRANSPORTATION INDUSTRIES,
1889-1946[a]
Thousand workers

	1889	1920	1929	1939	1946
Steam railroads[b]	749	2,076	1,694	1,007	1,378
Electric railways and city buslines[c]	71	316	280	184	203
Intercity buslines[d]	0	14	45	34	59
Intercity trucking, for-hire[e]	0	50	252	290	443
Pipelines[f]	0	16	25	22	27
Waterways[g]	97	178	126	106	151
Airlines[h]	0	0	2	15	82
TOTAL	917	2,650	2,424	1,658	2,343

[a] This table attempts to build up an employment series for transportation as a whole comparable with the output series already given. The data are intended to represent man-years, or equivalent full-time workers, but in this they only partly succeed. Most employment counts exaggerate the number of man-years: they give the peak payroll, the total number of individuals engaged at any time, or the average number employed during the active period of the year only. For instance estimates of employment in trucking often start from truck registrations, in waterways from the number of jobs to be filled in every vessel that sailed at any time during the year. Such counts plainly over-state the number of man-years of employment in the industry. For steam railroads in 1920 and later years and for other industries in 1929 and later years, averages of twelve monthly counts have been used, or the figures have been adjusted to a man-year basis in other ways. 1920 figures for industries other than steam railroads are substantially based on single counts and have not been adjusted to a man-year basis. However, the level of traffic in 1920 was so high, and periods of inactivity so brief, that the required adjustment would be slight and probably not exceed errors of estimation. Figures for 1889 (fiscal 1890 in the case of railroads) also rest on single counts: this too was a period of active business, and it may be that the adjustment necessary to convert the figures shown to a man-year basis would be small.
[b] Class I, II, and III line haul roads.
[c] 1889, electric railways, Census. 1920, electric railways, American Transit Association; local busline employment estimated at 7,000 on basis of number of buses. 1929, 1939 and 1946, full-time equivalent employees, National Income Table 24 (*Survey of Current Business*, July 1947, Supplement, and July 1948).
[d] 1920, based on number of buses. 1929 and 1939, full-time equivalent employees, unpublished tabulation by National Income Division of U. S. Bureau of Foreign and Domestic Commerce. 1946 extrapolation based on number of buses (see *Bus Facts*, annual publication of National Association of Motor Bus Operators).
[e] 1920, see Appendix F. 1929, 1939 and 1946, full-time equivalent employees, National Income Table 24.
[f] 1920, based on figure for 1921 in ICC Statement 4280 'Statistics of Oil Pipe Lines, 1921-1941' (Oct. 1942). 1929, 1939 and 1946, full-time equivalent employees, National Income Table 24.
[g] Vessel employees only. See Appendix Table H-7.
[h] See Appendix Table I-1.

viewpoints. First, how much confidence do we have that the result
is genuine, and not due to some optical illusion or statistical quirk?
To a minor extent the expansion of output reflects a shift of
passenger traffic from agencies with low to agencies with high
revenue per passenger or per passenger-mile, and of freight traffic
from agencies with low to agencies with high revenue per ton-
mile. Yet this factor is quite unimportant, for if the effects of such
shifts of traffic between agencies are eliminated,[2] 1939 output on
an 1889 base becomes 530 instead of 540 as reported in Table 12.

Table 12

ALL TRANSPORTATION: OUTPUT, EMPLOYMENT, AND
PRODUCTIVITY, 1889-1946
1889 : 100

	1889	1920	1929	1939	1946
Output (Table 5)	100	560	600	540	1,040
Number of workers (Table 11)	100	290	260	180	260
Output per worker	100	190	230	300	400

Again, our use of the 1889 Census of Waterways may have understated local traffic on rivers and canals, but in that case a corresponding undercount of employees would apparently prevent any
bias from this cause in the productivity index. Finally, it is true
that employment figures for intercity buslines and intercity trucking are very uncertain. To be on the safe side, let us double them.
For 1939 this would raise the employment index in Table 12 to
around 230 and cut output per worker from 290 to 240. Even so,
the average annual increase in output per worker (Table 13) for
transportation would be reduced only from 2.2 to 1.8 percent, the
figure for manufacturing. To balance the hypothetical upward
bias just mentioned, a definite downward bias must be pointed
out. The output of local transportation (streetcars and buslines)
is perforce measured by number of passengers. But as cities have
grown and urban transportation networks have been expanded

[2] To eliminate the influence of such shifts, passengers (for electric railways
and city buslines), passenger-miles (elsewhere), and freight ton-miles were
respectively summed over all agencies. The three totals were then weighted by
aggregate passenger revenue in 1939 on electric railways and city buslines,
passenger revenue elsewhere, and freight revenue, respectively.

the average journey has undoubtedly lengthened. Could we report the output of buses and streetcars on a passenger-mile basis, our output and productivity indexes for transportation as a whole would rise more rapidly than they do.

So much for possibilities of error in the measurement of output. Yet suppose that output, although correctly measured, has shifted from low to high productivity agencies? 'High productivity' in this context denotes a high value of product per worker, product being valued in some constant set of prices. It need not denote

Table 13

AVERAGE ANNUAL RATES OF CHANGE IN OUTPUT PER
WORKER IN TRANSPORTATION AND OTHER INDUSTRIES

	Period Covered	Average Annual % Increase
Transportation[a]	1889-1939	2.2
Manufacturing[b]	1899-1939	1.8
Mining, including oil and gas wells[c]	1902-1939	2.8
Mining, excluding oil and gas wells[c]	1902-1939	1.6
Agriculture[d]	1890-1940	1.6

[a] See Table 12. Based on a comparison of 1939 with 1889.
[b] Fabricant, *Employment in Manufacturing*, p. 10.
[c] Barger and Schurr, *The Mining Industries*, Table 11.
[d] Barger and Landsberg, *American Agriculture*, Table 39.

greater efficiency of individuals working under comparable conditions. It may reflect more capital per worker in one industry than in another, or a larger consumption of materials, or a stronger bargaining position in marketing the transportation service produced.

To what extent can shifts of this sort be held responsible for the relatively rapid rise reported for output per worker in transportation as a whole? To test this question, per worker product, measured in 1939 prices, was computed for the five divisions of transportation shown in Table 14.

We may notice, first, that the two industries with higher-than-average productivity (in the above sense) appear to be waterways and pipelines. Although the growth in pipeline traffic has been rapid, the percentage share in total traffic neither of pipelines nor of waterways increased sufficiently to offer a ready explanation of the relatively high annual increment in the productivity of total transportation. In fact highways, toward which notoriously the largest diversion of traffic from older agencies occurred, has actually had a lower-than-average product per worker.

Table 14

PRODUCT (IN 1939 PRICES) PER WORKER IN THE
TRANSPORTATION INDUSTRIES[a]
Thousand dollars

	1889	1920	1929	1939	1946
Steam railroads	1.3	2.4	3.0	3.7	5.1
Highways[b]	2.0	2.6	2.3	3.8	4.9
Pipelines	....	1.9	5.4	8.5	11.7
Waterways	1.3	5.1	7.0	7.2	10.0
Airlines	....	....	1.0	3.9	5.5
MEAN	1.4	2.6	3.0	4.0	5.4

[a] Computed from Tables 3, 4, 5, 8, 11, and 37.
[b] Electric railways, city and intercity buslines, and for-hire intercity trucking.

The matter may be further tested as follows. If we take the per worker product, measured in 1939 prices, for steam railroads, highways and waterways, weighted by the number of workers in each industry in 1889, we find that the average change in output per worker between 1889 and 1939 is the same as that reported for all transportation in Table 12, i.e., a rise from 100 to 300, or about 2.2 percent yearly. In other words, shifts in the relative share of traffic, including the advent of high-productivity pipelines and low-productivity airlines, approximately offset each other, so far as concerns the level of output per worker in transportation as a whole. On the other hand, if the same calculation is performed, using per worker product in 1939 prices, and also 1939 (instead of 1889) employment to weight the quotients, the average change in productivity for railroads, highways, and waterways works out (on an 1889 base) at 260 for 1939 (instead of 300).[3] The lower figure is due to the heavier weight given to

[3] Further calculations, for instance valuing product in 1889 prices, cannot be made for lack of data.

highways whose per worker product rose less rapidly than that of railroads or waterways. On this showing productivity would still have risen — in the absence of shifts in relative shares of traffic — more than 1.9 percent per annum.

A critique of the statistical basis for the estimate of 2.2 percent per annum as the average rate of growth of productivity in transportation is therefore reassuring. This high rate of growth can scarcely be due to faulty estimates of output or employment. Nor can it be explained to an appreciable degree, either by shifts from low- to high-value forms of output, or by shifts from low- to high-productivity industries. To an unknown but probably not very large degree it may reflect the reduction in railroad employment consequent upon the cessation of new construction, and possibly undermaintenance of existing railroad equipment (see Chapter 4). We may conclude that most of the reported rise in productivity reflects a real increase — real in the sense that it does not depend upon the weighting system used to combine the outputs of different agencies.

In contrast to output, to judge from the few observations recorded in Table 12, output per worker grew without retardation during our period. Average annual growth rates were 2.1 percent during 1889-1920 and 1920-29, 2.7 percent during 1929-39, and 4.2 percent during 1939-46. Unusually intensive utilization of equipment raised productivity in 1946.

The relatively more rapid rise of output per worker in transportation than elsewhere offers a partial explanation of its declining share of national income and employment, reported in Chapter 1. In part, at least since 1920, transportation output seems to have lagged — especially through diversion to the automobile and the private truck. Yet advances in productivity, more rapid than in other sectors of the economy, probably helped to cut transportation's percentage shares of the labor force and of national income.

INDIVIDUAL INDUSTRIES

It would be pleasant to offer indexes of output per employee, not only for the five groups shown in Table 14, but also for different

Chart 9
OUTPUT PER WORKER

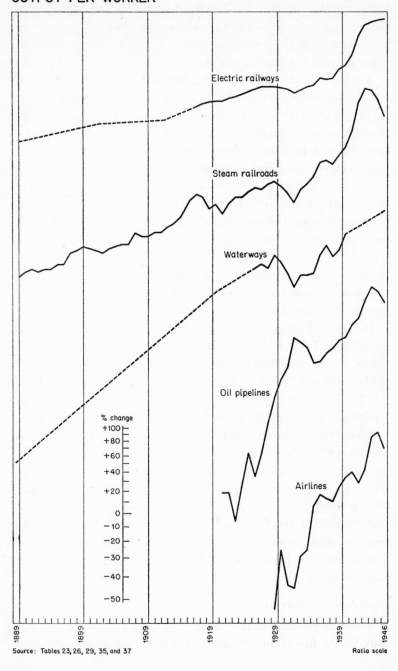

Electric railways

Steam railroads

Waterways

Oil pipelines

Airlines

% change
+100
+80
+60
+40
+20
0
−10
−20
−30
−40
−50

1889 1899 1909 1919 1929 1939 1946

Source: Tables 23, 26, 29, 35, and 37   Ratio scale

types of highway transportation and different kinds of waterway. Unfortunately the data do not allow any more detailed analysis than that sketched. For instance, employment figures for buslines and trucking have been inserted in Table 11 to complete the totals, but they do not inspire sufficient confidence to enable us to offer separate productivity indexes for those industries. Obviously the discussion of trends in employment and productivity must be confined to the few industries for which adequate data exist. Accordingly Part Two deals only with steam railroads, electric railways, pipelines, waterways and — for a few recent years — airlines. In addition, some aspects of the motor trucking industry (for which productivity trends can only be guessed at) are treated in Appendix F.

Trends in output per worker for the five industries for which the ratio can be computed are brought together in Chart 9. Electric railways had the slowest growth of productivity. Young at the opening of our period, at its close the industry had passed its peak and all but disappeared. Somewhat larger gains in output per worker were recorded by steam railroads and waterways, old industries still vigorous. The sharpest rises in productivity were reserved for the two still youthful forms of carriage — oil pipelines and airlines. If we discard electric railways as anomalous in behavior, these results roughly confirm Fabricant's observation for manufacturing, i.e., that the sharpest gains in output per worker tend to be recorded by the most youthful, or at least the fastest growing, industries.[4] The individual trends will be discussed and interpreted in the chapters that follow.

[4] *Employment in Manufacturing,* Chapter 4.

Part Two

Individual Transportation Industries

Chapter 4

Steam Railroads

Despite some use of electric traction and the recent adoption of
Diesel power on a fairly large scale, all rail carriers — except only
wholly electrified local systems — are still officially described as
'steam railroads'. This usage will be followed here.

Steam railroads move more than half the passenger and nearly
two-thirds of the freight traffic carried by intercity transportation
agencies. Of two million transportation workers within the United
States and on ocean-borne American-flag vessels, about half are
employed by our railroads.

Relatively speaking the railroads are old, for among forms of
carriage considered in this book only waterways have a longer
history. Moreover, railroads are distinguished from all other transportation agencies in that they constitute, from the physical and
traffic standpoints, a unified system. Although operated by several
hundred distinct companies, they have long enjoyed standard
track and loading gauges, interchangeable locomotives and cars,
and uniform couplers and air brakes. From the traffic viewpoint,
joint rates and through routes allow passenger travel and freight
shipments from one end of the country to the other.

Our definition of the steam railway industry includes the line-
haul roads, the switching and terminal companies, the Pullman
Company, and the Railway Express Agency or its predecessor
companies.[1] Since 1911 the ICC has classified line-haul companies on the basis of operating revenues, those of class I having
annual revenues above $1,000,000, class II above $100,000 but

[1] Excluded activities which might possibly be considered part of the industry
are buslines owned by railroads and freight-forwarding concerns. The former
are here considered part of the bus industry; data on the latter are scanty.

below $1,000,000, and class III below $100,000.[2] Line-haul
carriers provide most of the switching and terminal services
required by their operations; the remainder is furnished by specialized switching and terminal companies.[3] The functions of the
Pullman Company and the Railway Express Agency are familiar.
In 1939 line-haul companies constituted more than nine-tenths
of the entire steam railroad industry (Table 15).

Table 15

STEAM RAILROADS: VALUE OF PRODUCT AND
NUMBER OF EMPLOYEES, 1939[a]

	Operating Revenue in 1939 (mil. $)	Percentage of Total	Employees in 1939 (th.)	Percentage of Total
All line haul companies	4,050	93.9	1,007	90.5
Class I	3,995	92.6	988	88.8
Class II	47	1.1	15	1.4
Class III	8	0.2	4	0.3
Switching & terminal companies	90	2.1	42	3.8
Class I	61	1.4	30	2.7
Class II and III	29	0.7	12	1.1
Pullman Company	61	1.4	21	1.9
Railway Express Agency	112	2.6	42	3.8
TOTAL, ALL COMPANIES	4,313	100.0	1,112	100.0

[a] Interstate Commerce Commission, *Statistics of Railways in the United States, 1939.*

THE CONCEPT OF PHYSICAL OUTPUT

The output of any industry, with minor exceptions, is sold on the
market. By appealing to the judgment of the market place we can
combine the outputs of different commodities (or units of trans-

[2] The relative importance of class I line-haul carriers has slightly expanded
since 1911, in which year they contributed 96.5 percent of the operating
revenues of all line-haul companies; corresponding percentages were 98.6 for
1939 and 98.8 for 1946. Any index of output based on class I statistics, as ours
must be in some years of the period, therefore requires a small adjustment to
eliminate a slight upward bias.
[3] Switching and terminal companies may also operate bridges and ferries and
transport regular freight and passenger traffic, although such activity on their
part is small.

portation service, as in the present instance) in a reasonably unambiguous fashion. We add apples and oranges by summing their values in constant prices; that is, by valuing physical quantities in terms of a system of prices derived from the market place. The prices chosen are constant in the sense that their time reference is the same, not only for all commodities in the summation, but for output at all dates for which any given comparison is made. The time reference in question is called the 'weight base', and may be a single year or group of years. In this study within the railroad industry we have used the Edgeworth formula, which rests on the average price of the commodity (e.g., average revenue per passenger-mile) for each pair of years considered. In combining the outputs of the various transportation industries we have used 1939 weights.

So long as we are willing to accept its judgments, the phenomena of the market place also afford criteria for testing the adequacy of any unit, or system of units, we may select for measuring the output of a single commodity.[4] It is convenient to regard amounts of output, produced simultaneously, as equivalent to each other when the value the market sets upon them is the same. A simple extension of this notion leads to the requirement that the physical unit we choose, in measuring output from one period to another, shall satisfy the following condition: namely, that quantities of output measured in terms of this unit shall, at any given moment, be proportional to the money values assigned to them by the market. The use of this criterion of course leads to results that are a function of the institutional character of the market itself. For instance, where the price of output is administered, or where monopoly conditions prevail, the result may be quite different from that under conditions of perfect competition. We have no certain knowledge as to how price and output would behave if the character of the market were different

---

[4] If no conceivable system of units will satisfy the test to be proposed, we are bound to regard the output in question not as a single commodity but as a group of distinct commodities. If the classification is sufficiently fine, we can presumably always find units that meet the test: in that case the problem is reduced to one of the availability of statistical detail and of the patience of the computer.

from what it is: consequently the criterion just outlined appears to furnish the sole objective basis available for distinguishing between different possible physical units of measurement.

The strict application of this principle would force us to take full account of product differentiation wherever the latter gives rise to price differentials. Not only variations in quality, but quantity discounts, and varying conditions of service or delivery, would force us to classify as separate commodities portions of output that are otherwise similar. However, in the case of most concrete goods it is not hard to find an attribute, such as weight or volume, for which the condition indicated — a proportional relationship between quantity and value — is approximately fulfilled. In considering the output of services, it is often much more difficult to find a satisfactory unit. The product is intangible; and peculiarities of pricing may cast doubt upon procedures that in other industries would appear acceptable. In particular, transportation services are sold in a market that, although somewhat more competitive than it once was, is still highly monopolistic at some points, and in which prices are frequently settled by *fiat*. The use of such prices for weighting an index of transportation output, as in this book, perhaps needs explicit justification. The points at issue are discussed at greater length in Appendix A.

The units of passenger and freight output adopted here are the passenger-mile and ton-mile respectively. In the case of passenger traffic we are comparatively fortunate. For years since 1922 the available statistics allow us to divide the sum total of passenger-miles among (1) parlor and sleeping car, (2) coach (noncommutation), and (3) commutation traffic. For any given year revenues per passenger-mile differ sharply between these three classes, but within each are practically constant and do not depend on length of journey.[5] Accordingly, we have constructed our index of output for passenger transportation by combining the three passenger-mile series mentioned, using revenues per passenger-mile as weights.

[5] However, since 1932 coach passengers have paid lower rates in the south than elsewhere, and reductions for round-trip tickets have been instituted in many parts of the country. Some traffic also moves at tourist or excursion rates.

In the case of freight traffic the situation is much less favorable. Except for the isolated year 1932, we have no breakdown of ton-miles, by revenue per ton-mile or by commodity. The statistics treat a ton of fresh vegetables shipped a hundred miles as the equivalent of a ton of coal shipped a like distance. Yet we know that fresh vegetables earn a higher revenue per ton-mile than coal. Equally the summation of ton-miles gives to a single ton carried a hundred miles the same significance as a hundred tons carried one mile, although revenue per ton-mile is commonly lower for long than for short hauls. Evidently two quanta of transportation, each comprising one hundred ton-miles, may sell for widely differing prices. No definite, least of all any proportional, relationship exists between the amount of output and its value. This difficulty could be overcome only through the use of ton-mile figures classified simultaneously by commodity and by length of haul, but no such statistics exist.[6]

This deficiency in the ton-mile suggested the possible use of the ton originated (i.e., shipped) as an alternative unit for measuring freight traffic. Unlike ton-miles, tons originated (and revenue per ton originated) are available by individual commodities. In using these data, therefore, it would be possible to take account of *differences* in rate per ton-mile and length of haul *between commodities*. On the other hand, an index based on tonnage originated can pay no attention to *changes* in the length of haul — a substantial factor. For this reason we rejected tons originated as a basic measure of freight output. We preferred to base our measures on a summation of (unweighted) ton-miles, making subsidiary calculations to suggest the bias introduced by the lack of an appropriate weighting system.[7] In these calculations it is shown, for example, that — on plausible assumptions — our (unweighted) ton-mile index understates by some 5 to 10 percent the decline in freight traffic between 1919 and 1939 that would

[6] The error introduced into our index of freight traffic by our failure to discriminate *between* groups of commodities can be estimated, granted certain assumptions; see Appendix C.

[7] Still another alternative might possibly be deflation of freight revenue by an index of freight rates; however the worth of the result would be difficult to appraise.

be reported by an appropriately weighted index, i.e. the un-weighted index has an upward bias during the years indicated.[8]

We turn now to the actual indexes, first for passenger traffic, then for freight traffic, and finally for railroad transportation as a whole.

PASSENGER TRAFFIC

Railway passenger traffic falls into three well defined categories: (1) commutation, (2) other coach, and (3) parlor and sleeping car service. Commutation traffic is the smallest of the three, con-tributing less than 18 percent of passenger-mileage and only 9 percent of passenger revenue in 1939. Coach travel is quanti-tatively the largest, making up about one-half of total passenger-miles in 1939; its revenue contribution, however, was somewhat less than that of parlor and sleeping car service, which accounted for nearly half of the revenue total but only one-third of total passenger-miles (Table 16).

Table 16

STEAM RAILROADS: PASSENGER TRAFFIC, 1939[a]

	Passengers (mil.)	Passenger-miles (bil.)	Revenue ($ mil.)	Revenue per Passenger-mile (cents)
Commutation	231	4.01	41	1.02
Coach (other than commutation)	200	11.12	200	1.80
Parlor and sleeping car	20	7.53	224	2.98
TOTAL	451	22.66	465	2.05

[a] *Statistics of Railways;* see also Appendix Table B-3. Figures relate to class I roads only. Parlor and sleeping car revenue includes Pullman charges.

The index of passenger traffic (Table 17 and Chart 10) is con-structed in three segments. For years after 1922 it employs the tri-partite division just noted. For 1911-22 it is based on a simple division between coach (including commutation) traffic on the

[8] The choice between ton-miles and tons originated as a basis for the measure-ment of freight traffic is explored more fully in Appendix C, where the calcu-lations mentioned are given in detail.

one hand, and parlor and sleeping car traffic on the other. Prior
to 1911 the index represents unweighted passenger-miles. The
difference in movement between weighted and unweighted
indexes, for the period for which both can be computed, is slight.

Trends in Passenger Traffic

Rail passenger traffic reached peak levels in 1919 and 1920 —
levels which were not surpassed until World War II (Chart 10).
The movement over the five decades 1889-1939 suggests a rather
clear case of retardation in growth. Indeed an upward trend prior
to World War I seems to have given place to a downward trend
during the interwar period. The significance of the change in trend
which occurred about 1920 is clear enough. During World War I
automobile production first attained a really large scale.[9] Not
until the war was over did the full impact of the private automobile and the unfolding public highway network make itself
felt.[10] Once wartime shortages were safely in the past, and the
brief but sharp business collapse of 1920-21 had been surmounted,
the private passenger automobile quickly became the chief competitor of rail passenger service. Nor must we overlook the motorbus and the airplane. Buslines, which had hastened the decline of
electric railways, came in the 1920's to compete with rail coach
traffic, as their range of operations widened. Finally, commercial
airlines, whose seeds were to be found in the expansion of aviation
during World War I, emerged in the 1930's as a competitor of
rail parlor and sleeping car traffic. Some of these rival transport
agencies will be considered in later chapters.

Against this background, the vast expansion of passenger traffic
during World War II may be viewed as a partial and temporary
return to an earlier output trend — the trend which had prevailed
before World War I. During 1942-46 private automobile travel
was severely restricted by rubber and gasoline shortages; and the
expansion of intercity buses and commercial airlines was checked.
As a result, the smaller railroad mileage of 1944 carried far more

[9] Almost 2 million cars and trucks were produced in 1917, about ten times as
many as in 1910.
[10] See Joseph L. White, *Transportation and Defense* (University of Pennsylvania Press, 1941), p. 21.

Table 17

STEAM RAILROADS: INDEXES OF PASSENGER,
FREIGHT, AND TOTAL TRAFFIC, 1890-1946[a]
1939 : 100

Year Ending June 30	Passenger	Freight	Total	Calendar Year	Passenger	Freight	Total
1890	50.4	22.7	27.1	1920	207	123.4	136.7
1891	54.9	24.5	29.3	1921	164.2	92.3	103.9
1892	56.5	26.5	31.3	1922	157.9	102.0	110.8
1893	59.9	28.1	33.2	1923	169.9	124.1	131.0
1894	60.1	24.2	29.8	1924	161.4	116.9	123.6
1895	51.8	25.9	30.1	1925	161.3	124.5	129.9
1896	55.3	29.0	33.3	1926	159.6	133.4	136.9
1897	52.0	28.8	32.6	1927	150.7	128.8	131.5
1898	56.6	34.6	38.3	1928	141.3	130.0	131.2
1899	61.6	37.5	41.6	1929	138.2	134.2	133.7
1900	67.6	42.8	47.0	1930	117.8	115.0	114.6
1901	73.0	44.3	49.2	1931	94.3	92.8	92.5
1902	82.8	47.4	53.3	1932	71.1	70.2	70.0
1903	88.0	52.1	58.2	1933	69.2	74.7	73.6
1904	92.7	52.6	59.3	1934	77.8	80.6	79.8
1905	100.8	56.3	63.7	1935	80.3	84.6	83.7
1906	106.6	65.2	72.2	1936	98.2	101.7	100.9
1907	117.3	71.4	79.2	1937	108.7	108.2	108.1
1908	122.6	65.3	74.8	1938	95.5	87.0	88.1
1909	122.5	65.4	74.8	1939	100.0	100.0	100.0
1910	136.0	76.1	86.1	1940	103.6	111.9	111.0
1911	139.6	75.7	86.3	1941	129.5	142.4	140.5
1912	139.8	78.7	88.9	1942	243	191.1	195.4
1913	146.2	90.0	99.0	1943	390	218	236
1914	149.2	86.1	96.1	1944	425	221	244
1915	138.1	82.6	91.3	1945	409	204	229
1916	146.6	102.4	109.1	1946	288	177.4	192.9

Calendar Year			
1916	151.1	109.2	115.4
1917	172.7	118.8	127.2
1918	184.4	121.9	131.0
1919	204	109.5	124.1

[a] Based on data in Appendix B. The freight index represents unweighted ton-miles on class I, II and III roads. For 1890-1911 the passenger index represents unweighted passenger-miles on class I, II and III roads. For 1911-46 the passenger index shows weighted passenger-miles on class I roads and the Pullman Company. Wherever two or more series are combined, the Edgeworth method was used (i.e., weights are average unit revenues for each pair of years compared). For any segment, the terminal years were compared, and the results of year-to-year comparisons were adjusted to the terminal year comparison by distributing of the small discrepancy. In constructing the passenger index 1911-22, 1922-29 and 1929-39 were treated as such segments. (Thus the

comparison between 1922 and 1931 involves three Edgeworth comparisons: 1922-29, 1929-30 and 1930-31, the two latter including the small adjustment mentioned.) The passenger index prior to 1911 and the freight index throughout are simple aggregates. The passenger and freight indexes were combined using segments: 1890-99, 1899-1909, 1909-19, 1919-29, 1929-39. Comparisons for years after 1939 use 1939 unit revenues as weights (Laspeyres' index). In order to include uniformly all line haul, and switching and terminal companies, the Pullman Company and the express companies, the index was multiplied by an index of coverage (which varied only slightly from 100 percent) based on the ratio of operating revenues of all companies to revenues of companies included in the index before adjustment for coverage.

————

traffic than moved in 1920. Indeed growth of railroad passenger traffic between 1920 and 1944 (omitting the intervening years) was almost as rapid as it had been before 1920 (Chart 10). The practical cessation of growth after 1920 in peacetime passenger traffic must evidently be attributed mainly to the rise of newer modes of travel.

No breakdown of passenger traffic is available for the first decade of the century, but it is likely that all classes of traffic shared in the general expansion. At the turn of the century fears had indeed been expressed that the rapid rise of the electric railway might retard the future expansion of the passenger traffic of steam railroads; the difficulties of the rail passenger service in the previous decade when, especially in the 1893-97 depression, passenger-mileage declined sharply, had been attributed to this factor.[11] However, with the purchase of new equipment and the electrification of suburban trackage, the railroads successfully met what proved to be but the first of several new competitive threats. Commutation traffic was first reported separately from other coach traffic in 1922, when it amounted to 6 billion — or about one-sixth of total — passenger-miles (Chart 11). It rose moderately throughout the 'twenties to nearly 7 billion passenger-miles in 1929; meanwhile other coach traffic was already declining rather sharply.

Coach travel (other than commutation) fell nearly 7 billion

[11] See *Statistics of Railways*, 1897, p. 61, and 1898, p. 68. On the effects of electric railway competition, see also Thomas Conway, Jr., 'Traffic Problems of Interurban Electric Railroads', *Journal of Accountancy*, Oct. 1908, pp. 427-8; and Edward S. Mason, *The Street Railway in Massachusetts* (Harvard University Press, 1932), pp. 63-4.

Chart 10
STEAM RAILROADS:
PASSENGER, FREIGHT, AND COMBINED TRAFFIC

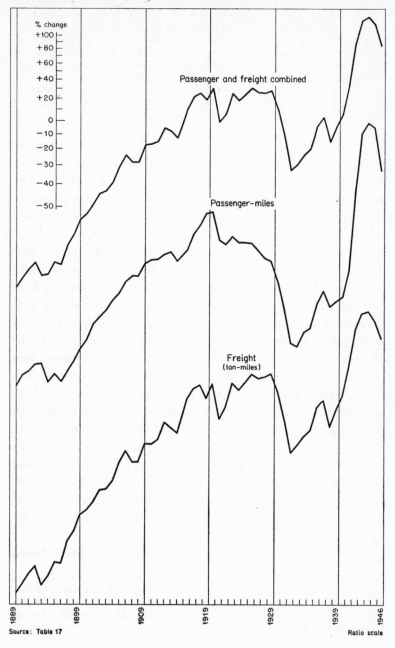

% change

Passenger and freight combined

Passenger-miles

Freight
(ton-miles)

Source: Table 17

Ratio scale

passenger-miles between 1922 and 1929, and measured about the same in 1939 as in 1929. It is plain that the private automobile, furnishing several hundred billion passenger-miles of travel annually, has mainly called forth 'new business' which never could have moved by rail. Doubtless a substantial part of intercity bus travel (10 billion passenger-miles in 1939) consists of coach traffic lost by the railroads, but it too must have reached layers of demand not tapped by rail transportation. If the newer agencies have

Chart 11
STEAM RAILROADS: PASSENGER TRAFFIC

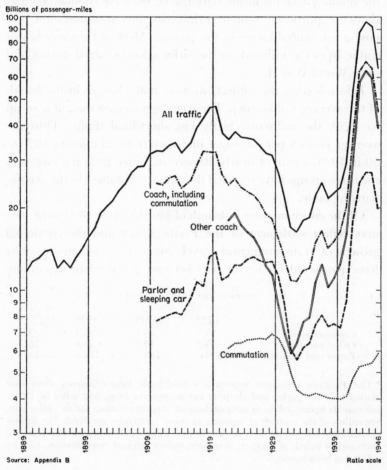

Billions of passenger-miles

All traffic

Coach, including commutation

Other coach

Parlor and sleeping car

Commutation

Source: Appendix B   Ratio scale

predominantly encouraged travel which the railroads could not or would not develop, it seems certain that the cessation of growth in railroad coach travel must be attributed to the automobile and intercity busline.

Small amounts of Pullman traffic, which quantitatively had begun to outrank coach by 1929, were lost to the commercial airlines during the 1930's. Yet in 1939 airlines still accounted for well under a billion passenger-miles, although rail Pullman service had apparently lost six or seven times that amount of traffic during the decade. Obviously the privately owned passenger car had become the dominant factor in intercity travel, both for commercial and domestic purposes; moreover intercity bus transportation was now a substantial factor in the picture. Most of the diversion of traffic from the railroads to the airlines has occurred during and since World War II.

Before leaving the subject, we may note changes in the length of the average rail journey. These changes suggest that, at least up to 1939, the railroads chiefly lost short-haul traffic. Thus the average journey per passenger increased from 28 miles in 1899 to 50 in 1939, a gain of nearly 80 percent. Since 1922 passengers in the three groups have traveled the average distances in the accompanying table.

Of the entire increase in length of journey since 1899 some part may reflect settlement of the Pacific Coast and the continued growth of transcontinental travel. Since 1922 commuters may have journeyed further in part because of suburban expansion.

AVERAGE JOURNEY* (miles)

	1922	1929	1939	% gain 1922-39
Commutation	14.3	15.1	17.4	22
Other coach	35.7	40.2	55.6	56
Parlor and sleeping car	259	288	379	45

---

* The Pullman Company reports a considerably longer journey than that shown here for parlor and sleeping car passengers (e.g., 542 miles in 1939) because its figures relate to the purchase of accommodations for an entire trip, regardless of the number of separate railroad companies involved. The figures quoted here refer to the average journey over any single railroad. The reported increases in length of journey, therefore, reflect railroad consolidation, but the effect has been minor.

Yet it seems plain that the growth of the average length of the rail journey mainly reflects greater diversion to other agencies of short than of long distance traffic.

To summarize: railroad passenger traffic reached a peak in 1919-20, a peak surpassed only by the rush of business during World War II. During the 1920's regular-fare coach traffic declined rapidly but commutation and parlor and sleeping car traffic remained remarkably stable. Although all forms of traffic fell off during the depression, coach traffic suffered no further net decline during the 1930's. But commutation traffic did not recover from depression levels, and parlor and sleeping car traffic also stood lower in 1939 than in 1929. Because of loss of short haul traffic, and for other reasons, the average journey steadily lengthened.

FREIGHT TRAFFIC

The ideal measure of freight traffic would involve a summation of shipments (i.e., tons originated), each shipment being weighted by the revenue it earned during some base period. That is, all shipments of commodity A between points X and Y (or, less accurately, all shipments of commodity A with a specified length of haul) — but no larger aggregate — should be treated as homogeneous. The resulting total (whether of tons or ton-miles is unimportant) would then be weighted by its average revenue in the base period. This is a counsel of perfection. Shipments are not classified by length of haul; and — except for the isolated (and atypical) year 1932 — no division of the ton-mile aggregate by commodities is available. Yet if we wish to allow for changes in length of haul — and there is ample evidence that hauls are longer than they used to be — then we must use the ton-mile as our unit, despite the fact that we have no means of segregating high revenue from low revenue ton-miles. Accordingly, our basic index for railroad freight traffic is a simple (unweighted) ton-mile aggregate. (Tables 17 and 18 and Chart 12.) Unlike passenger traffic, which reached a peak in 1919-20 and then declined, freight traffic continued to grow, reaching its pre-1940 peak in 1929. Between 1889 and 1929 ton-miles rose not quite sixfold, declined some

Table 18

STEAM RAILROADS: INDEXES OF FREIGHT TRAFFIC, 1890-1940
1929 : 100

Year Ending June 30	Basic Index Ton-miles, unweighted[a]	Alternative Indexes	
		Tons originated, unweighted[b]	Tons originated, weighted[c]
1890	16.9	....	....
1891	18.0	....	....
1892	19.6	....	....
1893	20.8	....	....
1894	17.8	....	....
1895	18.9	....	....
1896	21.2	....	....
1897	21.1	....	....
1898	25.3	....	....
1899	27.5	35.3	37.8
1900	31.4	41.1	43.0
1901	32.7	41.1	43.4
1902	34.9	46.3	48.4
1903	38.5	50.4	53.5
1904	38.8	50.3	53.4
1905	41.4	55.3	57.1
1906	47.9	63.1	64.9
1907	52.5	68.9	70.3
1908	48.5	61.3	61.6
1909	48.6	62.1	62.6
1910	56.6	72.3	71.3
1911	56.4	70.7	71.9
1912	58.7	72.7	73.9
1913	67.0	83.3	84.1
1914	64.1	79.6	80.2
1915	61.6	72.1	76.5
1916	76.3	89.0	91.2

Calendar Year

1916	81.3	92.8	95.0
1917	88.5	97.4	97.7
1918	90.8	97.0	97.8
1919	81.6	83.8	89.0
1920	91.9	96.0	97.1
1921	68.8	71.7	75.3
1922	76.0	78.3	83.0
1923	92.5	97.8	97.5
1924	87.1	90.7	92.5
1925	92.7	95.2	96.2
1926	99.4	101.4	100.2
1927	96.0	96.7	96.2
1928	96.9	96.6	97.4
1929	100.0	100.0	100.0

Calendar Year	Basic Index Ton-miles, unweighted[a]	Alternative Indexes	
		Tons originated, unweighted[b]	Tons originated, weighted[c]
1930	85.7	86.0	85.2
1931	69.1	66.6	68.2
1932	52.3	47.8	50.6
1933	55.7	51.7	53.2
1934	60.0	56.5	57.9
1935	63.0	58.6	59.9
1936	75.8	71.3	70.9
1937	80.6	75.8	74.9
1938	64.8	57.8	60.0
1939	74.5	67.3	67.5
1940	83.4	75.3	73.4

[a] Data from *Statistics of Railways;* see Appendix Table B-1. Index covers class I, II, and III line-haul companies for 1907-39; and the same, together with switching and terminal companies, for 1890-1907. This index is the same as that shown in Table 17, except that data have not been adjusted for coverage prior to 1911.

[b] Data from *Statistics of Railways;* not available prior to 1899. Index covers class I, II, and III line-haul companies; for 1899-1907, some small amounts of tonnage originating on switching and terminal companies may be included, but no adjustment was possible on this account.

[c] Data from *Statistics of Railways;* not available prior to 1899. Index is based on commodity breakdown for class I traffic, as follows; 6 classes, 1899-1924; 66 classes, 1924-28; 157 classes, 1928-40. Comparisons used revenues per originating ton as follows: 1899-1928, 1928; 1928-29, average 1928 and 1929; 1929-40, average 1929 and 1937. Revenue data were used to adjust the index to include traffic on class II and III roads, the assumption being that the ratio of revenue per ton on class I to revenue per ton on class II and III roads did not alter.

25 percent on balance between 1929 and 1939, then more than doubled during World War II.

Trends in Freight Traffic

Although for the reason indicated the ton-mile aggregate will be treated as basic, indexes derived from tons originated are also shown (Table 18). The latter appear to be biased downward, since they do not take account of the lengthening average haul. Thus over the period 1899-1939 the average annual increase is only 1.6 percent for tons originated but 2.3 percent for ton-miles. In discussing the changing composition of railroad freight traffic, we shall have to use originating tonnage series and bear this bias in mind.

It is obvious that freight traffic, like passenger traffic, has been subject to marked retardation of growth, at least over the period 1889-1939 (Chart 10).

The substantial advance of railroad ton-mileage in the first two decades of the century accompanied the expansion of the national market. The railroad network, now approaching completion, served to connect manufacturing centers with the source of raw materials, and urban consumers with areas of food supply. The pre-World War I era was generally characterized by a business optimism engendered by a steadily rising commodity price level, increasing industrial and agricultural production, and the opening of new markets at home and abroad. In this era, the railroads enjoyed an unchallenged position in the country's transportation system. Preceding decades had seen the virtual supersession of rivers and canals by the railroad, while mechanical highway transportation was still in its infancy.

Already evidence of the railroad industry's maturity was to be found in the falling off in the construction of new lines. Total rail mileage under operation (excluding switching and terminal companies) stood at 188,000 in 1899 and rose at an average annual rate of 2 percent to a peak in 1916; thereafter it maintained itself at a level of 260,000 until 1930, when an average annual decline of one-half percent set in. During the period after 1916, the small construction of new lines balanced the abandonment of unprofitable lines. The construction of additional trackage and sidings continued throughout the 'twenties, although this too declined after 1930. Railroad investment in the period under review tended more and more toward amplification rather than extension of the existing network.

Yet during World War II the railroads carried more freight traffic than ever before. As in the case of passenger traffic, though in lesser degree, we may regard the wartime peak in freight traffic as a partial and temporary return to a previous trend. The practical cessation of growth of freight traffic after 1920 (the peak did not actually come till 1929) is not due to any single factor: the growth of motor trucking and pipelines played a part; so did the bulk transportation by water of such products as petroleum.

During World War II trucking and coastwise shipping were sharply inhibited. As a result freight traffic in 1944 approached, but did not reach, the level it would have done, had the rate of growth before 1920 continued thereafter.

Chart 12
RAILROAD FREIGHT TRAFFIC:
TONS ORIGINATED AND TON-MILES

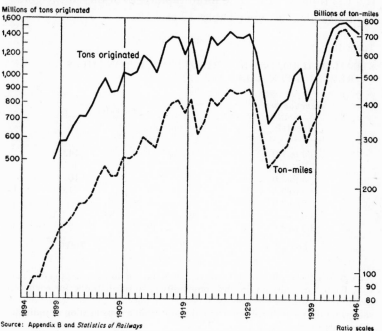

Source: Appendix B and *Statistics of Railways*   Ratio scales

The preceding remarks are based upon the movement of the (unweighted) ton-mileage aggregate which, as already explained, is our basic measure. Data for the computation of a weighted ton-mile index do not exist. Yet we still can inquire how our unweighted index would be modified, were we able to weight each ton-mile by its revenue in constant prices.

The Federal Coordinator of Transportation arranged for a classification by commodities of the entire carload ton-mileage total for 1932. A summary of this breakdown (Table 19) shows considerable dispersion among mean revenues per ton-mile for different commodities.[12] The existence of this dispersion makes for the possibility that a weighted ton-mile index would show a different result from that indicated by the unweighted index. In fact, the railroads have lost to competitors especially less-than-carload and other freight customarily moving at a rather high rate per ton-mile. Such reasoning suggests that a weighted index would rise less rapidly, or decline more rapidly, than the (unweighted) ton-mile index shown in Tables 17 and 18.

Table 19

STEAM RAILROADS: DISTRIBUTION OF TON-MILES
BY REVENUE PER TON-MILE, 1932[a]

Revenue per Ton-mile (cents)	Ton-miles	
	(million)	%
0.5 to 1.0	108,977	44.9
1.0 to 1.5	84,713	37.2
1.5 to 2.0	23,468	10.3
2.0 to 2.5	3,129	1.4
2.5 to 3.0	52	c
3.0 to 3.5	0	0
3.5 to 4.0	7,239[b]	3.2
TOTAL	227,578	100.0

[a] See Appendix Table C-2; for coverage of data, see note a to Appendix Table C-1. Based on a distribution by commodities; since all traffic for each commodity was assigned the average revenue per ton-mile for that commodity, a somewhat different distribution would result from a classification of individual shipments by revenue per ton-mile.
[b] Includes 6,590 million ton-miles of less-than-carload freight.
[c] Less than 0.05.

Another unit which provides an alternative measure of freight traffic volume is the ton originated, or ton of traffic shipped by rail. Available for years since 1899, the total number of tons originated is represented by the index in the second column of

[12] The tabulations published by the Federal Coordinator do not tell us anything about the corresponding dispersion for a single commodity, occasioned by the varying length of haul among shipments of that commodity. But even a slight acquaintance with rate scales suggests that this dispersion, too, must be considerable.

Table 18. It is obvious on casual inspection that this index does not rise as rapidly between 1899 and 1929 as our ton-mileage total, and that between 1929 and 1940 it declines further than does the latter. The evidence shows that the average haul, which can be calculated by dividing ton-miles by tons originated, increased rather steadily, at least during the first four decades of the present century. Whether this trend reflects a general lengthening of the distance individual commodities are hauled, or a shift from short haul to long haul commodities, we shall inquire presently.

Table 20

STEAM RAILROADS: DISTRIBUTION OF FREIGHT
TONNAGE ORIGINATED BY LENGTH OF HAUL, 1932[a]

Haul (miles)	Tonnage Originated	
	(th. tons)	%
0 to 200	159,628	24.9
200 to 400	333,080	51.9
400 to 600	102,060[b]	15.9
600 to 800	28,938	4.5
800 to 1,000	7,462	1.2
1,000 to 1,200	3,342	.5
1,200 to 1,400	1,115	.2
1,400 to 1,600	194	c
1,600 to 1,800	458	.1
1,800 to 2,000	273	c
2,000 to 2,200	3,470	.5
2,200 to 2,400	225	c
2,400 to 2,600	948	.1
Total	641,193	100.0

[a] Computed from Appendix Table C-1; for coverage of data see note a to that table. Based on a distribution by commodities; since all traffic for each commodity was assigned the average length of haul for that commodity, a somewhat different distribution would result from a classification of individual shipments by length of haul.
[b] Includes 15,115 th. tons of less-than-carload freight.
[c] Less than 0.05.

Unlike the ton-mileage total, which cannot be broken down except for the single year 1932, the number of tons originated is distributed each year among commodities transported. The classification has gradually become more detailed, and in 1928 extended

to 157 commodity groups. Using these data to weight tons originated by the revenue received per ton, we can allow for differences
between one commodity and another, not only in rate per ton-
mile, but also in length of haul. (Some idea of the dispersion of the
latter may be gained from Table 20). For most years the weighted
index constructed in this manner differs only slightly from the
corresponding unweighted index (Table 18). This is not altogether
surprising, for the composition of traffic, at least by broad commodity classes, has not changed greatly during our period (Chart
13). Moreover, although it takes some account of variations in the
relative importance of short and long haul commodities, the
weighted originated-ton index makes no more allowance for
changes in the length of haul of individual commodities than does
the corresponding unweighted index. Like that index, it shows a
downward movement in relation to the ton-mile index.

The Composition of Freight Traffic

Just as we can think of the growth or contraction of railroad
freight traffic in terms either of ton-miles or of tonnage originated,
so the same choice is open to us in appraising its composition. However, 1932 is the only year for which we can compare the two
classifications (Table 21).[13]

The first four classes listed — Products of Agriculture, Animals
and Products, Products of Mines, and Products of Forests —
include many raw or unprocessed commodities, although there
also appear such processed goods as flour and other mill products,

[13] Identified with the nadir of the depression, 1932 was in many respects an
unrepresentative year. Thus the relative importance of farm products was
greater, and of forest products and manufactures was less, in 1932 than in other
years. This may be seen if the distribution of tonnage originated for 1932 (see
Table 21) is compared with its average distribution for 1929-38.

	PERCENTAGE DISTRIBUTION OF TONNAGE ORIGINATED	
	1932	*Average 1929-38*
Products of Agriculture	13.0	10.1
Animals and Products	2.8	2.1
Products of Mines	55.1	55.8
Forest Products	4.3	5.5
Manufactures and Miscellaneous	22.5	24.3
Less-than-carload	2.4	2.2

Table 21

STEAM RAILROADS: FREIGHT TRAFFIC,
BY COMMODITIES, 1932*

	Tons Originated		Ton-miles		Freight Revenue		Revenue per Ton-mile	Average Haul
	(mil.)	%	(bil.)	%	($ mil.)	%	(cents)	(miles)
Products of Agriculture	83	13.0	43.0	18.9	480	19.0	1.12	517
Animals and Products	18	2.8	11.4	5.0	191	7.5	1.68	625
Products of Mines	353	55.1	98.7	43.4	732	28.9	.74	279
Forest Products	27	4.3	12.4	5.5	108	4.3	.87	455
Manufactures and Misc.	144	22.5	55.4	24.4	768	30.4	1.39	385
Less-than-carload	15	2.4	6.6	2.9	251	9.9	3.81	436
TOTAL	641	100.0	227.6	100.0	2,529	100.0	1.11	355

* See Appendix Table C-1; for coverage of data, see note a to that table.

leather, meats and lumber products. By contrast, Manufactures and Miscellaneous and Less-than-carload freight are predominantly fabricated, although unprocessed items such as cotton sometimes fall in the latter category. The distinction between low- and high-grade traffic is somewhat less clear. In the sense that the revenue per ton-mile obtained from their transportation is relatively low, minerals and forest products, and to some degree farm products, can be called low-grade traffic. On the other hand live animals, many manufactures, and less-than-carload freight move at a relatively high rate per ton-mile. Judged by this standard, the lowest-grade traffic — bituminous coal, metallic ores, flour and meal[14] — yields 0.6 or 0.7 cents a ton-mile. The highest grade of freight consists of manufactures or of less-than-carload traffic: for instance, furniture, 2.4 cents; trucks, 2.8 cents; automobiles, 3.7 cents; explosives, 3.8 cents; and all less-than-carload traffic, 3.8 cents a ton-mile.[15]

[14] However, the haul of flour and meal is artificially lowered by the existence of in-transit privileges.
[15] See Appendix Table C-1. Unfortunately less-than-carload traffic cannot be classified by commodities even for the year 1932.

Chart 13
STEAM RAILROADS:
PERCENTAGE COMPOSITION OF FREIGHT TRAFFIC
Tons originated

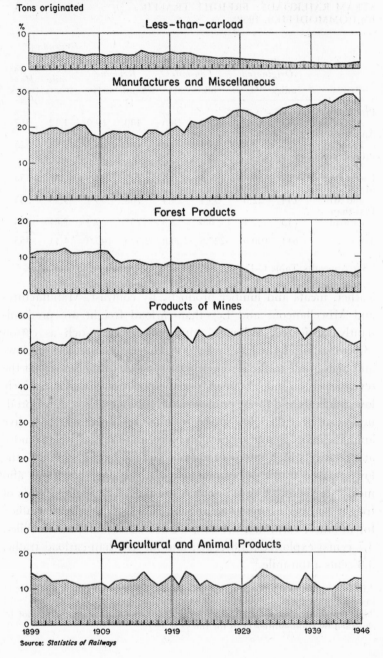

Source: *Statistics of Railways*

The distribution of traffic among the six classes of commodities shown in Table 21 differs markedly according to the criterion employed. Thus in terms of tonnage originated — i.e., amount of freight shipped — minerals contributed over half total freight traffic. But their haul tends to be short: under 300 miles on the average, compared with 355 miles for all commodities. Hence minerals contributed a much smaller fraction of total ton-miles than of tons originated. Since their revenue per ton-mile is also low, their contribution to total freight revenue is still smaller. For opposite reasons animals and animal products and less-than-carload freight — both less important than minerals by every criterion — contribute a larger fraction of revenue than of ton-miles, and a larger fraction of ton-miles than of tonnage originated.

How have the relative importance of these six broad commodity groups varied over time? Such a detailed analysis as that given for 1932 is possible for no other year. Nevertheless, we can compute the percentage contributions of different groups to tonnage originated for the period since 1899.[16] It will be seen from Chart 13 that changes have not been striking and that the nation's mines and quarries have for long been the most important source of railroad shipments. The products of American farms, mines and forests have apparently always constituted more than two-thirds of all tonnage shipped by rail, and at the beginning of our period comprised more than three-quarters of the total. On the whole the shares of forest products and of less-than-carload freight have declined, and the share of manufactures and miscellaneous has increased. The relative decline in the movement of lumber, and the increasing importance of manufactures doubtless reflect shifts visible elsewhere in the nation's domestic production and foreign commerce, shifts from primary production toward fabrication. In the case of lumber, too, the rise of production in the Pacific Northwest and the opening of the Panama Canal allowed movement by

[16] The percentages for the years prior to 1918 may be subject to some slight error because of fluctuations in coverage. In 1899 only 88 percent of total tonnage originated was distributed into commodity groups, although the proportion rose to 96 percent in 1911 for all operating roads. Data for years after 1911 relate to class I roads only, and for this group coverage rose from 96 percent in 1911 to 100 percent in 1917 and later years.

water. However, agricultural products have pretty well maintained their relative position. The decline in less-than-carload traffic dates only from 1921, and is clearly associated with the rise of motor trucking. Some decline in the animals group is also apparent in recent years, and this, too, must be attributed to diversion to highway transport, rather than — as with lumber — a decline in the importance of the commodity in the transportation picture as a whole.

Length of Haul

As we have seen, the unit of output adopted here for the measurement of freight transportation — the ton-mile — is a resultant of the amount of tonnage offered to the rails by shippers and the length of haul associated with each shipment of goods; thus, tonnage shipped being given, changes in the average length of haul have a significant effect on trends in rail output.[17]

The average haul for a ton of freight increased, for all steam railroads, from 247 miles in 1899 to 351 miles in 1939, i.e., by some 42 percent (Chart 14).[18] No significant rise occurred during the first decade of the century, but an upward movement set in during the second decade, particularly during the war years. Thus in 1919 the average haul stood at 309 miles, or 23 percent above the 1909 figure (251 miles). The ICC attributed the lengthened haul, especially the marked increase after 1914, to "fundamental economic changes, such as the development of the Western States,

---

[17] When the national ton-mileage total is divided by the total amount of *tonnage originated,* an average haul figure is obtained for all carriers considered as a system. This should be distinguished from the (less significant) average haul for individual railways obtained when the total of all *tons carried* is used as a divisor. Changes in both averages reflect the impact of such economic factors as the expansion of market areas and the shift in centers of production and consumption, but the movement of the latter average reflects also a slight tendency toward consolidation within the railroad industry, a factor unrelated to the volume of rail output, which is our primary concern here. Accordingly, we shall center our attention on the movements of the average haul for the rail network as a single system.

[18] Length of haul for class I railroads, not available for years before 1911, is slightly above the figure for all roads, being 370 miles in 1939. Data for originated tons were not collected prior to 1899; but, on the basis of tons carried, average haul for all roads regarded as one system may be estimated at 225 miles in 1890.

growth of exports, and shifting of centers of production and consumption."[19]

Chart 14
RAILROAD FREIGHT TRAFFIC: LENGTH OF HAUL
Class I, II, and III roads regarded as one system

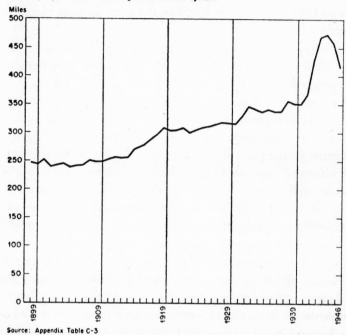

Source: Appendix Table C-3

The principal ways in which average haul may lengthen we
can safely group into three categories. First, greater dependence on
distant markets for the purchase of materials or the sale of a
product must have been rather generally experienced as the nation
spread across the continent and became more fully industrialized.
Second, some tendencies toward greater regional specialization led
to the rise of articles specifically designed for consumption in areas

[19] *Statistics of Railways, 1921*, p. XXXV. It may be noted that in the previous
year, the Commission had suggested that part of the increase in haul may have
been accounted for by the "extension of through billing," referring to the
possibility that originated tonnage totals are subject to duplication because
rebilled carloads may be reported as originating a second time. The elimination
of rebilling may have accounted for some increase in the average haul figure;
such a change does not of course reflect a real lengthening of the haul.

remote from the point of production. This can be documented by noting the growing traffic in certain commodities with long average hauls: citrus fruits (2,154 miles) and other fresh fruits (1,442 miles) and vegetables (1,744 miles), poultry (1,225 miles) and eggs (1,353 miles).[20] Third, diversion of short-haul traffic to truck transportation will plainly lengthen the average haul of railroad freight traffic.

To what extent can we distinguish statistically between these three kinds of influence? We can test how far the lengthening of the average haul for all commodities is associated with (1) a general increase in the hauls of all or most commodities, or (2) a shift in the composition of traffic in favor of those commodities with long average hauls. This classification does not exactly fit the categories of the preceding paragraph. Yet we would expect the first influence (geographical widening of the market) to affect short as well as long haul commodities, and so roughly to correspond with (1). By contrast the second influence (growth of commodities specially designed for distant markets) should be reflected mainly under (2). Again, although transcontinental truck lines are not unknown, mainly short haul traffic has been lost to the highways. Such lost traffic could have included short haul shipments of commodities with a wide dispersion of haul, or representative shipments of commodities with a short average haul. The former kind of shift would figure under (1), the latter under (2) above. What we know of truck traffic suggests that the latter may have outweighed the former.[21]

These considerations lead to the hypothesis that lengthening of haul during the earlier part of our period was due primarily to a general increase in the hauls of individual commodities, but that this gave way to a lengthening from a shift in traffic composition as the period advanced. There is no real doubt that the lengthening of haul in the first two decades of this century repre-

[20] Hauls quoted are for 1932, the only year for which ton-mile data for individual commodities have been collected. See Appendix Table C-1.

[21] That the latter factor will explain *cyclical* changes in the average length of haul, has been ingeniously demonstrated by Thor Hultgren, at least for recent cycles ('Railway Freight Traffic in Prosperity and Depression', *Occasional Paper 5*, NBER, 1942, pp. 40-43; *American Transportation in Prosperity and Depression*, NBER, 1948, pp. 17-18).

sented a general increase in average distances most commodities were hauled. The question is how the further lengthening of haul during the third and fourth decades is to be explained.

Almost the whole of the increase in average haul since the close of the first World War occurred during the decade 1929-39. Let us therefore begin by comparing the terminal years of this decade. If we apply the hauls observed in 1932 to the actual tonnage of individual commodities originated in 1929 and in 1939, we find that the average haul for freight traffic as a whole would have increased about 4 percent, even if the average haul for each of the 157 commodity classes had remained at the 1932 level through-

Table 22

STEAM RAILROADS: AVERAGE HAULS, 1929 AND 1939, AS COMPUTED FROM 1932 DATA AND AS ACTUALLY OBSERVED

| | Average Haul (miles) | | % Change |
	1929	1939	
Computed[a]			
Products of agriculture	498	502	+1
Animals and products	585	658	+12
Products of mines	255	270	+6
Forest products	410	401	−2
Manufactures and miscellaneous	370	383	+4
Less-than-carload traffic[b]	436	436	....
ALL COMMODITIES	326	339	+4
Observed			
ACTUAL AVERAGE HAUL, ALL COMMODITIES	334	370	+11

[a] Class I roads only. Computed on the assumption that the average haul for each of the 157 commodities distinguished in the statistics was the same, both in 1929 and 1939, as in 1932. Thus the actual number of tons originated in 1929 (or 1939) were converted into ton-miles using the 1932 hauls, and the ton-mileage totals so obtained were divided by the corresponding tons originated to yield the hypothetical hauls shown in the table. The changes resulting reflect only shifts in the relative importance, measured in tons originated, of different commodities.

[b] In the official statistics less-than-carload traffic is treated as a single commodity. Consequently it is impossible to report the change in average haul (if any) associated with shifts within this classification.

out the decade. This calculation gives us a measure of the increase in haul associated with shifts in the character of railroad freight traffic from short to long haul commodities (Table 22).

Amounts of tonnage originated were in general lower in 1939 than in 1929, and numerous changes occurred in the relative importance of shipments of different types of freight. The greater decline in the shipments of short- than of long-haul commodities undoubtedly reflects, at least in good part, the unequal results of motor truck competition. For example, the 12 percent lengthening that would have occurred in the average haul of animals and products, even with constant hauls for individual commodities, reflects a relative decline of live animal shipments (which have short hauls) and a corresponding growth of shipments of meat and poultry products (which have long hauls). We know that the movement of livestock to market has shifted from the railroad to the highway to a larger extent than any other form of traffic, except possibly, less-than-carload freight. In the case of the other groups also, some at least of the decline in the relative importance of short haul traffic must be attributed to diversion from railroad to highway. Obviously forest products form an exception to the general tendency, for here traffic would have registered a slight decline in average haul, had hauls for individual commodities remained unchanged. Where other groups lost short haul, forest products lost significant amounts of long haul traffic to other agencies.

In brief, something under one-half of the 11 percent rise which actually occurred between 1929 and 1939 in average haul can be imputed, in the manner indicated, to shifts in the relative importance of different commodities or commodity groups. But it would be unsafe to regard this as even the roughest measure of the degree to which short haul traffic has been lost to other transportation agencies. In the foregoing calculation we were able to take account only of the effect of shifts between commodities. The lengthening of haul not so accounted for, we must plainly impute to longer hauls of individual commodities. Since 1932 is the only year for which we can measure the haul commodity by commodity, we have no means of discovering which items moved longer distances (on the average) and which did not. Nonetheless it is plain that the average haul of a given commodity may lengthen, not only through a general lengthening of the customary haul of individual shipments, but also through the loss to rival agencies of short haul traffic in that commodity.

We should also remember that we have no breakdown of less-than-carload tonnage. This traffic is not of course a homogeneous category from any viewpoint. It includes commodities drawn from almost the entire freight classification, although less-than-carload shipments are relatively high grade and long haul in nature in comparison with the general run of carload traffic. Our knowledge of the drastic losses to motor trucking suffered by the less-than-carload traffic of the railroads suggests that its average haul has probably increased greatly.[22]

The presumption that the increase in average haul in recent years is due in large measure to shifts in the composition of rail traffic rather than to general expansion of market areas is further strengthened by the fact that the method of Table 22, if applied to the interval 1920-29, reveals a somewhat different picture. In this period the average haul of all class I freight increased from 327 miles to 334 miles, or just over 2 percent. Applying the known 1932 hauls to the tonnage originated in those commodity classes in 1920 and 1929 which are comparable,[23] we obtain average hauls for all carload traffic that show a *decrease* of 1.2 percent. Obviously the changes are too small to warrant definite conclusions except of a negative sort. If a significant lengthening of haul

[22] Tonnage of less-than-carload traffic originated between 1929 and 1939 declined nearly 60 percent. How much of this decline represents a diversion of traffic to other transportation agencies is difficult to determine, for it must be attributed in part to the development of 'forwarding' agencies during the 'thirties. These agencies consolidate small shipments at various points into full carloads to obtain carload rates, and usually also provide 'store-door' delivery. While most forwarder shipments are carried by the railroads, motor trucks and inland waterways are also employed by these agencies. See K. T. Healy, *Economics of Transportation* (Ronald, 1940), p. 28.

[23] The ICC commodity classification was revised in 1928 to exhibit greater detail, but to retain comparability we had to use the cruder 1920 classification for our 1920-29 comparison. The latter is therefore less precise than the 1929-39 comparison, based on the more detailed classification, whose results are reported in Table 22.

occurred during the 1920's it was a very small increase; nor can it be explained by shifts in traffic composition.

To summarize, length of haul was about the same in 1914 as in 1899. Between 1914 and 1919 it increased sharply. This increase appears to have been due to a widening of the market, perhaps associated with industrial expansion during World War I. Between 1919 and 1929 average haul increased only slightly. The widening of the market slowed down or came to an end, but appreciable amounts of short haul traffic were not yet diverted to the highway. Between 1929 and 1939 a further substantial lengthening of haul occurred, due chiefly to loss of short haul traffic to competing agencies.

RAILROAD TRAFFIC AS A WHOLE

The measure of total railroad traffic (Table 17) required two further steps. First, the indexes already constructed for freight and passenger traffic respectively were combined. Second, a small adjustment was made for variations in coverage.

To combine freight and passenger output, we used revenue per ton-mile and per passenger-mile as weights in the Edgeworth formula, changing the weights appropriately for each comparison. The coverage of the completed index, which can readily be assessed in terms of revenue, varies slightly over the period. Accordingly a small adjustment was made in order that the series should consistently represent the output of all line-haul roads and switching and terminal companies, of the Pullman Company, and of the Railway Express Agency, i.e., the entire steam railroad industry.[24]

As was to be expected, the index of total rail output (Table 17

[24] For a detailed account of the procedure, see note a to Table 17. Previous indexes of total rail output have been based on a fixed relationship between the passenger-mile and ton-mile. Thus, Witt Bowden in 'Productivity, Hours, and Compensation of Railroad Labor' (Monthly Labor Review, Dec. 1933, pp. 1277-8) equated one revenue passenger-mile to 2.6 revenue ton-miles, the latter figure representing the average ratio of receipts per passenger-mile to receipts per ton-mile over the period 1916-32. For that period the change in the ratio was not great enough (ranging from 2.9 in 1916 to 2.1 in 1932) to introduce any significant divergence between the Bowden index and our own. The use of a fixed weight even for the entire period 1899-1939 would not have resulted in a wide divergence, mainly because of the dominating influence of the ton-mileage component.

and Chart 10) does not diverge greatly from that of freight output, its dominant component. One effect of the inclusion of passenger traffic is to emphasize the element of retardation. The pre-1940 peak in total rail output is seen to have occurred in 1926, three years prior to the peak in freight output. However, the 1926 level is not significantly higher than the figure for total output attained in 1920, when rail passenger travel had marked an all-time high. Like its components, the total index shows rather clear retardation of growth, at least during 1889-1939, and an all-time peak in 1944.

EMPLOYMENT AND PRODUCTIVITY

In 1939 the railroad industry employed about one million persons. Rail employment reached an all-time peak in 1920, when class I railroads alone employed over 2 million persons; thereafter a decline set in that brought rail employment down to the level obtaining at the turn of the century. Peak employment during World War II, about 1.4 million, was still well below the level of the 1920's.

Many different factors have influenced the draft made by railroads upon the nation's labor force. First and foremost are variations in rail output. Yet other factors have been important also. Throughout railroad history technology has scored noteworthy advances. During our period the decline and practical cessation of new railroad construction probably lessened the need for labor in the 'way and structures' departments.[25] Again, consolidation of railroads, for instance in the combination of terminal facilities, made for economies in labor. It is probable, too, that the efficiency of the average railroad employee has varied, not only through technological change, but for other reasons also. Apart from the slow increase of education and formal training among the general population from which railroad workers are recruited, declining employment in the industry has led to the practice of retaining men with the longest service. It has been argued that the

[25] Although extensions of line practically ceased around 1915, intensive construction continued; moreover it is possible that contractors were less used than formerly. These reasons mitigated the net decline in construction activity by the railroads themselves.

Chart 15
STEAM RAILROADS:
OUTPUT, EMPLOYMENT, AND PRODUCTIVITY

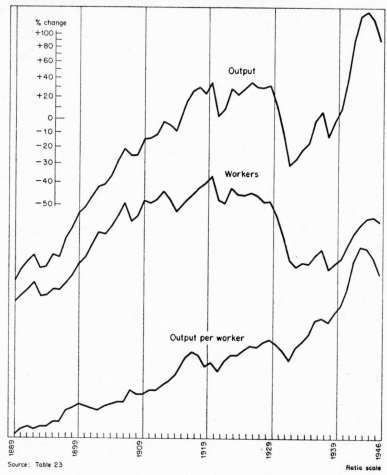

Source: Table 23

Ratio scale

application of the principle of seniority, endorsed by both labor and management, has raised the level of experience of the average worker, and thereby also his competence.[26] On the other hand it frequently is alleged that restrictions by unions on the use of labor by management, particularly those embodied in the so-called

[26] See testimony of Byrl A. Whitney, *Temporary National Economic Committee, Hearings* (1940), Part 30, p. 16903.

'featherbed rules', have to some extent lowered the worker's effectiveness.

The net outcome of these various influences was to leave the number of workers in 1939 about the same as in 1899: but these workers worked fewer hours[27] and produced far more — about twice as much — output.

This comparison conceals the fact that both output and employment rose to a peak during our period from which they then declined; while the upward movement of output per worker, although by no means perfectly steady, continued throughout the four decades considered. In fact to say that output per worker doubled is to understate the rise which has occurred in the productivity of labor. In 1900 the railroads were still expanding. Not only had they to be fully maintained; some employment was no doubt concerned with adding to plant and equipment — additions which of course nowhere appear in our measure of output. At the end of our period, on the other hand, few new facilities were under construction, and some track and equipment were candidates for abandonment, perhaps inducing a temptation toward under-maintenance. For these reasons, the indicated increase seems a minimum estimate for the change in output per worker over four decades.

Output per worker increased rather steadily at an average rate of 1.9 percent per annum (Chart 15), compared with 2.2 percent for transportation as a whole (Table 13 above).

Reasons have sometimes been advanced for anticipating a slackening of the rate of productivity growth as the age of an industry advances.[28] Such might be the case if the rate of technological change were slower, or the opportunities for technological advance more restricted, in an old industry than in a young one. However, the trend in output per worker, measured logarithmically, does not vary significantly from a straight line. Output per worker in the

[27] Data on average weekly hours in the railroad industry do not appear to exist even for recent years. Average annual hours (computed from Appendix Table B-1) declined from 3,100 in 1916 to 2,500 in 1921, and have since fluctuated between 2,200 (in 1932-33) and 2,600 (in 1943-45).

[28] Solomon Fabricant, 'Factory Employment and Output since 1899', *Occasional Paper 4*, NBER, 1941).

Table 23

STEAM RAILROADS: OUTPUT, EMPLOYMENT,
AND PRODUCTIVITY, 1890-1946
1929 : 100

Year Ending June 30	Output Comparable with Workers[a]	Number of Workers[b]	Output per Worker	Output Comparable with Manhours[c]	Man-hours[c]	Output per Manhour
1890	20.4	44.3	46	....	....	....
1891	22.1	46.4	48	....	....	....
1892	23.6	48.6	49	....	....	....
1893	25.0	51.6	48	....	....	....
1894	22.5	46.1	49	....	....	....
1895	22.7	46.4	49	....	....	....
1896	25.1	48.9	51	....	....	....
1897	24.6	48.7	51	....	....	....
1898	28.9	51.7	56	....	....	....
1899	31.3	54.9	57	....	....	....
1900	35.4	60.2	59	....	....	....
1901	37.0	63.3	58	....	....	....
1902	40.2	70.3	57	....	....	....
1903	43.8	77.6	56	....	....	....
1904	44.6	76.6	58	....	....	....
1905	48.0	81.7	59	....	....	....
1906	54.3	89.9	60	....	....	....
1907	59.6	98.9	60	....	....	....
1908	56.3	84.9	66	....	....	....
1909	56.4	88.8	64	....	....	....
1910	64.8	100.5	64	....	....	....
1911	65.0	98.7	66	....	....	....
1912	66.9	101.5	66	....	....	....
1913	74.6	108.6	69	....	....	....
1914	72.5	101.4	71	....	....	....
1915	68.9	91.8	75	....	....	....
1916	82.2	98.0	84	80.7	118.1	68

Calendar Year

1916	86.9	100.7	86	85.3	123.5	69
1917	95.5	105.8	90	93.9	129.5	73
1918	98.7	111.9	88	97.4	135.5	72
1919	93.3	116.1	80	92.1	119.7	77
1920	102.4	123.0	83	101.1	129.5	78
1921	77.7	101.2	77	76.7	97.4	79
1922	82.8	98.5	84	82.1	99.8	82
1923	97.9	111.6	88	97.3	114.3	85
1924	92.5	105.6	88	91.7	105.4	87
1925	97.1	105.3	92	96.5	105.2	92
1926	102.4	107.3	95	101.9	107.8	95
1927	98.4	104.6	94	98.0	104.2	94
1928	98.1	99.8	98	97.7	99.2	98
1929	100.0	100.0	100	100.0	100.0	100

Calendar Year	Output Comparable with Workers[a]	Number of Workers[b]	Output per Worker	Output Comparable with Manhours[c]	Man-hours[c]	Output per Manhour
1930	85.7	89.6	96	85.6	86.3	99
1931	69.2	75.9	91	69.0	69.6	99
1932	52.3	62.2	84	52.2	54.2	96
1933	55.0	58.7	94	54.9	50.8	108
1934	59.7	60.9	98	59.5	54.4	109
1935	62.6	60.3	104	62.3	54.4	115
1936	75.5	64.7	117	75.1	60.8	124
1937	80.8	67.8	119	80.3	63.6	126
1938	65.9	57.5	115	65.4	52.8	124
1939	74.8	60.4	124	74.2	56.3	132
1940	83.0	62.8	132	82.3	59.1	139
1941	105.1	69.6	151	104.5	67.6	155
1942	146.2	77.4	189	146.8	77.2	190
1943	176.8	83.1	213	178.0	86.0	207
1944	182.7	87.6	209	183.3	89.9	204
1945	171.2	88.2	194	170.9	89.0	192
1946	144.3	84.9	170	142.2	81.0	176

[a] 1921-39, adjusted to cover class I, II, and III line-haul roads, switching and terminal companies, the Pullman Company, and the Railway Express Agency. Prior to 1921 we do not have employment data for switching and terminal companies, and the Railway Express Agency (or its predecessor companies). Therefore, for 1899-1921 the index here shown is adjusted only to include class I, II, and III line-haul roads and the Pullman Company.

[b] Comparisons 1921-39 cover class I, II, and III line-haul roads, switching and terminal companies, the Pullman Company and the Railway Express Agency. Comparisons 1911-21 include class I, II, and III line-haul roads and the Pullman Company. Comparisons 1890-1911 are based on class I, II, and III line-haul roads. For recent years data are mainly averages of monthly counts; for earlier years, employment on June 30 (see note d to Appendix Table B-1).

[c] Data relate to class I line-haul roads and the Pullman Company.

railroad industry does not appear to be subject to retardation — at least to the present time.

Manhour Productivity

For manhours, as distinct from number of workers, we have data only since 1916. In that year the average workday was about ten hours. It fell sharply as a result of the Adamson Act (1918) and again during the 1930's. As a consequence output per manhour increased considerably faster than output per worker (see Table 23 and Chart 16). On a 1916 base comparison may be made as follows:

Year Ending	Output per Worker	Output per Manhour
June 30, 1916	100	100
Calendar Year		
1920	99	114
1929	119	146
1939	148	193
1946	202	259

Chart 16
STEAM RAILROADS:
OUTPUT PER WORKER AND PER MANHOUR

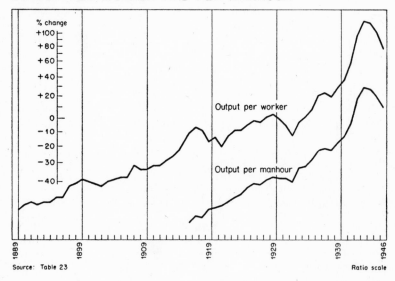

Source: Table 23   Ratio scale

THE AMOUNT OF EQUIPMENT

We have seen that output increased more rapidly than employment. We should like to examine also the relation between output
and the amount of capital used by the railroads. In any comprehensive sense the latter is difficult to measure, and we shall content
ourselves by noticing some changes in the amount and capacity of
movable equipment employed.

The stock of equipment units (locomotives, passenger cars, and
freight cars) weighted by the average cost of each type was larger
in 1920 than in 1903 (earlier data are not available), but in 1939
and 1946 had fallen back almost to the level at the opening of the

century (Table 24). The number of equipment units, that is to say, changed in roughly the same fashion as employment. Output per equipment unit rose with roughly the same speed as output per worker. Evidently the equipment became more efficient in producing transportation, although it still needed about the same amount of manpower to operate each unit. Locomotives are known to have become more powerful, and freight cars to have larger capacities than formerly; we have no record of any change in the size of passenger cars (although they now offer greater comfort).

Let us approximately allow for these changes by measuring the

Table 24

STEAM RAILROADS: OUTPUT, EMPLOYMENT, AND
THE VOLUME OF EQUIPMENT, 1903-1946[a]
1903 : 100

	Year Ending June 30		Calendar Year			
	1903	1916	1920	1929	1939	1946
Output: Passenger & freight traffic combined	100.0	187.6	235.1	229.9	172.0	331.8
Number of equipment units (weighted)[b]	100.0	142.8	148.3	140.3	102.1	105.4
Output per equipment unit	100	131	159	164	168	315
Aggregate equipment capacity (weighted)[c]	100.0	192.8	213.0	226.2	178.4	191.7
Output ÷ equipment capacity	100	97	110	102	96	173
Number of workers	100.0	126.3	158.5	128.9	77.8	109.4
Equipment units per worker	100	113	94	109	131	96
Equipment capacity per worker	100	153	134	175	229	175
Output per worker	100	149	148	178	221	303

[a] Data cover all line-haul and switching and terminal companies. For indexes of output and employment, see Table 23; figures for the number and capacity of equipment units come from general summaries in the *Statistics of Railways*.
[b] Index represents numbers of locomotives ($17,321), passenger cars ($7,883), and freight cars ($973), weighted by the unit values in parentheses. These unit values are the average cost of equipment owned on June 30, 1916 shown in ICC valuation reports for the following roads: Pennsylvania, New York Central, Southern, Santa Fe, New Haven, Northern Pacific, Chesapeake and Ohio, Burlington, and Boston and Maine.
[c] Index represents aggregate locomotive tractive effort ($.535 per lb.), number of passenger cars ($7,883), and aggregate freight car capacity ($24.0 per ton), weighted by the unit values in parentheses. For source of unit values see note b.

locomotive stock by its aggregate tractive power and of freight
cars by their aggregate capacity; passenger cars we shall measure
as before by number. The resulting index of capacity (instead of
units) of equipment roughly doubled during the period. By and
large the same amount of labor is needed to operate a large as a
small piece of equipment. In fact the doubling of equipment, in
terms of capacity, compares with a threefold expansion of output
and also of output per worker. We may say therefore that larger
equipment contributed to the growth in output per worker and
per manhour, but does not completely account for this growth.
To be sure, more powerful locomotives could pull heavier trains;
but, as we shall see in the next section, many other technological
changes, unconnected with capacity of equipment, also helped to
save labor.

CHANGES IN TECHNOLOGY AND THEIR EFFECTS

Among factors influencing the amount of labor required to produce a unit of railroad output, changes in technology obviously
rank high. I shall first discuss some cases where the influence of
such changes upon particular branches of railroad employment
can be traced, and then take up the question of railroad technology from a more general standpoint.

Table 25 shows percentage changes in the number of railroad
workers by seven broad divisions. The decline from 1923 to 1939
was especially marked in maintenance personnel. Thus, in the
period 1923-39 losses in maintenance employment were of the
order of 53 percent, as compared with 40 percent for transportation service employees and administrative personnel. This could
indicate either that technological displacement affected maintenance employment most severely, or that the industry as a whole
has been characterized by undermaintenance.

During 1923-29 employment declined nearly 11 percent. Administrative employment suffered least; indeed, the number of
executives, officials, and staff assistants increased slightly. Profes-
sional, clerical and general employment, however, declined by 5.9
percent, perhaps reflecting the extended use in this period of office
machines — a trend characteristic of all business activity. In the

railroad industry the introduction of office machinery has been closely connected with the trend toward office centralization.[29]

Table 25

RAILROAD TRAFFIC AND EMPLOYMENT, 1923-1939[a]

	Employees 1923 (thousand)	PERCENTAGE CHANGE		
		1923-1929	1929-1939	1923-1939
Passenger and Freight Traffic Combined	....	+2.8	−25.8	−23.7
Total Employment	1,858	−10.6	−40.5	−46.8
Administrative Personnel, total	299	−5.4	−38.1	−41.5
Executives, Officials, staff assistants, etc.	16	+3.8	−29.7	−27.0
Professional, clerical and general	282	−5.9	−38.7	−42.3
Maintenance Personnel, total	983	−12.8	−45.6	−52.6
Way and structures	398	+2.2	−50.4	−49.3
Equipment and stores	585	−23.0	−41.4	−54.8
Transportation Service, total	576	−9.6	−33.4	−39.8
Other than train, engine and yard	213	−9.4	−35.4	−41.5
Yardmasters, switch tenders, and hostlers	26	−17.8	−42.2	−52.5
Train and engine service	337	−9.1	−31.6	−37.8

[a] Class I line haul roads.

Maintenance employment, as we have indicated, declined most. The drop of 13 percent in the period 1923-29 is to be attributed to declines in the employment of men charged with the maintenance of equipment and stores. The number of men engaged in the maintenance of way and structures increased somewhat, reflecting in part the nature of railway investment in this period. While relatively little new mileage was added to the rail network in the 'twenties, there was a considerable amount of construction activity,

[29] In testimony before the Temporary National Economic Committee in 1940, Mr. George Harrison, president of the Brotherhood of Railway Clerks, commented on this point as follows: "The machine could not be utilized under the old method. When the machine was introduced it was necessary to centralize the work, and so the work has been removed from many offices along the railroad line and consolidated and centralized in, ordinarily, the headquarters or general office building of the railroad." See TNEC, *Hearings*, Part 30, p. 16613.

reflected in increased employment in maintenance of way and structures.[30] Some transcontinental mileage was double-tracked; also additional yard track and sidings were built, terminal facilities were extended, and considerable sums were spent on the relocation or improvement of existing trackage.[31] To some extent heavier equipment and faster speeds made higher standards of maintenance necessary.

Among the technological improvements on which maintenance employees were engaged in the 'twenties were the laying of heavier rails, the introduction of chemically treated ties, and the use of improved ballast and tie-plates. In large part, this activity reduced future maintenance requirements, as indicated rather vividly by the fact that such employment was cut in half in the succeeding decade, although some of the latter decline may have been due to more or less deliberate undermaintenance rather than technological displacement. Most of the technological advances associated with the 41 percent decline in employment on the maintenance of equipment and stores in the period 1929-39 were designed to increase the running time of locomotives and cars in relation to time and labor required for service repairs. This was accomplished by the application of metallurgical advances to locomotive construction, the adoption of cast-steel frames integral with the cylinders, the chemical treatment of locomotive water supply, better lubrication, the gradual introduction of roller bearings, and the introduction of longer-lived, rust-resisting steel cars. In addition, in the railroad shops very considerable savings of labor were accomplished by the introduction of such modern

[30] Most such construction doubtless was undertaken by contractors, yet some additions and betterments probably were built by railroad maintenance employees. Whether built by contract or not, subsequent responsibility for maintenance fell upon railroad employees.

[31] Among western roads to which sections of second main track were added may be mentioned: the Union Pacific in Idaho and Wyoming between 1917 and 1922; the Santa Fe in New Mexico, Arizona and California in 1923; and the Southern Pacific across the Sierra Nevada in 1926. After 1930, not only did traffic decline, but construction of second track was rendered less necessary, for the development of centralized traffic control allowed the capacity of busy sections of single track to be increased sharply. Since 1930 construction has been practically confined to the relocation of existing trackage, to the reduction of grades or curves, or to the elimination of grade crossings.

machine tool apparatus as multiple planers, improved drill presses, and tapping machines, and by the more efficient use of the assembly line system for locomotive and car repair.[32]

Some of the same technological advances that have reduced the need for maintenance have also displaced employees in the train and engine service; for example, the advent of the modern locomotive which requires less servicing and has higher tractive power. The more significant advances affecting employees engaged in transportation service, however, are those relating to dispatching, communications, freight handling, etc. The installation of automatic block signal devices facilitating the automatic control of train movements has been one of the most significant innovations in rail transportation technique.

Among employees performing transportation service, the small group comprising yardmasters, switch tenders and hostlers has contracted most sharply since 1923. Many of these workers have been displaced through the progressive mechanization of switching operations. 'Hump yards' have a long history, but their further elaboration in recent years has significantly affected the employment of this class of rail worker. Here must be included the centralized control of switching operations and the general introduction of car-retarding devices.

SOME TECHNOLOGICAL ADVANCES

Looking back over the past half century we can see that railroad technology has undergone numerous changes. It is not easy to summarize these changes briefly; still less easy is it to indicate accurately either the contribution to efficiency each has made or the degree to which each has become standard practice.

Most of the instances of technological advance we shall be able to cite can be brought within one or another of the following four broad categories: changes in design and organization that have taken place rather gradually and have merged into each other; economies of scale; rather straightforward instances of mechanization; and applications of chemical and metallurgical

[32] Cf. Redesign of the C.C.C. and St. L. shops at Beech Grove and the New Haven shops at Readville (*Railway Age*, Oct. 27, 1923, pp. 767-70).

discoveries, most of which originated in other industries. The sources of changes in railroad technology are therefore exceedingly diverse: some developments depend upon true inventions, of a kind potentially subject to patent rights; others are related rather to the mere passage of time, the growth of traffic, or the accumulation of experience both within and without the industry.

Instead of attempting to classify these changes directly along the lines just indicated, however, it is perhaps more convenient to adopt a functional approach, and to consider separately, first, the operation and maintenance of rolling stock; second, the maintenance of track and other fixed equipment; and third, the general organization and operation of the railroad undertaking as a whole. Of these the first — the application of power to the movement of passengers and freight — has undergone by far the most dramatic, and probably also the most quantitatively significant, series of changes.

Rolling Stock

Despite the gradual introduction of Diesel power, first for switching and later for main line work, at the end of our period the steam locomotive still remained by far the most important source of motive power.[33] But the steam locomotive itself had changed. Larger and more powerful units have rendered possible economies of scale through hauling longer and heavier trains — economies both of fuel and labor. The average tractive effort of all steam locomotives in service rose from 20,000 pounds in 1902 to 36,000 pounds in 1920 and 54,000 pounds in 1946.[34] It has been claimed that over a period of twenty years or so weight per horsepower was cut in half and thermal efficiency doubled: this statement of

[33] The distribution of available equipment in terms of tractive effort at the end of 1946 was: steam, 87.2 percent; electric, 2.1 percent; Diesel electric, 10.7 percent. Since the average utilization of Diesel power is more intensive than steam, these figures understate Diesel performance in terms of car-miles or ton-miles.

[34] Tractive effort is a theoretical measure of pulling power based on boiler pressure and cylinder and driving wheel dimensions. The mean tractive effort of all locomotives (including electric and Diesel) did not differ appreciably from that for steam locomotives alone.

course applies to locomotives available for replacement, not to the locomotive stock owned by the railroads at the two dates.[35]

Such economies represent more than the mere result of doing things in a bigger way. The increase in tractive effort has been associated with a long series of innovations, most notable of which are the superheater, the feed-water heater, the force-feed lubricator, the mechanical stoker, and power reverse gear. Some of these — especially the superheater and the feed-water heater — have also contributed economies in fuel consumption. All may be said to date from the period since 1899, and collectively they have made possible the large modern main line power plant.

While in most respects progress in design and the adoption of improvements in the steam locomotive have followed a continuous line of development, the history of compounding forms an interesting exception. There is no doubt that fuel consumption may be reduced through the multiple-expansion principle — by using the expansive properties of steam more than once in a series of cylinders: the universal use of compounding in the practice of marine reciprocating engines is sufficient evidence of this. In fact compound locomotives were introduced in the late 1880's, and by 1900 appeared to many likely to become standard practice in this country for main-line work. From about 1910, however, a reversion to the two-, three- or four-cylinder single expansion locomotive began. By the 1920's even articulated locomotives, traditionally built as compounds, were being designed for single expansion.

The rise and subsequent decline of compounding offers an interesting example of an innovation promising large economies, especially in fuel consumption and boiler repairs, that almost became standard practice, then virtually disappeared from the scene. For the eclipse of the compound locomotive no entirely convincing explanation is forthcoming, but it appears to have been connected with the elaboration and more extended use of superheating. The compounds of forty years ago used saturated steam and realized undoubted economies, especially in fuel and water consumption. But similar economies are available through the use

[35] National Resources Committee, *Technological Trends and National Policy* (1937), p. 192.

of superheated steam in a single set of cylinders by cutting off the supply of steam at a very early stage of the piston stroke. The expansibility of saturated steam is insufficient to allow of this: but if the steam is superheated it will continue expanding long after it is no longer being admitted to the cylinders. Consequently, if the steam is superheated, less of it is required per piston stroke. In theory no doubt, these economies should be cumulative, and one might regard the superheated compound locomotive as the acme of efficiency. In practice it appears that the effect of superheating — now almost universal — has been to supplant compounding rather than to be combined with it. Insofar as the two devices are regarded as alternatives by designers, it is easy to see why superheating should have been preferred, for unlike compounding it requires no additional moving parts. Higher boiler pressures — 300 instead of 200 pounds per square inch — also appear to have favored the superheater over the compound engine. Other disadvantages of compounding were high maintenance costs, and the excessive size to which the low pressure cylinders grew in a nonarticulated compound locomotive as its capacity was increased.

While therefore the steam engine has undergone very marked improvement in recent decades, and while it is still the principal form of motive power on the railroads, two newcomers should be mentioned — the electric locomotive and the Diesel engine. Electrification has so far been confined to areas of high density traffic or where peculiar operating conditions, such as tunnels (New York terminals of the Pennsylvania and New York Central) or sharp grades (Norfolk and Western), occur combined with dense traffic. Capital cost of equipment is high and, although fuel economies are marked, main line electrification has made little progress in this country. Diesel power was first introduced in the 1920's for switching and for the operation of rail motorcars. At first transmission difficulties limited power output; soon electrical transmissions, though expensive, removed this restriction. In 1934 the Burlington and the Union Pacific introduced Diesels for main line passenger work, and thereafter their use spread both for passenger and freight operation. Principal advantages are the ease with which several units can be combined, the long runs possible between stops for servicing, and the reduced wear on the track at high speeds due to the absence of heavy reciprocating parts.

Higher speeds and heavier trains — especially large-capacity freight cars — have been only partially offset by the use of aluminum and of metallurgical discoveries which lighten the weight of steel. While modern alloys have played a dramatic role in the advent of the streamlined passenger train, traveling at high speeds, often with Diesel power, the high cost of the new metals has prevented their use to date for ordinary freight car construction. Potential reduction in the weight of rolling stock through the use of the newer — but still more expensive — methods of construction is undoubtedly large, but has yet to be realized.[36]

Improvements in the maintenance and servicing of rolling stock have been no less considerable, if less dramatic, than in the equipment itself. The chemical treatment of feed water and the sludge remover have diminished the frequency with which boilers must be washed out and lengthened their life. Mechanical coaling equipment and conveyors for removing cinders have reduced the labor involved in servicing. Improved brakes and draft gear have lengthened the time between repairs; while within the last ten years better lubricants (as well as better-designed bearings and other factors) have cut sharply the risk of contracting a hot box.[37] Meantime technological developments in railroad repair shops have paralleled changes in machine shop practice elsewhere — for example in the general use of welding, of spraying machinery for painting, and in improvements in plant layout. Repairs have been concentrated in fewer and larger plants.[38] Partly through the less

[36] Cf. Evidence of J. H. Parmelee, TNEC, *Hearings*, Part 30, pp. 16602-3.

[37] On the Milwaukee the frequency of reported hot boxes was as follows:

| | THOUSAND MILES PER HOT BOX | |
	1929	1940
Freight cars	128	462
Passenger cars	242	1,166

(President's Emergency Board, 1941, 'Hearings', mimeo, p. 1975.)

[38] Cf. the concentration of repair work on the Delaware and Hudson in 1911-12 from Carbondale, Oneonta and Green Island to Colonie near Albany (*A Century of Progress: History of the Delaware and Hudson Company, 1823-1923*, J. B. Lyon, Albany, 1925, pp. 362-3). On the Pennsylvania between 1920

frequent need of repairs, partly through shortening a locomotive's stay in the shops, the proportion undergoing repair has been reduced.[39]

Track and Fixed Equipment

Rather striking improvements have been made in the maintenance of track and fixed equipment. The burden placed upon those concerned with permanent way has of course increased through heavier and faster trains: these have necessitated heavier rail,[40] strengthened bridges and relocated tracks. However, the reduction of grades and elimination of curves involved in the relocation of track have made for operating economies, while the installation of automatic highway crossing signals and the elimination of grade crossings have reduced the need for watchmen. In the maintenance of existing track — a continuous operation that must be carried on year in, year out — substantial improvements have also been effected. As recently as the early 1920's less than half of all replacement ties were chemically treated: treated ties, which may last three times as long as untreated, now comprise more than four-fifths of all ties laid.[41] The use of longer rails and the heat treatment of rail ends to withstand battering also decrease the need for maintenance. Finally in the actual operations of relaying track and replacing ballast a high degree of mechanization has been achieved.[42]

and 1934 locomotive repair shops were reduced from 26 to 3, passenger car shops from 12 to 3, and freight car shops from 16 to 11 (George H. Burgess and M. C. Kennedy, *Centennial History of the Pennsylvania Railroad Company*, P.R.R., 1949, p. 597).

[39] Cf. Charles B. Going, *Methods of the Santa Fe* (The Engineering Magazine, 1909), pp. 57-8; Henry S. Haines, *Efficient Railway Operation* (Macmillan, 1919), pp. 63, 73. See also evidence of J. H. Parmelee, TNEC, *Hearings*, Part 30, pp. 16601-2.

[40] On class I roads the average weight of rail per yard of main track rose from 82 pounds in 1920 to 95 pounds in 1939 and 99 pounds in 1946. The percentage of all track with rail heavier than 100 pounds per yard rose from 13 percent in 1920 to 50 percent in 1946, *(Statistics of Railways)*.

[41] TNEC, *Hearings*, Part 30, p. 16563; President's Emergency Board, p. 1903; P. Harvey Middleton, *Railways and the Equipment and Supply Industry*, (Railway Business Association, Chicago, 1940), pp. 18-9.

[42] Cf. TNEC, *Hearings*, Part 30, pp. 16594-16601. Power machinery is available for adzing ties, drilling rails, tightening bolts, driving and pulling spikes, and cleaning ballast (President's Emergency Board, p. 1977). Rail laying, tie renewal, ballast work, and ditching have been largely taken away from regular section gangs and given to gangs specially mechanized for these purposes.

General Operation and Maintenance

As in the case of equipment and track, in the field of general operation and maintenance the railroads have partly borrowed from the experience of other industries and partly developed specialized devices to meet their own peculiar problems. In accounting and office routine they have shared in developments that mainly originated elsewhere; and the same might be said of the improvement of communications but for the very special role played by the telegraph and telephone in railroad operation. The transmission of information concerning train movements was indeed one of the earliest applications of electrical communication. The installation of block signal systems, designed to enforce a space interval between trains, was primarily a contribution to safety. It belongs, as do the first interlocking machines, to the very beginning of our period. The function of interlocking is of course to harmonize the movements of signals and switches and to prevent the giving of contradictory indications. In their original form these inventions were purely mechanical in character, although operated in conjunction with the electric telegraph. Before long, however, electricity was applied to block signaling itself. First, from about 1879, the track circuit began to be used in conjunction with interlocking. Human operation of signals and switches still was necessary, but it could now be made physically impossible to direct traffic onto a section of track already occupied. Second, fully automatic block signaling, already widely adopted for main line operation by about 1910, was due originally to city subway practice.[43] Now for the first time the signals were directly controlled by the trains themselves. During the 1920's fully automatic interlocking plants to protect crossings began to be installed.[44] Finally, where manually operated signaling remains indispensable — as at junctions and terminals — switches and signals alike may be remotely controlled over great distances. Closely allied and sometimes combined with these developments must be mentioned centralized traffic control. It consists in directing from a single point all traffic movements over a wide area of railroad territory

[43] On the introduction of automatic block signaling, see *Railway Age,* March 20, 1903, pp. 536-8 and Jan. 15, 1909, pp. 118-9.

[44] Cf. *Railway Age,* Dec. 12, 1931, pp. 890-2.

and eliminates the ordinary business of dispatching by means of train orders. That is to say, train movements are directed entirely by signal indication, the signals being operated from a central point, so that operators at way stations are eliminated. Train movements are reported on an indicator board which may cover thirty, forty or more miles of track; all switches and signals are controlled from a single desk. The function of CTC is not only to eliminate local control of signals (from towers or otherwise), but also enormously to enlarge the elasticity of the time table by rerouting and rearranging traffic at a central headquarters to suit the conditions of the moment. By increasing the effective capacity of equipment and track, CTC has produced large economies in many cases. Perfected originally on eastern roads with dense traffic, it has been applied even to such single-track sectors as those of the Missouri Pacific, Denver and Rio Grande Western, and Southern Pacific: in the last case it is said to have increased track capacity by as much as 50 percent.[45] Perhaps the most notable installation to date is that consisting of four sections of the Union Pacific aggregating some 600 miles between Los Angeles and Salt Lake City. Yet CTC is fairly expensive to install and in 1942 was used to control only about 3,000 miles or perhaps $1\frac{1}{2}$ percent of all main track.

TECHNOLOGY AND OUTPUT PER WORKER

Enough has been said to show that technological changes on the railroads are numerous and diverse, and that they have a complex history. Accurately to date the general introduction of any individual innovation is difficult; to appraise quantitatively its labor-saving value would require elaborate and specialized study. Yet the combined influence of these many changes (not all of which are here listed) conditioned the rise in output per worker and per manhour (Chart 16).

Perhaps the most remarkable aspect of the upward trend of labor productivity in the railroad industry is its continuity and persistence. The average technological situation in such an industry as the railroads, the representative way of doing things, changes

[45] *Fortune,* June, 1942; see also *Railway Age,* Sept. 12, 1931, pp. 388-90.

only slowly. Sharp rises in output per worker, or its relative stagnation for a few years, must be traced to varying degrees of utilization
of working force and fixed equipment, or to short term variations
in maintenance activity. The steadiness and persistence of the
influence of technological change, as evidenced by the practically
linear movement of output per worker (measured on a ratio scale)
over more than half a century can be attributed to two characteristics. In the first place, most innovations are themselves gradual
in nature. Modern Diesel power or the hump classification yard as
we know it today — to pick two instances — each embody numerous features successively introduced over a time span of several
decades. In the second place the introduction into general practice
even of a perfected and seasoned improvement must inevitably be
a gradual affair. Not only must the idea be sold to many separate
managements; often its introduction must await replacement.
Continuous rail or treated ties may be worth installing, but only
if replacement is anyhow in prospect.

Such considerations go far to explain the continuity of the
upward trend of productivity; they do not explain the lack of
evidence of any slackening of growth. Why the rate of technological
change in the railroad industry — or at least of its measurable
effects — should vary so little from decade to decade poses an
interesting problem for the solution of which little evidence is at
hand.

Chapter 5

Electric Railways

The term 'electric railways' includes street and interurban railway systems and city subways but does not cover the electrified divisions of steam railroads. The industry carries vast numbers of short distance passengers. Although they have numbered ten to twenty times those carried by steam railroads, neither the revenues nor the employees of electric railways have ever exceeded one-fifth the corresponding figure for steam railroads.

The first streetcars were drawn by animals. Cable systems were installed as early as 1873. Electric traction, introduced in 1884, had superseded all other types of motive power by 1907. The electrification of existing street railways was accompanied, especially during the first decade of this century, by the construction of interurban roads and city subways.[1]

The industry reached a peak in passengers, revenues and employees shortly after World War I. Thereafter the competition of the motorbus and private automobile bit deeply into electric railway operations. The story therefore resembles that of steam railroads, except that electric railways started much later and rose more rapidly to prominence, and — after their peak — declined more sharply.[2]

---

[1] See *Census of Street and Electric Railways,* 1902 and 1907. On the early history of street railways, see especially the historical chapter by Thomas C. Martin (Part II, Ch. I) in the 1902 Census.

[2] Within the past 25 years electric railway companies have in many cases converted a part or the whole of their systems to bus operation, the same management and employees furnishing similar service with radically different equipment. In this study we have chosen to exclude bus (but not trolley bus) operations from the electric railway industry, and to consider them separately. It follows that a recorded decline in electric railway operations is frequently matched by an expansion of the bus industry.

ALL ELECTRIC RAILWAYS

Between 1890 and 1920 the number of passengers carried by all electric railways (urban and interurban) grew roughly sixfold (Table 26 and Chart 17). No doubt passenger-miles grew even more rapidly as the average journey lengthened with the extension of urban networks and the growth of interurban systems. Peak output occurred in 1923 with 12½ billion passengers. Thereafter a decline set in and traffic in 1941 about equalled the 1906 level. The burst of activity during World War II failed to carry output back even to the levels of the 1920's. Indeed, for it to have done so would have been virtually impossible, for the physical plant of the industry had shrunk sharply in the interval: miles of route in operation fell from 31,000 in 1922 to 14,000 in 1937.

At its peak the industry employed nearly a quarter of a million workers. Employment has moved rather closely with output, and output per worker has risen rather slowly — by about 80 percent in half a century. Its average rate of growth was less than 1.2 percent annually over the fifty-year period, compared with about 2.2 percent for transportation as a whole (Table 13 above). As already suggested, series for number of passengers are biased downward, for if we could report passenger-miles a different picture might unfold. A productivity measure based on passenger-miles per worker would certainly rise faster than 1.2 percent per annum.

INTERURBAN ELECTRIC RAILWAYS

With respect to location and to character of traffic, the electric railway industry falls rather sharply into urban and interurban segments. In fact urban railways have always formed much the larger component, and Table 26 and Chart 17 are dominated by the experience of the city street and elevated railway and the subway. Leading statistics for the two branches of the industry are shown for census years in Table 27. To urban — as distinct from interurban — railways no further reference will be made except for a brief paragraph at the end of this chapter.

Table 26

ELECTRIC RAILWAYS, URBAN AND INTERURBAN:
OUTPUT, EMPLOYMENT, AND PRODUCTIVITY, 1890-1946
1929 : 100

	Output (no. of passengers)[b]	Employment (no. of workers)	Output per Worker
1890[c]	17.9	28.2	64
1902	42.2	56.7	74
1907	65.8	87.7	75
1908	66.4	....	....
1909	70.8	....	....
1910	75.6	....	....
1911	79.9	....	....
1912	84.5	111.9	76
1913	88.3	....	....
1914	88.5	....	....
1915	87.6	....	....
1916	94.1	....	....
1917	100.0	117.1	85
1918	98.9	114.3	87
1919	103.6	118.3	88
1920	108.6	122.6	89
1921	101.9	113.9	89
1922	108.0	119.0	91
1923	110.4	119.4	92
1924	108.4	115.1	94
1925	107.0	111.1	96
1926	107.1	109.5	98
1927	104.8	105.2	100
1928	101.3	101.2	100
1929	100.0	100.0	100
1930	91.6	92.9	99
1931	81.3	82.9	98
1932	68.9	72.2	95
1933	64.5	66.3	97
1934	67.2	67.5	100
1935	66.2	65.8	101
1936	68.5	64.0	107
1937	65.8	62.0	106
1938	62.1	58.1	107
1939	61.6	53.7	115
1940	60.9	51.2	119
1941	62.8	48.5	129
1942	73.5	48.6	151
1943	91.6	55.6	165
1944	94.1	55.7	169
1945	94.1	54.6	172
1946	92.9	53.6	173

[a] Appendix Table D-1. Includes trolley buses.
[b] This index appears on a 1939 base in Table 7.
[c] Year ending June 30.

(The interurban segment of the industry is worth further study because it affords a rare example of a form of enterprise that grew, reached maturity, declined, and virtually disappeared within the brief space of a few decades.) From the industrial experience of the United States we can draw some other examples of industries that

Table 27

ELECTRIC RAILWAYS: URBAN AND INTERURBAN
SEGMENTS, CENSUS YEAR 1922-1937ᵃ

	1922	1927	1932	1937
Passengers (million)				
Urban	10,658	11,126	7,588	7,359
Interurban	2,009	1,049	338	159
TOTAL	12,667	12,175	7,926	7,519
Passenger revenue ($ thousand)				
Urban	701	731	481	453
Interurban	155	104	35	20
TOTAL	856	836	516	473
Employees (thousand)				
Urban	209	206	156	136
Interurban	92	58	26	18
TOTAL	300	265	182	153

ᵃ The 'total' is taken from the *Census of Electrical Industries* (see Appendix Table D-1; figures for passengers do not check exactly, because the coverage of the annual series shown there is incomplete). 'Interurban' data are from the ICC (see Appendix Table D-2). 'Urban' data were obtained by difference.

seem to have completed an entire life cycle: the natural ice industry and some now obsolete types of manufacturing. Unfortunately in most such cases the statistical picture cannot be filled out. The rise and decline of the interurban segment of the electric railway industry, however, is documented in statistics collected by the Interstate Commerce Commission.[3] Already they have a nostalgic flavor.

[3] The coverage of the ICC figures appears to be rather complete. In 1932 the Bureau of the Census reported that electric railways operated 31,548 miles of track of which it classified 11,039 miles as 'interurban.' In that year railways reporting to the ICC, and regarded by us as interurban, operated 10,750 miles of track (ICC, 'Electric Railway Statistics 1890-1934', Statement 35101, Sept. 1935, p. 22). The interurban railways of this section comprise all those reporting to the ICC except the Hudson and Manhattan (regarded as urban) and three companies whose railway and power operations cannot be separated.

Chart 17
ELECTRIC RAILWAYS, URBAN AND INTERURBAN: OUTPUT, EMPLOYMENT, AND PRODUCTIVITY

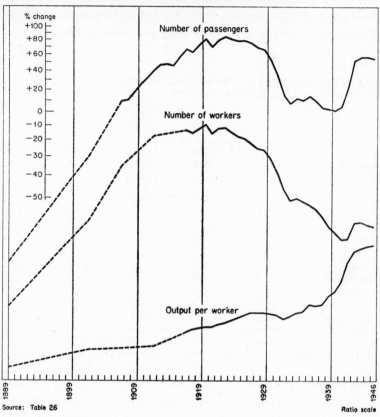

Source: Table 26   Ratio scale

In the present advanced stage of the industry's decay, the scope and social significance of the 'interurban' at the height of its development is not easy for us to realize. A relatively new tractive agent — electricity — actually was harnessed to provide cheap and fast interurban and local rural travel in many eastern and northern states and on the Pacific Coast. All this occurred in an age when the automobile and bus as we now know them still lay in the future. A real effort of the imagination is needed to recapture the enthusiasm that accompanied the construction boom of the first decade of the present century. Some idea of the role played by interurban electric railways at the peak of their prosperity may be gleaned from a few selected facts.[4]

By 1912 it was possible to travel between St. Louis, Missouri, or Sheboygan, Wisconsin and Buffalo, New York entirely by interurban electric railway. A contemporary account of the latter trip is worth quoting:

Starting from Sheboygan, the passenger bound eastward for New York state would travel to Milwaukee over the Milwaukee Northern Railway. . . . From Milwaukee the trip south 75 miles to Evanston is made over the Chicago and Milwaukee Electric Railroad, which has an electric service over a double-track line in Wisconsin and over a four-track one between Waukegan and Evanston, and which at Evanston has a joint terminal with the Northwestern Elevated Railroad Company. The next link is a double-track surface line of the Chicago, Milwaukee and St. Paul Railway . . . thus furnishing the elevated road with a surface extension between Evanston and the Wilson Avenue terminal. Arrived in Chicago, the passenger has many alternative routes by which to reach Hammond, Ind., where is located the terminal of the Chicago, Lake Shore and South Bend Railway, with a heavily built, high-speed, single-phase electric-railway system of modern design, built in 1907-8. Starting from Hammond, or from Pullman, Ill., the route of this line extends along the shore of Lake Michigan and continues across the state of Indiana, the passenger reaching the eastern terminus at South Bend, after having passed through a number of important points, including Gary, the new steel center. From South Bend to Warsaw, Ind., the passenger can continue his eastern trip over the Chicago, South Bend and Northern Indiana Railway and the Winona Interurban Railway system, the latter of which has recently built an extension from Warsaw to Peru, Ind. . . . At Peru, Ind., limited cars of the Winona Interurban connect with the limited service of the Fort Wayne and Wabash Valley Traction Company, operating between LaFayette and Fort Wayne, and from Fort Wayne the Ohio Electric Railway system covers the ground to Lima. Arrived at Lima, either of two routes can be taken to Toledo and from that city the limited service of the Lake Shore Electric Railway Company (Ohio) continues to Cleveland over a route of 121 miles. From Cleveland the route lies eastward through Painesville, Ashtabula, Conneaut, and Erie, over the systems of the Cleveland, Painesville and Eastern Railroad Company, Pennsylvania and Ohio Railway Company, the Conneaut and Erie Traction Company (Pa.) and the Buffalo and Lake Erie Traction Company, at last reaching Buffalo.[5]

Except for the lines into and out of Chicago, all the railways mentioned are now defunct.

Mention of journeys that could be made entirely by electric railway help to indicate the scope of the interurban network at the height of its development. Yet the interurban never constituted a

[4] Most of the information given here is taken from the *Census of Street and Electric Railways,* 1902, Part I, Chapter VII and Part II, Chapter IV; and 1907, Part II, Chapter IV. See also files of the *Electric Railway Journal.*
[5] U. S. Bureau of the Census, *Street and Electric Railways, 1907,* pp. 265-6.

unified system. Through cars, tickets or even timetables were uncommon,[6] and effective competition with steam roads usually extended only over the 50, 100 or 150 miles operated by a single electric company. Thus a continuous journey was possible from New York to Portland, Me. via Springfield and Worcester, and Lowell or Boston: but the travel time would have been 29 hours and the journey would have occupied two if not three days.[7]

The elaborate network of interurban roads that existed in 1910 carried mail and express, and even carload freight traffic, as well as passengers. Many companies brought milk from the country to urban areas. Some operated traveling post offices and refrigerator cars, and possessed their own freight houses and express agencies. Passengers were accommodated in buffet and even sleeping cars — as on the overnight trip between St. Louis and Peoria (Illinois Traction). A few lines built special equipment to handle funeral traffic.

(The interurban roads owed their initial success to the fact that construction costs were lower, and that service could be more frequent, than on steam roads. In rural areas tracks were commonly laid on private rights of way (particularly in the West) and in the towns on city streets, but the problem of gaining entrance to the larger cities was solved only with difficulty, and the solutions often were unsatisfactory. For instance the Illinois Traction company had to build its own bridge across the Mississippi to enter St. Louis; the Aurora, Elgin and Chicago made a not entirely happy arrangement with a city elevated line whose trains ran much more slowly than its own; and the New York, Westchester and Boston never did secure a Manhattan terminal. (Yet the prime reason for their later difficulties was the obvious fact that the interurban lines were far more vulnerable to the competition of the private automobile than were the steam roads.) It is not too much to say that the duration of the industry's activity and its peak volume of traffic were both determined by the time which happened to elapse between the introduction of the electric motor

[6] Cf. Thomas Conway, Jr., 'Traffic Problems of Interurban Electric Railroads,' *Journal of Accountancy,* Oct. 1908, p. 430.

[7] *Electric Railway Journal,* September 4, 1909, pp. 364-5.

and the invention of the gasoline engine. Had the automobile developed a quarter of a century earlier or the electric motor been delayed for a like space, there would have been no 'interurban'. Had the reverse happened, the industry might have reached a still greater extension and had a longer — but still limited — life.

The few lines that still operate scarcely conform to the popular notion of an interurban of thirty years ago. They fall mainly into two classes: glorified suburban roads handling traffic into and out of large metropolitan areas — Chicago, Aurora and Elgin; Chicago, South Shore and South Bend; Pacific Electric (Los Angeles); or roads that depend mainly upon some specialized type of freight traffic — St. Louis and Belleville (coal); Butte, Anaconda and Pacific (copper ore). A few — very few — lines continue to operate rail passenger cars between cities and through rural areas in the manner of the interurban of yore.

Indexes of output, employment and productivity for interurban electric railways are shown in Table 28 and Chart 18. Unfortunately figures for interurban roads are given separately only in the 1902 Census of Electric Railways, while the Interstate Commerce Commission tabulations do not begin until the 1920's. Hence no statistics for interurban railways are available between 1902 and 1922. We may assume that the number of passengers and the level of employment reached a peak about the year 1922, as did the corresponding quantities for electric railways as a whole. Although the picture is fragmentary, it is plain that we are observing the history of an industry which within a quarter of a century of its establishment rose to a peak and after another quarter of a century was almost extinct. If our measures are correct, output per worker declined about 15 percent between 1902 and 1929. Data on hours worked are not available, but the reduction in the work week was probably of the same order of magnitude, so that output per manhour can scarcely have changed during this period. The fluctuations in output per worker after 1929 are rather clearly associated with changes in output and appear to reflect variations in the degree of utilization of equipment.

Table 28

INTERURBAN ELECTRIC RAILWAYS: OUTPUT,
EMPLOYMENT, AND PRODUCTIVITY, 1902-1946
1929 : 100

	Output[a]	Employment (no. of workers)	Output per Worker
1902	52.5	44.6	118
1922	200.4	193.0	104
1926	137.4	136.5	101
1927	126.5	122.7	103
1928	112.5	111.5	101
1929	100.0	100.0	100
1930	83.6	83.3	100
1931	61.8	67.5	92
1932	47.3	56.6	84
1933	35.1	44.2	80
1934	36.4	40.0	91
1935	34.1	39.1	87
1936	34.6	37.6	92
1937	33.8	37.0	91
1938	27.0	34.5	78
1939	26.9	29.9	90
1940	27.8	29.6	94
1941	29.9	29.8	100
1942	34.0	30.8	110
1943	41.3	34.5	119
1944	44.7	35.1	127
1945	42.2	35.4	119
1946	36.5	34.3	107

[a] Weighted index of number of passengers and freight car-miles.

The tendency for industries with declining output to exhibit
little change in output per manhour, and sometimes to experience
actual contraction of output per worker, has been noted by Fabricant in the field of manufacturing.[8] Such findings do not necessarily imply an actual reversal or abandonment of technological
changes previously adopted. On interurban railroads we have no
evidence of a secular decline in output per manhour; all we can
say is that the results of any advance in technology were swamped
by a cut in hours of labor. No doubt the incentive to technological
change was weakened by the decline in demand for the industry's
product. A downward trend in the degree of utilization of equip-

[8] Fabricant, *Employment in Manufacturing*, Ch. 4.

ment — sharply reversed during World War II — may also have inhibited the expansion of output per worker.

Chart 18
INTERURBAN ELECTRIC RAILWAYS:
OUTPUT, EMPLOYMENT, AND PRODUCTIVITY

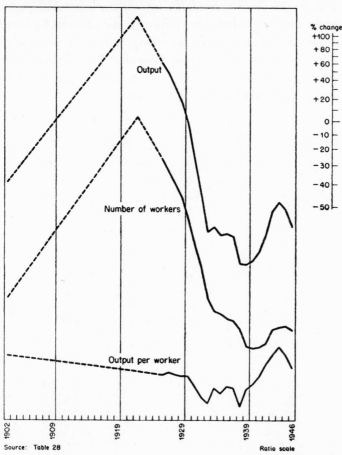

Source: Table 28   Ratio scale

URBAN ELECTRIC RAILWAYS

Urban were always far more important quantitatively than interurban railways (Table 27). Except for 1902 no separate statistics for urban railways are available; but possibly output and employment could be estimated by deducting figures for interurban lines

(ICC) from figures for all lines (Census and American Transit Association). (However, the picture for urban railways taken separately would not differ greatly from that presented in Table 26 and Chart 17 for all electric railways. The main difference would be a slightly more rapid rise in output per worker, a decided contrast to the decline shown by interurban lines. Although the urban sector of the industry has shown greater capacity for survival than the interurban, surface lines frequently have given way to bus operation. It may be that only those electric railways ultimately will survive that operate on elevated or subway tracks, or have otherwise obtained their own rights of way.)

Chapter 6

Pipelines[1]

The first considerable pipeline was laid in 1875. Some 60 miles long, it connected Pennsylvanian oil wells with Pittsburgh. Growth during the 1880's was rapid and by 1892 about 3,000 miles of trunk lines had been built.[2] Their construction resulted in a general removal of refinery capacity from oilfields to consuming centers. Under the Hepburn Act of 1906 pipelines were not finally declared to be common carriers subject to the Interstate Commerce Commission until 1914.[3] The Commission did not begin to collect statistics systematically until 1920, at which time about 25,000 miles of trunk lines were subject to its jurisdiction. Since 1920 ICC trunk lines have increased, through additional construction, to about 70,000 miles.[4]

The industry was therefore already well developed at the earliest date for which we have traffic and employment figures. The traffic figures in Table 29 and Chart 19 are for interstate trunk lines only and therefore cover less than half the industry's total pipeline mileage, but four-fifths of all trunk-line mileage. Traffic per mile of trunk is much greater than per mile of gathering line, and we may say confidently that the traffic figures (Appendix Table G-1) upon which our indexes are based account for much more than half of the entire industry. Whatever the

[1] For a description of how pipelines are constructed and operated, see David D. Leven, *Done in Oil* (Ranger, 1941), Chapter XXII; technological changes in pipeline transportation are reviewed in O. E. Kiessling and others, *Technology, Employment, and Output per Man in Petroleum and Natural-Gas Production* (National Research Project, Philadelphia, 1939), Chapter IX.

[2] Federal Trade Commission, *Report on Pipe-Line Transportation of Petroleum* (1916), p. 47.

[3] U. S. *v.* Ohio Co. et al. (234 U. S. 548).

[4] The inclusion of intrastate and gathering line mileage would roughly double each of the totals mentioned.

Table 29

OIL PIPELINES: OUTPUT, EMPLOYMENT,
AND PRODUCTIVITY, 1921-1946[a]
1939 : 100

	Output[b] (ton-miles)	Employment (no. of workers)	Output per Worker
1921	18	62.6	29
1922	25	83.9	29
1923	27	116.0	23
1924	34	108.3	31
1925	40	99.8	40
1926	43	131.8	33
1927	54	137.0	40
1928	62	121.8	51
1929	72	113.1	63
1930	77	105.8	73
1931	77	95.7	80
1932	80	78.5	102
1933	89	91.0	98
1934	95	100.5	94
1935	86	103.7	83
1936	93.6	112.0	84
1937	104.8	116.7	90
1938	99.0	105.0	94
1939	100.0	100.0	100
1940	105.7	104.0	102
1941	121.3	107.8	113
1942	132.5	111.6	119
1943	155.7	113.0	138
1944	174.3	113.3	154
1945	169.9	114.5	148
1946	167.5	124.4	135

[a] Covers only lines reporting to the ICC. Throughout the period ICC trunk lines represented between 80 and 83 percent of all trunk line mileage. Based on Appendix Table G-1.

[b] Trunk line movement only. Same series is given for 1920-1946 in Table 8.

exact fraction is, it probably remained fairly steady during the period covered, for we know that ICC as a proportion of total mileage did not vary much;[5] and that substantially all oil gathered has to move over trunk lines.

The employment figures are not exactly comparable with output. That is to say, they cover interstate lines only, but include

[5] ICC trunk line mileage was 82.2 percent of total trunk line mileage in 1924, and 81.8 percent in 1945.

work on gathering as well as trunk lines. The preponderance of trunk line movement suggests that this is not a serious qualification.[6]

During the 25 years ending in 1946 output (ton-miles of transportation) grew very nearly tenfold, and output per worker about fivefold. The employment figures include an unknown proportion of construction workers, in addition to the regular operating and maintenance forces. The rather sharp fluctuations in employment and output per worker are consequently to be explained by variations in the amount of new construction or major replacement.

Yet the upward trend in output per worker during the period observed is striking, and must be assumed to reflect mainly an improvement in ton-miles per operating employee. Among factors

[6] ICC trunk line mileage rose from 50.0 percent of total ICC mileage in 1924 to 61.5 percent in 1946. These figures suggest that our indexes of output and productivity may have a slight upward bias; however, traffic per mile of gathering is so much less than traffic per mile of trunkline that the bias can hardly be important.

Chart 19
OIL PIPELINES:
OUTPUT, EMPLOYMENT,
AND PRODUCTIVITY

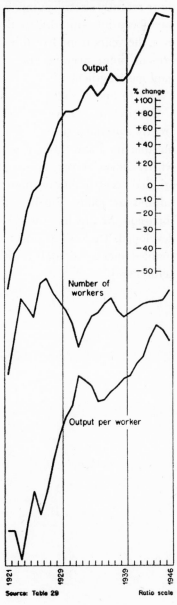

Output

% change
+100
+80
+60
+40
+20
0
-10
-20
-30
-40
-50

Number of workers

Output per worker

1921   1929   1939   1946

Source: Table 29   Ratio scale

responsible may be mentioned more efficient pumping machinery, pipe of larger diameter, and perhaps longer hauls. In recent years Diesel engines have received wide application for pumping. Still more recently electric pumps operating on the centrifugal principle have been introduced. The diameter of trunk lines has increased over the years from 4 or 6 inches to as much as 16 inches at the present time: average diameter now exceeds 8 inches. Average haul has lengthened from about 200 miles at the beginning of the 1920's to about 350 miles today.

Other changes have also occurred. Maintenance work has been greatly simplified through the introduction of more reliable and durable lines, and through newer methods of finding and dealing with failures. From about 1925 oxyacetylene welding in the original construction of lines began greatly to reduce subsequent failures at joints. Further, the control of electrolysis reduced corrosion. Meanwhile the use of aircraft for locating failures was developed. In 1928 an ingenious application of electric welding enabled lines to be patched without the necessity of emptying them beforehand.

Chapter 7

Waterways

Among the transportation agencies considered in this book, waterways are by far the oldest. In colonial times water surely played a
far larger role than land transportation. Early accounts indicate
that this was true both for passengers and for freight. Trade and
travel between the colonies was almost exclusively by sea. The
westward movement took advantage of lakes and rivers, soon
supplemented by canals. As the nineteenth century advanced and
the railroad came, the relative importance of waterways in the
total transportation picture must have declined steadily. At what
date this decline ceased it is impossible to say. All we know
definitely is that between 1889 and 1939 waterway traffic grew
at about the same rate as the traffic of all agencies combined. Its
relative position in the total transportation picture scarcely
changed in fifty years.[1] Yet the composition of total waterway
traffic changed markedly.

WATERWAYS IN 1939

Waterways (including ferries) had but half as many passengers
as steam railroads, and less than one-fifth as much passenger
revenue. A comparison based on freight traffic is somewhat more
favorable to water transportation. Indeed the 410 billion ton-
miles reported by us for waterway freight traffic in 1939 was
substantially larger than the 335 billion furnished by steam railroads. However, waterways earned less than one-quarter the
gross revenues collected by steam railroads (Chapter 1 above).

[1] However, if 'total transportation' is broadened to include private automobile
travel, and traffic in trucks operated by owners of the freight carried, then we
have to modify this statement. In that case, the share (of waterways in the
total) declined between 1889 and 1939. (Freight carried in ships operated
by owners of the freight is included in all our measures of waterway traffic, and
cannot be segregated; private automobile and private freight traffic is not
included in our measures of highway transportation.) For further discussion
see Chapter 2 above.

Table 30

WATERWAYS: PASSENGER AND FREIGHT TRAFFIC, 1939ᵃ

Short tons, statute miles

	PASSENGER TRAFFIC				FREIGHT TRAFFIC					Total Transportation Revenue ($ mil.)	%
	Revenue passengersᵇ (mil.)	Revenue passenger-milesᶜ (bil.)	Average journeyᵈ (miles)	Passenger revenueᶜ ($ mil.)	Revenue freight shippedᵈ (mil. s.t.)	Revenue ton-milesᵉ (bil.)	Average haulᵉ (miles)	Freight revenueᶠ ($ mil.)	Revenue per ton-mile (cents)		
Coastwise	17.7	n.a.	n.a.	4.7	141	174	1,230	225	0.13	230	29
Intercoastal	0.009	0.050	5,900	1.6	8.37	51.9	6,200	82	0.157	84	11
Great Lakes (domestic only)	5.35	1.5	n.a.	9.6	113	69.0	609	74	0.107	84	11
Inland	12.7		n.a.	8.5	329	19.9	61	82	0.4	90	11
Noncontiguous	0.131	0.218	1,660	10	6.13	15.7	2,560	80	0.5	90	11
International, American-flag	0.384	0.927	2,410	41.8	23.0	79.5	3,460	167	0.200	209	26
Ferries	223	n.a.	n.a.	7	....	....	....	....	....	7	1
TOTAL	259	n.a.	n.a.	83	622	410	660	710	0.17	793	100
International, foreign-flag	.745	2.314	3,110	93.9	80.7	360	4,460	575	0.160	....	....

n.a.: not available

ᵃ The various waterways are defined in note c to Table 3 above; see also text of this chapter.

ᵇ Regular and excursion passengers were 19.0 mil. for Atlantic, Gulf, and Pacific coasts and 5.41 mil. for Great Lakes (U. S. Army, Chief of Engineers, *Annual Report, 1940*, Part 2, p. 30). According to correspondence with the War Department these figures include 'all passengers embarking and disembarking at United States ports and those traveling on the waterways'. To obtain totals for coastwise and Great Lakes (domestic), we therefore deducted foreign and noncontiguous arrivals and departures (all flags) numbering 1.3 mil. and 0.06 mil. respectively (U. S. Maritime Commission Report 2610, 'Water-Borne Foreign and Noncontiguous Commerce and Passenger Traffic', for 1939). The extent to which the resulting totals include both arrivals and departures (i.e., double counting of passengers) in domestic traffic is not clear. Intercoastal passengers were extrapolated from the 1937 figure (22 thousand: see U. S. Maritime Commission Report 157, 'Water-Borne Passenger Traffic', for 1937) using passenger revenue (U. S. Board of Investigation and Research, *Comparison of Rail, Motor and Water Carrier Costs*, 79th Cong. 1st Sess. Senate Document 84, p. 209). Source for inland waterways and ferries was U. S. Army as above, and for noncontiguous and international, U. S. Maritime Commission Report 2610.

ᶜ For intercoastal, noncontiguous, and American-flag international, see Appendix Table H-2 and notes to that table. Intercoastal passenger-miles were extrapolated by means of passenger revenue (see note b above). Estimate for Great Lakes and inland waterways is by the ICC (see *55th Annual Report*, p. 9). For foreign-flag international, the same sources and methods were used as for American-flag.

ᵈ Data for coastwise, Great Lakes, and inland traffic based on unpublished estimates by the National Income Division, U. S. Bureau of Foreign and Domestic Commerce. For intercoastal, see note b above. American-flag and foreign-flag international, unpublished estimates by the Office of Business Economics, as above. Figure for noncontiguous assumes same revenue per passenger-mile as American-flag international. Ferries, *Survey of Current Business*, July 1947, National Income Supplement, Table 30.

ᵉ See Appendix Table H-1 and notes to that table. Figures for foreign-flag were obtained in the same way as figures for American-flag international.

ᶠ See discussion in text; also Table 31.

The seven kinds of waterway for which traffic and gross revenues can be estimated for 1939 are shown in Table 30. Only about one-tenth of all waterway revenues, according to our estimates, was contributed by passengers. Ferries, which carried four-fifths of all waterway passengers, furnished but one percent of gross revenues. The two largest divisions, in revenue terms, are coastwise and American-flag international shipping. The latter contributed roughly half waterway passenger revenues, but the former owes its importance almost entirely to freight traffic. The remaining divisions — Great Lakes, inland, intercoastal, and noncontiguous — are also freight rather than passenger carriers. The seven divisions vary greatly in other respects also, average haul of freight, for instance, running all the way from 61 miles for inland waterways to over 6,000 miles for intercoastal traffic. The average for all waterways — 660 miles — was almost twice the average haul for all railroad freight (Table 4 above).

Average revenue per ton-mile (.17 cents) for all waterway freight in 1939 was about one-sixth of the corresponding figure for steam railroads, and one twenty-fourth the figure for intercity trucking (Table 4). To be sure, as noted in Chapter 2, transportation by water is slower, as well as ordinarily more circuitous, than by land; there are longer handling delays and perhaps in some cases more risk of loss or damage. Yet a part of the differential must be attributed to the longer average haul; for equivalent distances the disparity would doubtless be smaller.

The remainder of this section describes how we estimated revenue per ton-mile in 1939, and explains some of the rather startling differences between the quotients obtained for different waterways.

Coastwise Traffic.[2] More than half our coastwise freight consists

[2] The U. S. Maritime Commission defines coastwise trade "as trade along the Atlantic, Gulf, and Pacific coasts, as well as trade between the continental United States ports and the noncontiguous American territories of Hawaii, Alaska and Puerto Rico" ('Economic Survey of Coastwise and Intercoastal Shipping,' U. S. Maritime Commission, 1939, p. 2). We exclude the traffic with noncontiguous territories from our definition of coastwise trade so as to permit comparisons with other domestic freight transport agencies. Following the Commission, we reserve the term 'intercoastal trade' to refer to traffic moving between the east and west coasts by way of the Panama Canal. Traffic moving between the Gulf and Atlantic coasts we include in 'coastwise' trade. The

Table 31

COMPOSITION OF COASTWISE FREIGHT TRAFFIC, 1939[a]

Short tons, statute miles

	Shipments (mil. tons)	Ton-miles (bil.)	Revenue per Ton-mile (cents)	Freight Revenue ($ mil.)
Petroleum and petroleum products	105	146	0.08	117
Dry cargo	37	28	0.38	108
Common carrier	13	10	0.66	69
Contract and private	23	18	0.22	39
TOTAL	141	174	0.13	225

[a] Tonnage shipped by coastal regions (U. S. Army, Chief of Engineers, *Annual Report,* Part 2) for 1939 was distributed between petroleum products and dry cargo, and the latter classified by type of carrier on the basis of the U. S. Maritime Commission's 'Economic Survey of Coastwise and Intercoastal Shipping' for 1937. Shipments by coastal regions, U. S. totals for which appear in the first column, were multiplied by average hauls for each region derived from Appendix Table H-3 to yield the ton-mile estimates in the second column. Derivation of the third column is described in the text and the fourth column follows immediately.

of petroleum shipments moving by tanker from the Gulf to Atlantic ports or along the Pacific coast. This accounts for its very low average revenue per ton-mile. Oil tankers are chiefly operated by the marine departments or transportation subsidiaries of large oil refining companies.[3] There is no common carrier tanker transport, but the transportation service of private oil carriers may be valued at the published rates for chartered tankers acting as contract carriers. These 'going charter rates' in 1939 averaged about 0.08 cents per ton-mile for crude and refined oil shipped from Gulf to North Atlantic ports not east of New York.[4]

statistics collected by the Army Engineers are also more comprehensive; they follow the legislative definition of coastwise trade, and include what we have called 'intercoastal' and 'noncontiguous' traffic: where necessary we adjusted such data to our definitions.

[3] The U. S. Maritime Commission found that 15 major oil companies own 84 percent of all oil tankers in operation (TNEC, *Hearings,* Part 14-A, p. 7730).

[4] 'Oil Price Handbook, 1939' (National Petroleum News), pp. 191-2. The rates here are given in terms of dollars per barrel, and were divided by 1,900 miles (taken as the average haul) and multiplied by suitable weight conversion factors to yield ton-mile rates. Tanker rates fluctuate rather widely and in 1939 were somewhat below the level in other years.

Among dry-cargo carriers in the coastwise trade we must distinguish between: (1) common carrier steamship lines operating over more or less regular routes in the transportation, at scheduled rates, of package and merchandise freight; and (2) private and so-called tramp or contract carriers. Ton-mile revenues for the former can be approximated from ICC figures ('Statistics of Carriers by Water', annual). Few of the latter report to the ICC; they are engaged in the transport of bulk commodities in cargo lots at rates far below those of common carriers. We have somewhat arbitrarily assumed ton-mile revenues for contract at one-third of corresponding revenues for common carriers.[5] The composition of coastwise freight traffic may be roughly estimated as in Table 31.

Intercoastal Traffic. All types of carriers (common, contract, and private) participate in intercoastal traffic, but in recent years common carriers have dominated the trade, and their rates have been reported regularly to the Maritime Commission.[6]

Great Lakes. Freight ton-miles between Great Lakes ports in 1939 were fewer than in the coastwise trade but many more than on rivers and canals. Revenue per ton-mile is estimated at little more than one-tenth of a cent.[7] Just as coastwise trade is dominated by petroleum, so traffic on the Great Lakes consists largely of other bulk commodities — wheat, iron ore and coal. A fairly long haul, combined with mechanized loading and unloading equipment, make their transportation very economical.

Inland Waterways. Revenues for river and canal traffic are estimated at 0.4 cents per ton-mile. This relatively high rate may

[5] See, for instance, Federal Coordinator of Transportation, *Freight Traffic Report* (1935), Vol. III, p. 152.

[6] See 'Economic Survey of Coastwise and Intercoastal Shipping.' In 1937 of 7 million short tons carried by all intercoastal vessels of 1,000 gross tons and over, common carriers accounted for nearly 6 million.

[7] The figure (.107 cents) relates to traffic passing through St. Mary's Falls Canal (Sault Ste. Marie), is due to U. S. Army Engineers, and will be found in the *Statistical Abstract of the United States.* The Canadian Bureau of Statistics in its *Report on the Grain Trade of Canada* (annual) gives a somewhat higher figure (.15 cents) for grain only shipped from Fort William — Port Arthur to Buffalo in Canadian as well as United States bottoms.

be explained in part by the shortness of the average haul. Mississippi traffic, which makes up the larger part of total river and canal traffic, is fairly well represented by that of the Federal Barge Lines, operated by the Inland Waterways Corporation, whose revenue receipts fluctuated between 3 and 4 mills per ton-mile in the late 1930's.[8]

The extent to which the rates charged by operators, especially on inland waterways, really measure the resources engaged has long been a source of controversy. Most investment in river and harbor improvements, which constitutes a significant portion of total waterway investment, has been financed by public agencies; and it has frequently been charged that unit cost figures of waterway operators do not adequately reflect the capital charges borne by government. Proponents of an expanded national waterway system, on the other hand, have claimed that waterway operators are sometimes saddled with "the cost of obsolete and superseded navigation works no longer used or useful" and with "the cost of uncompleted structures which cannot yet have aided present navigation."[9] In any case, the difficulty of distributing the cost of joint facilities between irrigation, flood control, power and navigation is obvious. This whole area of controversy was investigated by the Board of Investigation and Research appointed under the Transportation Act of 1940 with interesting but largely inconclusive results. For our present purpose the issues in question are secondary for, as elsewhere in this volume, we regard the charges actually paid (whether or not appropriate in a wider sense) as

[8] U. S. Army, Chief of Engineers, *Annual Report*, 1939, Part 2, p. 1447. Since such traffic is of a considerably longer haul than other river and canal traffic, we may have understated revenues for rivers and canals. On the other hand the Federal Barge Lines figure has indeed been characterized recently as a 'liberal' estimate merely for the line-haul cost of river transport (see Harold Kelso, 'Waterways Versus Railways,' *American Economic Review*, Sept. 1941, pp. 540-1). Yet in a study of contract carrier rates on the Mississippi system for eight basic commodities, the average unit revenue figure for all hauls was found to be 0.3 cents per ton-mile (*Transportation and National Policy*, National Resources Planning Board, 1942, p. 437). Presumably the rates to be imputed to private carriers, transporting especially coal, iron and steel along sections of the Mississippi River system, would be even lower. In the absence of more precise data we have used the figure of 0.4 cents per ton-mile.

[9] *Transportation and National Policy*, p. 454.

furnishing a suitable system of weights in combining our output indexes.[10]

Noncontiguous Traffic. The chief noncontiguous territories are of course Puerto Rico, Hawaii and Alaska. Trade between the United States and all such territories accounted for somewhat fewer ton-miles than did inland waterways in 1939 (Table 30). As data on revenues from this traffic appear to be completely lacking, we have used the same ton-mile rates, for dry cargo and tankers respectively, as in the coastwise trade.

Table 32

WATER-BORNE FREIGHT TRAFFIC BETWEEN THE UNITED STATES AND FOREIGN COUNTRIES, BY FLAG OF VESSEL, 1929, 1939, and 1946[a]

Short tons, statute miles

	American-flag	Foreign-flag	Total	Ratio: American-flag to Total
	(billion ton-miles)			%
1929	170	338	508	33
1939	80	360	440	18
1946	352	186	538	65

[a] Based upon receipts and shipments at United States ports (1929 and 1939, Maritime Commission; 1946, Bureau of the Census) and average hauls estimated by us; see Appendix H. Data for 1929 do not include Great Lakes traffic.

International Traffic. In 1939 ton-miles in American-flag vessels engaged in foreign trade exceeded traffic on the Great Lakes, but amounted to only about half the ton-mileage transported in the coastwise trade (Table 30). American- and foreign-flag carriers are of course in direct competition, and, as may be seen from Table 32, the recent history of American carriers has been chequered. The wartime expansion of the American merchant marine is measured by the fact that less than one-fifth of the ton-miles between the United States and foreign countries were carried in American-flag vessels in 1939, but two-thirds were so carried in 1946. Revenues have been estimated by the Maritime

[10] For a justification of this general procedure, see Appendix A.

Commission; they work out at 0.200 cents per ton-mile for American-flag and 0.160 cents for foreign-flag vessels.[11]

THE GROWTH OF WATERWAY TRAFFIC

Between 1889 and 1939 combined passenger and freight traffic grew six-fold (Table 5 and Chart 2 above). Passenger-miles multiplied two-and-a-half times, freight ton-miles sevenfold (Tables 7 and 8 above, and Chart 20). These ratios compare with a twofold growth in railroad passenger and a fivefold growth in railroad freight traffic. As in the case of railroads, growth was concentrated in the period before 1920. Ocean waterway, like railroad, passenger-miles showed a declining trend between 1920 and 1940.[12]

In Table 33 and Chart 21 the waterway freight traffic index is decomposed into its six constituents. Of course percentagewise intercoastal and noncontiguous traffic grew fastest. For in 1889 there was no Panama Canal; trade with Alaska was small and unimportant, and Hawaii and Puerto Rico were not yet under the American flag. Leaving these two minor — though fast-growing — components on one side, we see that the rapid rise in total waterway freight traffic is due primarily to the growth of the coastwise trade, which rose more than tenfold. This growth reflects especially the movement of petroleum by tanker from Gulf to Atlantic ports, and to a lesser extent from the southern to the northern Pacific Coast. The iron ore movement resulting from the opening of the Mesabi Range in 1893 caused the Great Lakes component to rise rapidly during the first three decades of our period, but further growth between 1920 and 1940 was slight. Over the entire five decades 1889-1939 ton-miles on the Great Lakes grew at about the same rate as all waterway freight traffic — roughly sixfold. The remaining components — Inland and American-flag international traffic — each grew about fourfold,

[11] I have to thank the Maritime Commission for an unpublished tabulation. Total revenues were estimated by applying average freight rates on principal trade routes to American and foreign cargo carryings. The Commission's figures were then divided by our own ton-mile estimates.

[12] Waterway passenger-miles cover only intercoastal, noncontiguous and American-flag international traffic, and are not available for years since 1940.

but their movement during the half century was quite dissimilar. Inland traffic was at about the same level in 1920 as in 1889, and then shot up partly, as with the coastwise trade, because of oil shipments. International traffic, on the other hand, grew tenfold between 1889 and the early 1920's and thereafter declined steadily until our participation in World War II: in 1946 it was four times the 1939 level.

The uncharacteristic behavior of our international traffic has already received comment in Chapter 2 (see especially Table 10). As indicated, waterway freight traffic grew sevenfold between 1889 and 1939; but if international traffic is excluded the growth is nearly ninefold. On the other hand international traffic in American vessels jumped sharply as a consequence of World War II; between 1889 and 1946, therefore, waterway freight ton-miles grew more than twelvefold if international traffic is included, but only ninefold if it is excluded.

The remainder of this section contains some notes on the composition of each major kind of waterway freight traffic. The following section will offer measures of productivity change for waterway traffic as a whole.

Coastwise and Intercoastal Freight Traffic. To a striking degree the expansion of the coastwise trade in recent decades reflects the movement of petroleum in tankers: in 1939 such traffic accounted for more than four-fifths of all coastwise ton-miles. Movement is principally from West Gulf[13] to Middle Atlantic ports. In addition to petroleum, West Gulf shipments include sulfur, copper, asphalt, flour, cotton, soda and chemicals.

In point of shipments the next most important coastal region is the Middle Atlantic: from here there is much relatively short haul coal traffic from Hampton Roads to northern ports, especially New England. Products of oil refineries in the Middle Atlantic region also move up and down the coast.

Other shipments were of phosphate and paper products from

[13] In Maritime Commission statistics the West Gulf region extends from New Orleans west; East Gulf ports include Mobile and ports east thereof. The South Atlantic region extends to the North Carolina-Virginia line, and the Middle Atlantic region thence to the New York-Connecticut line.

Chart 20
WATERWAYS:
PASSENGER, FREIGHT, AND COMBINED TRAFFIC

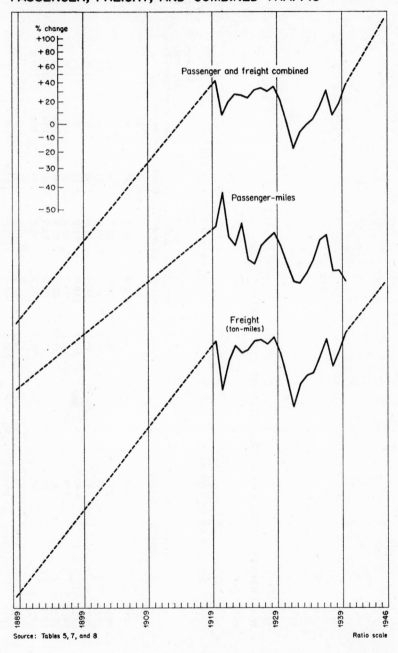

Source: Tables 5, 7, and 8

Ratio scale

Table 33

WATERWAYS: INDEXES OF TRAFFIC, 1889 AND 1920-1946ᵃ

1929 : 100

	PASSENGER-MILES			FREIGHT TON-MILES						All Waterways, Passenger & Freight Traffic Combinedᵇ
	Inter-coastal	Noncon-tiguous	Inter-national, American-flag	Coast-wise	Inter-coastal	Great Lakes (domestic)	Inland	Noncon-tiguous	Inter-national, American-flag	
1889		28		14.6	2.6	16.5	53	11		14.6
1920		104		36.8	29.4	82.7	58	93	165	104
1921		139		31.6	40.0	39.6	54	97	107	79
1922		97		45.7	68.4	64.6	52	91	118	89
1923		90		60.9	118.0	91.2	71	85	103	94
1924		108		65.1	95.2	68.4	80	90	108	93
1925		80		85.8	81.5	86.4	97.2	102	98	91
1926		78		87.7	95.6	93.5	110.2	105	104	97
1927		90		96.3	98.7	85.2	103.5	104	104.0	99
1928	84.4	74.9	100.5	97.0	88.9	86.8	106.4	109.4	97.2	95.9
1929	100.0	100.0	100.0	100.0	100.0	100.0	100.0	100.0	100.0	100.0

Year										
1930	92.4	72.8	92.8	96.3	85.7	77.8	104.9	104.2	86.9	89.4
1931	80.9	59.0	80.3	97.3	69.0	48.9	106.6	100.0	65.6	73.9
1932	74.0	44.4	70.9	90.6	54.3	22.8	91.3	97.8	50.4	60.4
1933	89.6	43.5	68.7	109.2	72.2	45.7	118.2	97.4	51.0	69.1
1934	108.7	57.0	71.8	110.3	80.5	47.8	108.8	104.8	57.0	73.6
1935	119.1	69.6	79.0	116.2	68.1	55.0	154.8	111.9	56.5	76.7
1936	96.9	74.3	98.6	143.3	63.4	79.6	177.7	121.2	55.5	85.0
1937	98.4	79.2	102.7	169.3	65.0	96.7	195.0	135.5	65.1	97.0
1938		82.1	73.5	159.5	55.2	47.6	205	117.4	48.6	79.1
1939		87.3	74.8	172.4	70.5	77.7	230	128.4	45.9	87.3
1940		95.4	65.1	181.0	63.4	98.7	259	143.9	68.2	100.9
1941		...	...	...	...	117.3	310	...	...	...
1942		...	...	...	...	126.6	305	...	...	...
1943		...	...	...	...	166.9	304	...	...	...
1944		...	...	...	...	119.0	362	...	...	...
1945		...	...	...	...	115.0	343	...	...	...
1946					120.5	98.1	323	212	203	171.9

a The waterways to which the columns refer are defined in note c to Table 3 above; see also text of this chapter. Figures are based on data in Appendix H, except as follows. Passenger-miles for years before 1928 were extrapolated on basis of arrivals plus departures at United States ports in vessels of all flags (August Maffry, 'Overseas Travel and Travel Expenditures', U. S. Bureau of Foreign and Domestic Commerce, Economic Series 4, 1939, Tables 3, 4, and 5)

adjusted by changes in the ratio of American-flag to all entrances and clearances (*Statistical Abstract of the United States*).

b Components weighted by average revenue. 1946 linked to 1940 on basis of freight traffic only. This index is the same as that shown on a 1939 base in Table 5. Indexes for total passenger and freight traffic respectively are given in Tables 7 and 9.

the East Gulf region; of citrus fruit, forest products and naval stores from South Atlantic ports. Shipments from New England, of pristine shipping fame, now yield less than 1 percent of all ton-miles in the coastwise trade.

On the Pacific Coast petroleum is again the leading commodity moved, although northern ports ship appreciable amounts of lumber, paper products, flour and grain. San Francicso distributes some manufactured products by coastal waterway.

In the intercoastal trade in 1939 east-bound shipments included lumber, paper stock and manufactures from the Pacific North-west; and petroleum products and canned fruits from California. Minor commodities were wheat flour, and wheat (from the Pacific Northwest), vegetables, fruits, canned fish and sugar. Of the west-bound traffic iron and steel products (mainly from the Middle Atlantic region) made up the greatest part. Other west-bound products were pigments, chemicals and manufactures, vegetables and products, refined petroleum and paper stock and manufactures.

Freight Traffic on the Great Lakes. The Great Lakes constitute one of the world's outstanding natural waterways, having a combined length of over 1,000 miles and a water surface area more than twice the size of the state of Pennsylvania. They are bordered by areas extremely rich in natural and industrial resources. Ice formation in the winter generally limits the navigation season to 8 or 9 months of the year. Although commonly classified as an inland waterway, transportation facilities and equipment on the Great Lakes are somewhat akin to those of ocean transport. However, the extremely heavy bulk freight traffic that moves through the Lakes during the limited season has given rise to a highly specialized type of bulk freighter that makes up the greater part of the present day Great Lakes fleet. These vessels are built with power plant and crew quarters at the stern and bow, all the intermediate space being unobstructed cargo hold, with no division into bulkheads or compartments. Many freighters are equipped with self-unloading devices, but the docks of the larger Lake ports have extensive specialized equipment for loading and unloading bulk freight, especially grain and iron ore.[14]

[14] U. S. Army, Corps of Engineers, *Transportation on the Great Lakes,* 1937.

Chart 21
WATERWAY FREIGHT TRAFFIC

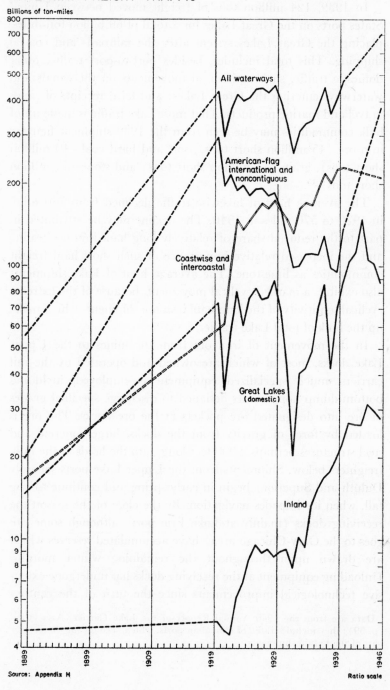

Billions of ton-miles

All waterways

American-flag
international and
noncontiguous

Coastwise and
intercoastal

Great Lakes
(domestic)

Inland

Source: Appendix H

Ratio scale

In 1939, 124 million tons of freight moved between United States ports on the Great Lakes for a total of 69 billion ton-miles, placing the Great Lakes system after the railroads and coastal shipping. This total includes, besides port-to-port traffic, other domestic traffic, such as internal movements on the canals and waterways entering the Great Lakes; and local receipts of sand, gravel and marine products. That most Lake traffic is made up of bulk commodities may be seen from the 1939 shipment figures: iron ore (45 million short tons), soft and hard coal (40 million short tons), grain (11 million short tons) and stone (12 million short tons).[15]

The average haul of lakewise traffic declined from 740 miles in 1920 to 570 miles in 1940. The decline may be attributed in part to the reduced share of relatively long haul iron ore traffic, and the increased relative importance of such short haul freight commodities as limestone. The average haul of Lake shipments also exhibits a marked cyclical movement, because of the extreme cyclical sensitivity of the long haul iron ore shipments which make up the bulk of total Lake traffic.

In the movement of iron ore from the mines to the Upper Lake docks, most of which are owned and operated by the rail carriers, much specialized equipment is employed, including bottom-dump hopper cars designed to discharge specified grades of ore into designated ore pockets at the ore docks. The ore is loaded by force of gravity from the docks, large concrete and steel structures perhaps 2,000 feet long, into the holds of the bulk freighters below. Shipments from the Upper Lake ports (mainly Duluth and Superior) begin in early spring and continue to late fall, when ice impedes navigation. By the close of the season the receiving docks (mainly at Lake Erie ports, although some ore goes to the Gary-Chicago area) have accumulated reserves which are drawn upon throughout the remaining winter months. Unloading equipment at the receiving docks has undergone extensive technological improvements since the turn of the century

[15] Data are from the 1940 Annual Report of the Lake Carriers Association (p. 39); they include traffic of Canadian ports, which account for the greater part of total grain shipments.

and today can handle 5 to 17 tons of ore at one operation, and can discharge a 10,000-ton vessel in 3 or 4 hours. The ore is then carried to interior blast furnaces in standard gondola and hopper cars; the rail hauls are relatively short, ranging below 100 miles.[16]

Eastbound bulk shipments of iron ore on the Great Lakes are conveniently offset by westbound movements of bituminous coal from the Appalachian mining districts of West Virginia, Pennsylvania, Kentucky and Tennessee. The coal moves to Lake Erie ports and thence by water to Duluth, Superior, Milwaukee and Chicago. The Lake coal is stored at Upper Lake ports for winter distribution to northern Michigan, Wisconsin and Minnesota; in the surrounding regions it comes into competition with all-rail coal from the midwestern coal regions of Illinois, Indiana and western Kentucky. Total Lake shipments of coal in 1939 had quadrupled since the beginning of the century.

After iron ore and coal come grain shipments. Like iron ore, grain moves from west to east. During the navigation season grain is shipped east principally by water: use of the more expensive all-rail route is made chiefly while the Lakes are closed to navigation. For 1939 total grain tonnage originated by rail in the United States amounted to some 40 million; in the same year nearly 6 million tons of grain were transported by all waterway routes, of which the larger part (131 million bushels or more than 4 million tons) was shipped by bulk freighter from Duluth, Superior, Chicago and Milwaukee.[17] Buffalo is the chief receiving center of Lake shipments of grain. While a good deal of wheat is consumed by Buffalo flour mills, most of the grain receipts are transferred to rail or water carriers for movement to points further east; some grain is transported by barge over the New York State Barge Canal and Hudson River. Great Lakes shipments of Canadian grain have increased rapidly since the beginning of the present century, but in 1939 grain movements in American-flag

[16] The foregoing description and much of the following discussion closely parallels the material presented in *Transportation on the Great Lakes,* pp. 257-305.

[17] Since the rail shipments include movement from the interior to lakeside these figures overstate the importance of rail transportation.

vessels from United States ports were about the same size as they had been forty years earlier.

Other bulk commodities moving in Great Lakes trade include lumber, stone, sand and gravel, and petroleum products. Limestone for the steel industry is handled by specialized loading and unloading equipment similar to that used for iron ore and coal traffic; as with iron ore, shipments tend to fluctuate with activity in the steel industry. Depletion of timber resources in the Great Lakes region has reduced lumber traffic; shipments of petroleum products have on the other hand risen steadily.

Inland Waterways. Unlike other waterways treated here, river and canal transportation relies heavily on barge and tugboat. According to the Census of 1926, for instance, 94 percent of the gross tonnage of vessels operating upon the Mississippi system and other inland waterways consisted of unrigged craft, that is, vessels without sails or mechanical power for independent propulsion. Extremely short haul in character, river and canal traffic made up nearly half the total tonnage shipped by water in 1939, but only 5 percent of all waterway ton-miles. About two-thirds of the traffic (in ton-miles) moves along the Mississippi River and its tributaries; the remainder consists mostly of relatively small amounts of traffic moving on numerous other rivers, canals and connecting channels.

On the Mississippi system shipments consist mainly of grain, coal, stone, sand and gravel, iron and steel, petroleum, and other bulk commodities. For instance steel mills in the Pittsburgh area ship iron and steel by water as far south as New Orleans. They have thus been able cheaply to reach rising markets, especially for steel pipe in southern and southwestern oil fields. Petroleum products move from the refining area around Baton Rouge northward, and also to New Orleans for reshipment by sea. The growth of the oil movement on inland waterways parallels that in the coastwise trade discussed above. Oil products have become a large component of Ohio river traffic, and in recent years have displaced grain as the leading commodity moving through the New York State Barge Canal.[18] Heavy, though short haul, shipments of coal

[18] Federal Coordinator of Transportation, *Public Aids to Transportation*, Vol. III, pp. 67, 113.

on the Monongahela River enjoy the distinction of being loaded
directly from the mine tipple; here is one of the few instances, other
than the movement of lumber and sand and gravel, in which
river transportation need not be 'fed' by other transport agencies.
Southbound grain traffic on the Mississippi revived after World
War I, in part through facilities of the federally operated common
carrier barge service which is said to have diverted to Gulf ports
grain shipments that formerly moved to the Atlantic seaboard by
rail.[19] Bauxite, sugar and cotton are other commodities that move
over the Mississippi system.

Freight traffic on other rivers and canals is mostly of a bulky
and short-haul character, consisting, especially on the smaller
waterways, mainly of lumber and sand and gravel. Indeed, sand
is often dredged from the very river over which it moves short
distances to its destination. In 1939 rivers of the Atlantic coast
contributed about 10 percent of inland waterway ton-mileage: the
principal routes are the Hudson, Delaware, Potomac and Connecticut rivers. About 3 percent moved over Gulf coast rivers
(other than the Mississippi system), especially the Mobile, Warrior
and Black Warrior rivers. Some 6 percent was contributed by
rivers of the Pacific coast, especially the Columbia and Willamette.

The sharp expansion of inland waterway traffic, which dates
only from 1920 (Chart 21), is undoubtedly in part the outcome
of federal policy. The transfer of freight traffic from waterways
to the spreading railroads during the decades following the Civil
War must have had every air of a permanent shift. To be sure,
coal traffic along the Ohio and Mississippi rivers had a short-
lived revival toward 1900, but even this movement was brought
to an end by the opening of the Southern coal fields in Alabama.
Public interest in waterways and their revival — by deliberate
stimulation, if necessary — dates roughly from the decision taken
in Albany in 1903 to enlarge the Erie Canal. Large scale appro-
priations for river and harbor improvements began shortly thereafter.[20] The Inland Waterway Commission, appointed by Theo-
dore Roosevelt, predicted in 1912 a future shortage of railroad
facilities. In fact, the federal government took over the operation

[19] *Transportation on the Great Lakes,* 1937, p. 117.
[20] In 1910-35 total expenditures reached $2.3 billion compared with $0.7
billion prior to 1910. See Federal Coordinator of Transportation, *op. cit.,* p. 12.

of barge traffic on the New York State Barge Canal and the Mississippi and Warrior rivers during World War I, and to some extent has been in the business ever since. The Inland Waterways Corporation, a federal agency, carries an appreciable fraction of all freight traffic moving over the Mississippi system.)

The Noncontiguous Trade. Nearly the whole of our noncontiguous trade is with the three territories Puerto Rico, Hawaii and Alaska. (Although the Philippine Islands were technically a dependent territory during most of our period, for the sake of comparability United States-Philippine trade has throughout been included with international traffic, of which it now forms a part.) Two-thirds of all noncontiguous ton-miles are carried between the United States and Hawaii, the most distant territory. Traffic with Puerto Rico is next largest (one-quarter) and with Alaska third in size (one-tenth of the total). Traffic with all three territories has grown slowly but rather steadily. Imports from Hawaii are dominated by sugar and fruit, especially in cans; from Puerto Rico sugar and from Alaska canned fish and copper ore are the main imports. In return are shipped to all three territories a wide range of manufactured goods.

International Traffic. As we have seen, the fraction of American waterborne foreign trade carried in American-flag vessels has fluctuated widely from one period to another. Although an accurate comparison between American- and foreign-flag traffic cannot be made until the 1920's, it may be supposed that in the early days of the Republic at least half the total was carried in American bottoms. As the nineteenth century advanced, relatively rosier prospects in other lines of economic endeavor prevented the merchant marine from expanding as rapidly as the rest of the economy grew, and led to the concentration in the protected coastwise and intercoastal trades of most of what ocean shipping survived. At any rate, data on entrances and clearances at American ports by flag of vessel suggest that one-fifth to one-quarter of the nation's waterborne foreign trade was carried in American vessels at the opening of our period in 1889, and that by the time the Census of 1906 was taken the fraction may have fallen to one-eighth.

Shipping subsidies have undoubtedly played a part in the latter day revival of the American merchant marine. Yet, as may be seen plainly from Chart 21, the outstanding factor influencing the volume of freight traffic has been the incidence of two World Wars. A sheer absence of statistics in World War I and wartime secretiveness on the part of government in World War II prevent us from measuring the peaks of wartime traffic movement. But in outline the picture is clear enough. In the years immediately following World War I, with relief shipments to Europe running high and the merchant fleets of many European competitors still paralyzed, our merchant marine furnished more than ten times as many ton-miles between United States ports and foreign countries than in 1889. During the 1920's one-third of our foreign trade was carried in American vessels (Table 32). Thereafter American participation in international freight traffic declined steadily until the proportion stood at one-sixth in 1939. World War II boosted the carrying power and performance of the American merchant marine and decimated the merchant fleets of some of our competitors. As a result American vessels carried two-thirds of our waterborne foreign trade in 1946.

International passenger traffic tells a rather different story. The American-flag share of total waterborne passenger-miles between the United States and foreign countries rose from 20 percent in 1929 to 29 percent in 1939. In the latter year one passenger in three used an American ship; but the average journey was somewhat shorter on American than on foreign vessels (Table 30). For 1946 no data have been published. As with freight traffic, foreign-flag revenues per passenger-mile were substantially below American.

Though American freighters ply all over the world, roughly half the traffic is with western hemisphere countries and half with other parts of the World (Table 34). The distribution in terms of tons of freight received and shipped through United States ports differs somewhat from the distribution in terms of ton-miles. Because of variations in the average length of haul, trade with Canada via the Great Lakes forms 15 percent of receipts and shipments but only 2 percent of ton-miles. Contrariwise, trade with Asia accounts for less than 10 percent of receipts and shipments but more than 20 percent of ton-miles.

Table 34

WATERWAYS: AMERICAN-FLAG INTERNATIONAL FREIGHT TRAFFIC, BY CONTINENTAL REGIONS, 1939[a]

Short tons, statute miles

Traffic between the U. S. and:	Receipts plus Shipments (mil. tons)	Ton-miles (bil.)	Average Haul (miles)	% DISTRIBUTION Receipts plus Shipments	Ton-miles
Canada, via Great Lakes	3.4	1.5	420	15.0	1.8
Americas, ocean-borne	12.8	34.0	2,700	55.7	42.8
Europe	4.3	22.0	5,100	18.8	27.6
Africa	.6	4.2	7,400	2.5	5.3
Australasia	.1	1.3	9,700	.6	1.6
Asia	1.7	16.6	9,600	7.5	20.8
TOTAL	23.0	79.5	3,500	100.0	100.0

[a] See Appendix Table H-6.

Besides the data on which these figures are based, the Maritime Commission prior to World War II issued elaborate tabulations by commodities. These show — as might be expected — that shipments from United States ports were predominantly manufactured goods and agricultural raw materials, while receipts included a wide range of raw products and (chiefly from Europe) some manufactures. Although not as important as in the coastwise trade, the movement of petroleum and petroleum products in tankers accounted for more than a quarter of all receipts and shipments in 1939, but for only about one-sixth of total ton-miles.

EMPLOYMENT AND PRODUCTIVITY

A perusal of Appendix Table H-7 and its notes will convince the reader that the employment data for waterways are very rough in character. Despite numerous census enquiries, the best series we could construct for years prior to 1929 takes account of vessel employment only and does not include stevedores or other harbor employees. Moreover attempts to distribute total employment among our six different waterways, and ferries, proved unsuccessful.

Table 35

ALL WATERWAYS: OUTPUT, EMPLOYMENT, AND PRODUCTIVITY, 1889-1946

1929 : 100

	Output[a]	No. of Workers[b]	Output per Worker
1889	14.6	77	19
1920	104	141	74
1926	97	108	90
1927	99	106	93
1928	95.9	106	90
1929	100.0	100	100
1930	89.4	95	94
1931	73.9	86	86
1932	60.4	78	77
1933	69.1	81	85
1934	73.6	87	85
1935	76.7	89	86
1936	85.0	85	100
1937	97.0	90	108
1938	79.1	80	99
1939	87.3	84	104
1940	100.9	85	119
1946[c]	171.9	120	143

[a] See Table 33.
[b] See Appendix Table H-7.
[c] Change in output between 1940 and 1946 is based on freight traffic only. For this reason the increases in output and productivity in 1946 compared with 1940 and earlier years are probably overstated. If passenger traffic is assumed to be zero in 1946, the output index becomes 162.2 and output per worker 135. Therefore it would seem that any overstatement cannot be large.

Employment increased about 80 percent between 1889 and 1920, fell back by the middle 'thirties roughly to the earlier level, but rose again by about 40 percent between 1939 and 1946[21] (Table 35 and Chart 22). These fluctuations were roughly parallel with changes in output, and output per worker rose rather

[21] Peak employment in 1945 was 176 percent of the 1939 level: see Appendix Table H-7. Unfortunately we do not have complete output data for 1941-45.

steadily. In fact the index, which represents combined passenger- and ton-miles per worker, grew roughly fourfold between 1889 and 1920, and doubled between 1920 and 1946. Between 1889 and 1939[22] output per worker increased at an average rate of 2.9 percent per annum — a rate which considerably exceeds the 2.2 percent yearly computed for transportation as a whole (Table 13). Undoubtedly this result reflects the increasing importance of bulk cargoes, especially petroleum moved by tanker and iron ore — that is, a shift in the character of output toward freight that can be moved in very large masses and can be loaded and unloaded mechanically. However, our employment index prior to 1929 is based on vessel employment only. Therefore, increased mechanization in loading and unloading is not reflected in our index of productivity prior to that year. Because of the trend toward mechanization of port equipment, and the shift toward bulk cargo — both tendencies began well before 1929 — our data may even understate the rise in output per worker in water transportation.

THE AMOUNT OF EQUIPMENT

For waterways as a whole output increased somewhat more rapidly than the gross tonnage of all vessels employed (Table 36). Gross tonnage per worker, in fact, rose nearly as fast as output per worker, and such influences as the trend toward bulk carriage of iron ore and petroleum doubtless are reflected in both quotients. Output and tonnage of vessels (but not employment) can be divided between domestic and international traffic. The contrast is striking. For combined coastwise, intercoastal, Great Lakes, and inland traffic, output rose far more rapidly than tonnage of vessels; these figures include iron ore and other bulk traffic on the Great Lakes, and the coastwise tanker trade. On the other hand for noncontiguous and American-flag international traffic, output rose at about the same rate as, or less rapidly than, vessel tonnage; no such shift toward bulk shipment is apparent.

Gross tonnage per worker rose more rapidly than gross tonnage per vessel. We may regard the rise in tonnage per worker as

[22] 1939 is chosen for the comparison rather than 1946 because, owing to the absence of passenger-traffic data, output and output per worker for the latter year may be overstated. See note c to Table 34.

Chart 22
WATERWAYS:
OUTPUT, EMPLOYMENT, AND PRODUCTIVITY

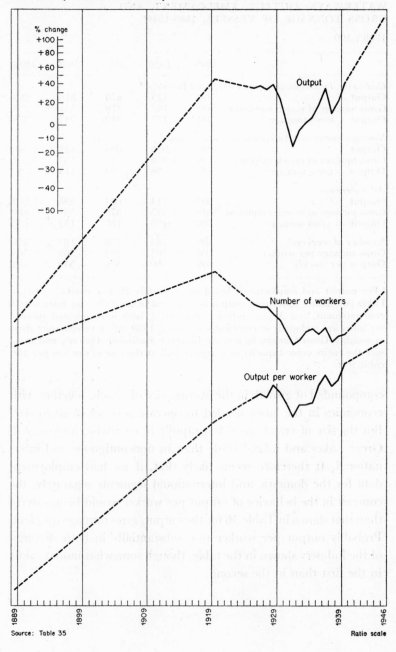

% change
+100
+80
+60
+40
+20
0
−10
−20
−30
−40
−50

Output

Number of workers

Output per worker

1889   1899   1909   1919   1929   1939   1946

Table 36

WATERWAYS: OUTPUT, EMPLOYMENT, AND
GROSS TONNAGE OF VESSELS, 1889-1946[a]

1889 : 100

	1889	1920	1929	1939	1946
Coastwise, Intercoastal, Great Lakes, and Inland					
Output	100	325	670	816	965
Gross tonnage of vessels employed	100	187	279	331	257
Output ÷ gross tonnage	100	174	240	247	375
Noncontiguous and American-flag international					
Output	100	1,028	696	423	1,346
Gross tonnage of vessels employed	100	1,070	744	357	3,204
Output ÷ gross tonnage	100	96	94	118	42
All waterways					
Output	100	714	684	598	1,177
Gross tonnage of vessels employed	100	375	379	337	888
Output ÷ gross tonnage	100	190	180	177	133
Number of workers	100	183	130	109	156
Gross tonnage per worker	100	205	292	309	569
Output per worker	100	390	526	549	754

[a] For output and employment, based on Appendix H. For coastwise, Great
Lakes and inland waterways, output is measured in ton-miles; for intercoastal
noncontiguous, and American-flag international, both ton-miles and passenger miles are included; in combining the data, 1939 unit revenues were used
as weights. Gross tonnage figures are from the *Statistical Abstract,* and measure the entire cubic capacity of a vessel's hull at the rate of one ton per 100
cubic feet.

compounded of growth in the average size of vessels, together with
economies in the labor needed to operate a vessel of given size.
But the size of vessels grew less rapidly in coastwise, intercoastal,
Great Lakes and inland trade than in noncontiguous and international. It therefore seems likely that, if we had employment
data for the domestic and international segments separately, the
contrast in the behavior of output per worker would be less sharp
than that shown in Table 36 for the output/gross tonnage quotient.
Probably output per worker rose substantially in both divisions
of the industry shown in the table, though somewhat more rapidly
in the first than in the second.

Chapter 8

Airlines

In 1946 domestic airlines furnished about six billion passenger-miles, compared with 59 billion for all railroad travel (other than commutation), or 20 billion for parlor and sleeping car travel only. In the same year American-flag international air carriers supplied a further billion passenger-miles; American-flag international waterway traffic is not available for 1946, but amounted to under a billion passenger-miles in 1939.[1] The industry has grown rapidly in output and employment, and also in output per worker (Table 37 and Charts 23 and 24). However, growth in productivity has been somewhat halting, particularly on the international lines. Because domestic operations are on a larger scale than international (see Appendix Table I-1) indexes for all airlines do not differ greatly from those for domestic only. In domestic operations (Chart 23) output grew steadily with no setback, rising roughly tenfold each decade; the growth in employment was somewhat less regular. International traffic (Chart 24) grew about as fast as domestic, but underwent setbacks in 1931 and 1936, and failed to advance appreciably in 1938 and 1943; except in 1942-43 employment expanded rather regularly.

This contrast suggests that international traffic is more subject to chance disturbances, and perhaps also to business cycle influences, than domestic. It suggests also that — in peacetime at least — the working force is somewhat less flexible, and less easily adjusted to traffic needs, in the case of international than in the case of domestic carriers. Perhaps this difference is connected with the smaller share of office workers, and the greater relative impor-

[1] Air traffic statistics quoted in this chapter cover scheduled or common-carrier operations only, and neglect unscheduled or contract flights. The latter are of unmeasured, but — as this is written — obviously substantial importance in the domestic field.

Table 37

AIRLINES: OUTPUT, EMPLOYMENT, AND PRODUCTIVITY, 1926-1946[a]

1939 : 100

	DOMESTIC			INTERNATIONAL, AMERICAN-FLAG			DOMESTIC AND INTERNATIONAL COMBINED		
	Output	No. of workers	Output per worker	Output	No. of workers	Output per worker	Output	No. of workers	Output per worker
1926	.16	...	...	...	...	...	...	...	...
1927	.25	...	...	...	...	...	...	...	...
1928	1.4	...	...	1.1	...	...	1.3	...	...
1929	4.6	...	...	8.9	...	...	4.9	13.2	37
1930	11.0	24.1	46	25.6	11.4	225	12.0	19.9	60
1931	13.8	36.1	38	19.5	21.5	91	14.0	31.3	45
1932	16.4	42.4	39	28.6	30.9	93	17.0	38.6	44
1933	22.5	42.7	53	34.4	36.9	93	23.1	40.8	57
1934	24.5	43.6	56	50.7	44.0	115	26.1	43.8	60
1935	42.5	51.6	82	63.4	49.1	129	43.8	50.8	86
1936	59.3	66.3	89	57.6	55.8	103	59.2	62.9	94
1937	66.7	74.6	89	74.0	72.5	102	67.2	73.9	91
1938	76.0	84.5	90	74.1	86.6	86	75.9	85.2	89
1939	100.0	100.0	100	100.0	100.0	100	100.0	100.0	100

1940	141.0	135.5	104	138.9	118.9	117	140.9	130.1	108
1941	185.5	179.2	104	227	139.4	163	188.1	166.2	113
1942	227	235	97	330	210	157	234	227	103
1943	309	288	107	340	235	145	311	271	115
1944	420	310	135	432	220	196	421	281	150
1945	591	415	142	624	308	203	593	380	156
1946	723	608	119	1,532	475	323	774	565	138

Passengers	$34.8 million
Express and freight	1.6 million
Mail	18.5 million

 Data cover scheduled (i.e. common carrier) airlines only. Based on Appendix Table I-1. Output data for domestic airlines were combined using 1939 revenues (Civil Aeronautics Administration, *Statistical Handbook of Civil Aviation*, 1948 issue):

Chart 23
DOMESTIC AIRLINES:
OUTPUT, EMPLOYMENT,
AND PRODUCTIVITY

Chart 24
AMERICAN-FLAG
INTERNATIONAL AIRLINES:
OUTPUT, EMPLOYMENT,
AND PRODUCTIVITY

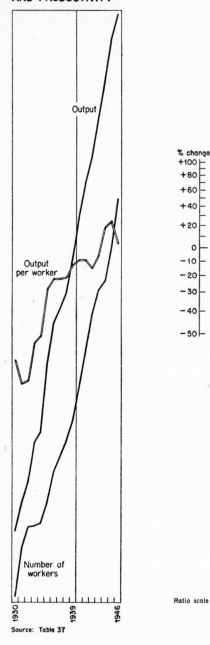

% change
+100
+80
+60
+40
+20
0
−10
−20
−30
−40
−50

Ratio scale

Output

Output
per worker

Number of
workers

1930
1939
1946

Source: Table 37

Output

Output
per worker

Number of
workers

1930
1939
1946

Source: Table 37

Table 38

DOMESTIC AIRLINES: PASSENGER-MILES, SEAT-MILES, AND PLANE-MILES PER WORKER, 1929-1946[a]

1939 : 100

	Revenue Passenger-miles	Passenger-miles per Worker	Passenger Seat-miles	Seat-miles per Worker	Revenue Plane-miles	Plane-miles per Worker
1930	10.7	44	n.a.	n.a.	39.4	163
1931	13.4	37	n.a.	n.a.	52.0	144
1932	16.0	38	25.0	59	55.3	131
1933	21.9	51	30.8	72	59.4	139
1934	23.8	55	30.3	69	50.1	115
1935	39.6	77	47.6	92	67.4	131
1936	55.0	83	56.5	85	77.5	117
1937	60.3	81	68.8	92	80.5	108
1938	70.3	83	78.3	93	82.7	98
1939	100.0	100	100.0	100	100.0	100
1940	154.1	114	149.5	110	132.8	98
1941	203	113	192.7	108	162.1	90
1942	208	89	161.6	69	134.3	57
1943	239	83	152.8	53	127.0	44
1944	319	103	201	65	167.3	54
1945	492	119	314	76	252	61
1946	871	143	622	102	374	62

n.a.: not available.
[a] All data from Civil Aeronautics Administration, *Statistical Handbook of Civil Aviation,* 1948 issue. For passenger-miles and workers, see Appendix Table I-1. Data cover scheduled (i.e., common carrier) airlines only.

tance of ground crews, among employees of international lines.[2] But reclassifications of the employment data make it impossible to substantiate this hypothesis.

The difference between domestic and international operations is further illustrated by figures for annual passenger-miles per employee — 100 thousand for domestic, 49 thousand for international, in 1946. The greater efficiency of the domestic carriers was exhibited despite a shorter average journey — 487 and 1,057 miles, respectively. We are apt to think that in transportation long hauls lead to economies not attainable with short; but long transocean flights require much fuel, and fuel cuts pay load.

[2] For instance, in 1940 for international and domestic carriers, ratios of office to all workers were 30 and 37 percent, and of all other ground employees to all workers 62 and 45 percent, respectively. See Civil Aeronautics Administration, *Statistical Handbook of Civil Aviation,* 1948 issue.

Chart 25
DOMESTIC AIRLINES:
PASSENGER-MILES, SEAT-MILES,
AND PLANE-MILES PER WORKER

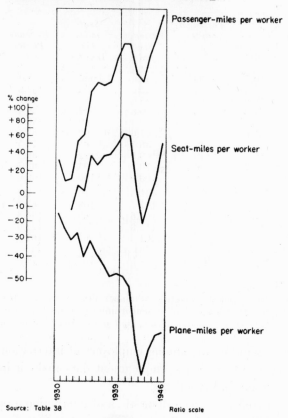

Passenger-miles per worker

Seat-miles per worker

Plane-miles per worker

% change
+100
+80
+60
+40
+20
0
−10
−20
−30
−40
−50

1930   1939   1946

Source: Table 38   Ratio scale

The fairly rapid rise in output per worker on domestic airlines can be analysed further. The indexes of output and output per worker (Table 37 and Chart 23), in the case of these carriers, include express, freight and mail ton-miles, as well as passenger-miles. Indeed transportation of property accounted for about one-third of total revenues in 1939, and its movement has a corresponding influence upon the index. Passenger-miles per worker (Table 38 and Chart 25) moves roughly in the same manner as total output per worker. We have also computed seat-miles per worker and plane-miles per worker.[3] It is evident that a large

[3] Plane-miles need no explanation; seat-miles are obtained by multiplying plane-miles by average seating capacity.

part of the rise in passenger-miles per worker between 1932 and 1941 is associated with a rise in seat-miles per worker. The average seating capacity of planes rose from 7 in 1932 to 18 in 1941, and the average journey increased from 268 to 360 miles. The remaining rise in passenger-miles per worker we may associate with an improved load factor (i.e., percentage of seats occupied).

On the other hand, between 1941 and 1946 seat-miles per worker declined on balance, despite a further rise in average plane capacity (to 25 seats) and a further lengthening of average journey (to 487 miles). The entire expansion in passenger-miles per worker over this period must be imputed to a further improvement in load factor (from 64 to 80 percent).

In fact, the rather steady *decline* in plane-miles per worker was no doubt partly due to the advent of larger planes which not only require larger crews, but also more manhours for servicing. The ratio of seat-miles per plane-mile is a function of the increasing size of plane, just as the ratio of passenger-miles per seat-mile is a measure of load factor. However, the extent to which passenger-miles per worker can continue to rise without a corresponding rise in seat-miles per worker is strictly limited by the impossibility of overloading: *average* load factor reached 91 percent in 1944, was 80 percent in 1946 and declined to 67 percent in 1947. Presumably the practically attainable load factor will be lower in peacetime than in wartime. At any rate it is obvious that appreciable further expansions in passenger-miles (and therefore in total output) per worker must reflect improvements in seat-miles per worker. Whether the latter ratio can be further increased through the adoption of larger planes remains to be seen. Certainly in the past the effects of increased seating capacity (i.e., larger planes) has been largely swamped by the rather steady decline in plane-miles per worker.

No doubt some of the decline in plane-miles per worker has come about — as suggested — through the heavier air and ground crew requirements of bigger planes. The remainder may have been associated partly with the introduction of labor-consuming safety devices, and partly with a reduction of hours of work. But the statistics needed to pursue this inquiry are not available.

Appendices

Appendix A

On the Measurement of the Physical Output of Public Utilities

Physical output might at first sight be considered a fairly simple notion; nevertheless it is a notion capable of a number of different interpretations, some of which must be distinguished briefly. Take for example the contrast between gross and net output. Not only is there some doubt as to just what deductions separate gross output from net, but in addition common usage employs the terms differently in relation to a single enterprise and to the economy as a whole.

CONCEPTS

Naturally for a single enterprise *gross* output comprises the entire product, without any deductions whatever. In such a case the entire output of the firm is treated as originating within the enterprise, irrespective of any input which the firm may obtain from elsewhere. *Net* output on the other hand is what remains after appropriate deductions are made. The comprehensiveness of these deductions varies with the purpose in hand. Thus we may subtract materials and fuel purchased elsewhere, and even the firm's consumption of its own capital. The intention is always to segregate the portion of its gross output that in some sense originates within the firm in question: the remainder — the firm's input — originates in other enterprises. In its strictest sense, therefore, net output includes only the contribution of the factors — natural resources, labor, and capital — peculiar to the enterprise in question. Conceptually it is identical with the real income originating within the enterprise. In this strict sense input, regarded as the difference between gross and net output, comprises not merely a firm's purchased materials, but everything necessary to maintain its capital intact. Conceptual and statistical difficulties connected with the maintenance of capital may lead us to prefer a rather less

163

strict, i.e., less comprehensive, definition of input, and an associated definition of net output in which only some of the appropriate deductions from gross output are made. Indeed the actual business of performing deductions of this kind is difficult enough, for in order to conform with our concepts it has to be performed in real rather than in money terms. But a discussion of concepts must precede any discussion of the measurement of their contents.

So much for the output of the individual enterprise. The physical output of the community as a whole also may be considered in either aspect, gross or net. The *gross* output of the community, not further qualified in common usage, remains a rather vague notion. It may mean simply the sum of the gross outputs of all the enterprises in the system. In that case it includes an amount of duplication which depends upon the business structure of the economy considered. Usually, however, gross output for the community means something narrower and less arbitrary than this. It means the sum of the *net* outputs of the various enterprises, the word 'net' being interpreted for this purpose *before* allowance for the consumption of capital and natural resources. The aggregate may be called the community's output 'gross of depreciation and depletion'. Unlike the preceding concept, it is independent of the business structure of the economy.

The *net* output of the community is plainly the sum of the net outputs of enterprises, 'net' being comprehensively interpreted to include deductions for depreciation of capital and depletion of natural resources. This is the concept that corresponds to our notions of 'real national income' or 'national dividend'. Again, since the appropriate deductions may be made with a greater or less degree of thoroughness, the aggregate so obtained may contain much or little duplication.

What purpose do such measures of output serve? In the long run, as a check upon deflated national income statistics they have perhaps some value. As a short run measure of real income, or of economic activity, such indexes as those compiled by the Federal Reserve Board in this country or the Board of Trade in Britain have obvious usefulness. But for the purpose of making comparisons over long periods of time, there is perhaps some risk of claiming more for indexes of output than they can actually perform. For example, unless we make a whole series of further assumptions, none of which is easy to justify, an index of output (regarded as the equivalent of a measure of real income) in fact tells us little about variations, either in the amount of resources engaged in production, or in the real satisfactions obtained from consumption. Fortunately we have other, more direct ways of measuring the employment of resources. Some may claim that indexes of physical output have a more direct bearing upon the question of consumer satisfaction. Even here, however, it may be argued that the supply of certain socially significant sample commodities, e.g., the number of bathtubs per head, tells us more about consumer satisfaction than do composite measures of output or real income. Nevertheless, it remains tempting to assume that net output and the level of consumer satisfaction do, in general, move in the same direction, even if we can know nothing about the quantitative relationship between them.[1] However this may be, the primary purpose of constructing indexes of output remains the less ambitious one of keeping tab on the over-all efficiency of the economy, or of segments of it: regarding this efficiency as a technological rather than as a psychological concept.

UNITS

Suppose that the entire output of an economic system comprised a single uniform product, let us say oranges of a certain specified size, weight, color, juiciness, and so forth. In these peculiar conditions, to measure the physical output of the economy would be simple. By merely counting the number of oranges harvested from year to year, or weighing them, or measuring their juice content, an index of output would at once be available free both from ambiguity and from arbitrariness. Nor would it matter in the least which measure was chosen, for as long as output remained homogeneous each would yield the same result, i.e., disclose the same pattern of temporal variation. Only in this very special case does the problem of measuring physical output admit of a unique solution.

For as soon as the community's output is no longer homogeneous

[1] Cf. A. C. Pigou, *Economics of Welfare* (London, 1929), Part I, especially Ch. VII.

in respect of its physical characteristics, the measurement of its physical magnitude ceases to admit of the easy and simple solution just indicated, and becomes instead a more or less complicated statistical problem. This lack of homogeneity assumes two forms. First, the oranges may vary in quality. Second, the community may produce not only oranges but apples as well. This distinction between variations in quality and variations in kind, although often of immense biological or physical significance, is by no means fundamental from an economic standpoint. Technical differences between one grade and another, which appear at first sight of minor moment, may turn out to have great economic importance. The consumer, ultimate or otherwise, is often exigent in quite unexpected directions. For one grade an altogether different commodity may be a better substitute than another grade of the same commodity. Nevertheless, the contrast between distinctions of grade within a single commodity on the one hand, and the differentiation of separate and distinct commodities on the other, is a convenient one, provided that we do not overrate its significance.

First, then, suppose still that oranges are the only kind of output, but let us allow their quality to vary. Two such sorts of variation are relevant: (a) in respect of weight, juiciness, sugar content, and other *measurable* characteristics; and (b) in respect of flavor, color, texture, and other attributes that cannot be measured.

Now, as regards (a) — measurable characteristics — it is evident that each variable provides a separate and distinct measure of physical output. Thus we can use the number of oranges in the crop, or their total weight, or their total juice or sugar content, or indeed any other measurable characteristic. Since output is no longer homogeneous with respect to these characteristics, it is only to be expected that each such computation will yield a different result. Obviously no unique measure of output is any longer available unless we decide that some *one* variable — e.g., number or weight — is more fundamental than any of the others. It is important to realize that this is an essentially arbitrary decision. There is no more reason why we should measure oranges by the thousand than by the case or by the ton. For simplicity of exposition we have chosen oranges. But that a point of substance is involved is easily seen if we consider for a moment the problem of interpreting the concept of a physical unit of output in such a field as transportation. Is the ton, the carload, the ton-mile, the carload-mile, a combination of these, or some altogether different measure to be taken as the fundamental unit of service rendered (i.e., of output) in the realm of freight transportation? For the moment this question is merely posed. At a later stage in the argument an approach to its solution will have to be attempted.

As regards (b) — nonmeasurable characteristics — the situation is different. Suppose the oranges vary in flavor. Such variations in quality between different units of output, where these cannot be quantitatively expressed, clearly cannot be made the basis for still further alternative measures of physical output. It is impossible to take account of them directly. What such variations in fact do, is to cast doubt upon the justification for choosing some other, measurable variable as the fundamental unit for measuring output. Suppose the oranges improve in flavor from year to year: unless this fact happens accidentally to be correlated with weight, or sugar content, or some other measurable characteristic, it will in no wise be reflected in any of the measures discussed above.

We come now to the second possibility just mentioned. So far the problems discussed already reach their full complexity in an economy producing what is ordinarily thought of as a single commodity, i.e., oranges. Suppose now that the community grows apples too. Having decided (with a greater or less degree of arbitrariness) what physical units to use for the measurement of oranges and apples separately, we are faced with the problem of combining them into a single measure representing the community's total output. It is obvious that this problem is different only in degree, not in kind, from the problem of dealing with the output of oranges, or other single commodity, when that output is not homogeneous. Still for the moment confining ourselves to variables of a purely physical nature, we might consider a single orange the equivalent of a single apple; or we might add tons of oranges and tons of apples; or we might perform the summation in terms of juice, or sugar content, or any one of an infinite number of more or less relevant and interesting physical characteristics. each time reaching a different result. Perhaps it might even be possible, with sufficient ingenuity, to conceive of a context in which each of these results would be appropriate.

The absurdity from the economic standpoint of any such procedure may be seen, not only in the essential arbitrariness of the decisions to be taken, but also in the rapid and complete disappearance of common physical characteristics among the commodities involved as we extend our purview. It remains possible, however inappropriate, to compare a ton of radium with a ton of lead. But a ton of lead, a unit of electricity, a ton-mile of transportation, and a telephone call have on the other hand no physical characteristics even superficially in common. Plainly an altogether different line of attack must be sought.

VALUE AS A COMMON DENOMINATOR

Let us suppose that output consists of two commodities — apples and oranges — each of which individually is homogeneous with respect to all of its physical characteristics. The object of our search is of course a ratio between apples and oranges (in terms of number, tons, cubic feet — or other physical unit) that has some meaning economically and is not merely an arbitrary ratio, and that will allow apples and oranges to be added in a manner which does not have to look to some special context for its justification.

Now the fundamental unit in economic measurement is of course the unit of money value. A dollar's worth of oranges and a dollar's worth of apples are equivalent in the sense that they can be exchanged for one another in the market. For making comparisons between different commodities therefore, the physical unit we may label 'a dollar's worth' has a significance that a ton, cubic foot, or carload lacks.

From the viewpoint of ordinary common sense, it is of course precisely the lack of correspondence between dollars' worth and tons that is responsible for our instinctive unwillingness to compare, for example, a ton of radium with a ton of lead. The arbitrariness, indeed the absurdity, of such a comparison disappears once the two commodities are reduced to common values — that is, to physical units (i.e., dollars' worth) of such a size that the market in fact treats them as equivalent. The process of summing amounts of different commodities in terms of dollars' worth is statistically equivalent to summing any arbitrarily chosen physical units, each weighted by its price.

While this solution is obviously of perfectly general application, and may be used for combining measures of physical output relating to any number of commodities, its requirements are not always easy to satisfy. Thus in order that a unique index of output shall emerge, the ratios between the market prices of given physical units of the various commodities must remain invariable. This is of course an impossible requirement. To put the matter otherwise, what we have in fact done is to assimilate the construction of an index of output to that of an index of prices. The record discloses both price changes and quantity changes. It is the business of an output index to abstract from the former, just as it is the business of a price index to abstract from the latter. No such abstraction can in the nature of things be performed unambiguously. It is not our purpose here to trace once more the familiar outlines of the 'index number problem'.[2] Choice of weight-base and formula will influence the outcome. The particular compromises embodied in the chronology and formulas used for computing purposes in the present study are described elsewhere.

Further, we have assumed each commodity to be homogeneous with respect to all of its physical characteristics. If, however, its output varies in quality at any given moment of time, either measurably or nonmeasurably, the difficulty can be overcome by grading, and treating each grade as a separate commodity. If this is done, account will be taken in the computation both of measurable and of nonmeasurable variations from one unit to another of the product, for both are equally reflected by the behavior of the market in setting prices. Specially large and specially flavorsome oranges both command a premium. So much — the reduction of physically nonmeasurable variations, as well as those which are measurable, to a common price basis — the use of market valuation does achieve, but only so far as these variations are contem-

---

[2] Cf. J. M. Keynes, *Treatise on Money* (London, 1930), Ch. 8; Irving Fisher, *The Making of Index Numbers* (Houghton Mifflin, 1922).

poraneous. Since abstraction is to be made from price changes
from one moment to another — this being the whole object of an
output index — no account can be taken of physical variation
through time (whether measurable or not). If the quality of a
commodity improves through an increase in the fraction of its
output concentrated in the better grades, at the expense of inferior
grades, this will be accurately reflected in the computation. If on
the other hand the quality of a given grade — or of a single
homogeneous commodity — improves with time, there is plainly
no way of recognizing the fact. We may be reasonably sure that,
especially in view of the comparatively coarse grading allowed
by the statistics, most quality changes in practice come about by
the latter method. We may be sure also that, on this account if
on no other, production indexes contain a rather serious downward bias, in that they take too little account of changes in quality.

It might perhaps be thought that quality changes are no concern
of an index of output. That it is not possible to place the quality
of the products on one side, and to confine attention to measures
of quantity which are independent of quality, may easily be
demonstrated, and is indeed already implicit in what has been
said above. Consider a single commodity whose output, though
homogeneous at any given moment, is subject to improvement in
quality through time. This improvement may be viewed as an
alteration in some or all of its physical attributes, or in the rela-
tions between them. The chemical becomes more nearly pure, the
automobile has more cylinders, the concrete lasts longer, the supply
of electricity is less frequently interrupted. No doubt we are prevented, for the most part, from incorporating these developments
in our output index. And yet, who will deny that *at any given
moment of time* pure chemicals command a premium; so also do
many-cylindered automobiles, long-lasting concrete, and electrical
installations of unusual reliability. To the extent that we appeal
to market valuation as a basis for the summations our measurements require, and weight products and grades according to their
prices, quality — as reflected in price-differentials — becomes
merely an aspect of quantity. The greater weight given to a
superior grade — as the market rules it to be superior at any

chosen moment — amounts to a tacit admission that quality and quantity are, in large degree, interchangeable concepts.

This fusion of the concepts of quality and quantity results of course directly from the appeal to market valuation. That in performing the summations necessary to the measurement of output such an appeal is inevitable, and the only available alternative to a chaos of arbitrary decisions, has already been shown. But to argue that the judgments of the market are invariably a true criterion of economic significance, or that such judgments are always unambiguous, would be a clear perversion of the facts. Since it is impossible to construct a measure of output without a weighting system, since the value concept is a convenient source of such a system, and since this concept underlies all our computations, it seems desirable to pursue the matter somewhat further.

THE LOGIC OF THE VALUE CONCEPT

The use of market values, or prices, as weights in computing the output index was suggested above primarily as a means of avoiding the need for arbitrary decisions. Since the market regards a dollar's worth of apples and a dollar's worth of oranges as equivalent or interchangeable, therefore — so the argument ran — we may regard them as equal physical quantities. What this leads to in practice is the aggregation of dollar volumes of different commodities at fixed prices per ton, per yard, or other commercial unit. By this procedure, the universal measure of physical output, applicable to all commodities without exception, becomes the dollar's worth — measured at the base date or over the base period.

Now under very special circumstances — circumstances which may roughly be labelled those of perfect competition — this procedure would have much more than merely pragmatic justification. Let us assume an unreal world in which perfect equality exists everywhere in the marginal significance attached to consumer expenditure in different directions, and at the same time perfect equivalence between market price and marginal cost of production; and further in which resources are remunerated according to their marginal productivity so interpreted, complete mobility existing among occupations. In such a world the phrase 'a dollar's worth' has a universal significance which is partially denied to it as things actually stand in the world as we know it. In such a world a dollar's worth, no matter of what commodity, comprises on the one hand, from the viewpoint of any given consumer, a standard amount of satisfaction. It measures at the same time on the other hand the product of a standard amount of resources. Furthermore, a dollar's worth of resources, no matter of what kind, will everywhere produce the same output as a dollar's worth of any other kind. The 'dollar's worth' therefore constitutes at any moment, in this ideal world, an unambiguous physical unit, not only of output, but of resources and satisfactions as well. This is of course true only at any given moment, for in making comparisons through time the ambiguities inherent in the 'index number problem' are in no way mitigated.

Consider then just what — in such a world — our appeal to the judgment of the market would have achieved. It would have provided us with a measure of output enabling us (apart from the index number problem, and apart also from possible deficiencies of coverage) to settle certain questions unambiguously. A rise in our index would be uniquely correlated with a rise in the community's aggregate level of satisfaction. If the community did not consume more of one thing, we would know that the community had chosen to consume more of something else. A rise in the index, unaccompanied by a corresponding rise in the amount of resources employed in production, would argue a real increase of economic efficiency. The economy could now produce as much as it produced previously, and still have resources over.

Evidently the significance of any output index we can actually construct will in large degree depend upon how closely the behavior of actual markets conforms to the ideal outlined above. Some consideration of actual market conditions is therefore called for.

THE CHARACTERISTICS OF MARKET VALUATION

Of the markets in which commodity output is sold the great majority are more or less imperfectly competitive. Perfect competition is probably as rare as outright monopoly. To some extent no doubt

the values of farm products, minerals, and manufactures differ
from the ideal values outlined above. Nevertheless, in the commodity field the difficulty is almost certainly less than in the production and sale of intangibles. Especially is this true of public
utilities. The prices at which transportation, gas, and electricity
are sold are notoriously the subject both of administrative control
and of monopolistic discrimination. How then do these facts affect
the construction and significance of our indexes of output?

Let us first consider the case of simple monopoly and see what
becomes of the argument of the foregoing section. An electric
utility, we will suppose, sells current at a price which, owing to
the absence both of competition and of effective rate control,
yields a particularly handsome return on its investment. The consumer pays more than the minimum necessary to attract and maintain resources in the industry, and purchases less current than he
would do were the price per unit lower. To any given consumer,
however, the significance of the marginal dollar's worth of electricity is still the same as the significance of the marginal dollar
devoted to the purchase of any other commodity. From the viewpoint of consumer satisfaction, therefore, the fact that a certain
commodity (electric current) is monopolized in no way invali-
dates our use of market prices as weights in the construction of an
output index. Whatever the structure of the market, the prices the
consumer pays are alone relevant to the measurement of output,
when output is regarded merely as a source of consumer satisfaction.

But output has to be related also to the resources employed in
its production. It is no longer true that a dollar's worth of electricity represents the product of the same amount of resources, in
any intelligible sense, as does a dollar's worth of other commodities not monopolized.[3] The price at which a kilowatt-hour sells
represents its cost to the consumer indeed, but to no one else. The
cost of a unit of electricity to the community, in terms of the
resources used up in its production, is measured by the sum for

[3] Unless of course monopoly power is itself regarded as a resource, whose
services are appropriately priced. But this does not seem a reasonable interpretation.

which that unit would sell if return on investment were normal and monopoly profit were absent. If therefore the units in which, in our index, we measure output are to represent (at the base date) the consumption of a defined amount of resources, rather than the provision to some given consumer of a defined amount of satisfaction, we must work with cost, including a normal return to investment, rather than with selling price. Where monopoly profit accrues, these two evidently diverge. It no longer is possible to construct a single output index, perfectly correlated both with the level of satisfaction to the community and with the consumption of real resources of a given efficiency.

These two systems of weights — one based on selling price, the other on cost — of course coincide in the world of ideal competitive behavior considered at the outset of this discussion. In the case of our electric utility it was not the fact of monopoly, but the existence of monopoly profit, that caused them to diverge. Had an efficient public service commission been in control of rates, such divergence might not have occurred. In asking ourselves how far existing market valuations really are appropriate for weighting an output index, or how far they conceal ambiguities of the kind indicated, the use made of monopoly power is more important than the fact of its existence.

The ambiguity — insofar as it relates to conditions of simple monopoly — is illustrated more concretely in the following example. The community's output consists of two commodities, A and B. A we will suppose monopolized, while B is produced and sold competitively. In two years A costs $1 to produce and sells for $2 a ton, whereas B costs and sells for $1 a ton. Let the outputs be as follows:

	Year I	Year II
A, tons	100	140
B, tons	100	50

Using the two alternative systems of weights, we have the following output indexes:

	Year I	Year II
Weighted by selling price:		
Price-sum	$300	$330
Index of output	100	110
Weighted by cost of production:		
Price-sum	$200	$190
Index of output	100	95

Evidently the question, Is the community better or worse off in Year II than in Year I? receives no immediate answer.

In terms of dollars' worth of *satisfaction,* measured at the margin, output is larger, and the community appears to be better off. But consumers' preferences have evidently so altered — they now take nearly three tons of A for every ton of B, instead of ton for ton, at unchanged prices — that any statement about the comparative satisfaction yielded by a dollar's expenditure in the two years appears unwarranted. The best we can do is to remark that *if* the marginal utility of the dollar has not declined, then the community is better off, in the sense that its level of satisfaction is higher, in Year II than in Year I.

In terms of dollars' worth of *resources,* on the other hand, also measured at the margin, output is smaller. Certainly it would seem that, if resources are mobile, and if their efficiency has not declined, the output of Year II can be obtained with fewer resources than that of Year I. In the use made of its resources, the community would seem to be worse off, or less efficient. How output would have behaved had there been no monopoly, had A been sold at its cost of $1 a ton (as B is sold), we have of course no means of knowing. However, under such conditions, no such ambiguity would develop in the measurement of output as that present in the instance cited.

The principle involved here is a perfectly general one. Evidently an ambiguity of this kind will appear whenever the demand price for a commodity differs from its cost of production. Cost has to be interpreted to include all payments necessary in the circumstances to attract resources and maintain them in a given occupation. The case of simple monopoly was discussed above merely because it provides a convenient illustration of the difficulty which arises when prices and costs do not correspond — when market price, that is, ceases to measure the amount of resources employed in production. Further important cases of the same difficulty include commodities subject to taxation,[4] or to price discrimination, and commodities jointly produced but inappropriately priced. The first of these, taxation, is important for certain manufactures,

---

[4] Taxation can of course be regarded as the price of services rendered to production by the state, but even so it would be hard to argue that such services are appropriately priced in each individual case.

e.g., beverages and tobacco products, but does not much affect the market for public utility services.

Price discrimination and joint supply are more in point for our purpose and may conveniently be considered together, since they merge into each other. The production of electric current has at one time or another been viewed as embodying both principles. It is, for example, a commonplace that current for domestic use is sold at higher prices than current for industrial purposes. So that if we regard a kilowatt-hour of electricity as a uniform commodity, irrespective of the character of the purchaser and the conditions surrounding its sale, it is evidently the practice of electric utilities to discriminate among their customers.

On the other hand the cost of supplying a kilowatt-hour differs considerably according to the load factor associated with, or embodied in the agreement for, its use, and with the quantity and type of equipment involved in supplying individual consumers. Moreover, the generation of current for some uses affects the cost of its supply for other uses. If we argue in this fashion, it would seem foolish to regard the total supply of kilowatt-hours as a single homogeneous commodity. In fact the provision of current for different uses would appear to possess many of the elements commonly associated with joint supply.

However we may prefer to analyze the situation, we know that apparently similar commodities, such as kilowatt-hours, are — like ton-miles of transportation — sold to different customers at widely different prices. What we wish to discover is whether, if we use these prices as weights in computing our output index, an ambiguity of the kind discussed above will ensue. Clearly such an ambiguity will be introduced insofar as price differences fail to correspond to differences of cost. This is the relevant criterion, and some attempt must be made to judge how far in their price policies public utilities and railroads do or do not conform to it.

The business of rate-making almost always leads in practice to a compromise between what is commonly called the 'value-of-service' principle (in other words, what the traffic will bear) on the one hand, and the 'cost-of-service' principle (that is, the cost of handling a particular shipment) on the other. To take the latter principle first: that each consumer of electricity or shipper of goods should bear at least the direct costs of the service he receives requires no special justification. That consumers are assessed, so far as general rules allow, with the cost of special equipment needed to serve them, or of specific charges entailed in handling their goods, is a well established principle of rate-making and need not detain us. Unfortunately, the costs common to the whole, or a large part, of the output of a utility or railroad are so considerable that the mere proviso that each consumer shall bear his own direct costs carries us only a very short distance. It does no more than set a floor below which individual rates must not be allowed to fall. To complete the schedule of rates (still for the time being adhering to the cost-of-service principle) it is necessary to distribute these common costs among the various classes of traffic. Authority exists for the statement that the proper interpretation of the cost-of-service principle results in distributing these common costs at a uniform rate per kilowatt-hour or per ton-mile, as the case may be.[5] To justify such a distribution we have to appeal to what would happen under simple competition. But such an appeal has little application in a field that is inevitably monopolized, and where competition may yield zero output. It would appear preferable to conclude that, if the cost-of-service principle alone were in question, the solution to the problem of railroad rate-making would be indeterminate.

According to the value-of-service principle, on the other hand, each consumer is charged whatever maximizes the net revenue of the enterprise. The prescription of the value-of-service principle therefore results in discriminating monopoly. Insofar as railroads and utilities follow this prescription — and there can be no doubt that they do so to a large extent — it might be thought the principle that prices and costs should correspond is reduced thereby to a mere pretence. That, even under a regime of discriminating monopoly, prices and costs are not *necessarily* unequal is best seen by reverting to the analysis of joint supply. Where several products come from a single process in unvarying proportions, the relationship between their selling prices in a competitive market will be

[5] Cf. A. C. Pigou, *Economics of Welfare*, Part II, Ch. XVIII.

such that the whole supply of each is absorbed without leaving unsatisfied customers. Provided that returns to the enterprise are normal, the aggregate proceeds will correspond to the aggregate costs of operation. While these costs cannot be imputed to particular products without reference to their selling prices, the price at which each product sells will of course measure its cost to the consumer, and in a real (if special) sense also its cost to the community at large, i.e., the amount of resources consumed in its production. Obviously true of all the products taken together, this statement is true also of each individual product, in the sense that only when these prices are charged is the market in equilibrium. In true cases of joint supply, therefore, the condition that price differences shall be such as to clear the market of each product, coupled with the further condition that the general level of these product prices shall secure normal returns to the enterprise — these two conditions taken together allow a complete determination of the costs of each and every product.

Unfortunately in the case of utilities and railroads so simple a solution does not exist. The provision of electric current or of transportation is not a true case of joint supply, because given quantities of service to one type of consumer do not imply stated quantities of service to another type. There is no such thing, for example, as clearing the market of any one kind of transport. In other words very considerable variations are technically possible in the relative degree to which a utility or railroad serves different classes of consumer. Nevertheless this problem equally is capable of a determinate solution, if we substitute for our previous condition, i.e., clearing the market, a new one, i.e., that the enterprise shall work as close to full capacity as is compatible with a normal return on its activities as a whole. This prescription may be described as a modification of the value-of-service principle, for the traffic is charged what it will bear in respect of the relation between rates, though not as regards their general level.[6]

[6] Neglecting prime costs, the condition is that the marginal revenues from each class of consumer shall be equal. If the monopoly dispenses service in two markets only, at prices y_1 and y_2 respectively, this is equivalent to the condition

$$\frac{y_1}{y_2} = \frac{e_1 \ (1 + e_2)}{e_2 \ (1 + e_1)}$$

In what sense can we say that such a plan keeps prices and costs equal to one another? Since returns are normal, there can be no doubt that the aggregate price paid for the services of the enterprise equals their aggregate cost. But there is no intelligible sense in which individual rates in the separate markets can be characterized as those which would prevail under competition. The most we can say is that the rate structure envisaged gives the community the maximum output it can obtain without a subsidy.[7] Any other set of rates would yield a smaller output and less efficient operation. Consumers in each market are charged, in the light of the elasticity of demand in that market, the minimum price necessary to cover normal returns. In this highly specialized sense, and in this sense only, can we say that prices and costs are equal, and that a weighting scheme which uses such prices is consequently appropriate.

In constructing our indexes of output for industries that practice monopoly pricing, we have presented more than one series. For railroads we have both weighted and unweighted ton-mile indexes, for electrical utilities both weighted and unweighted kilowatt-hour series. In some cases it does not much matter whether a weighting scheme is adopted or not; in others it makes a good deal of difference. Where monopolistic discrimination is practiced, it remains to ask, in terms of the preceding discussion, what degree of significance is to be attached to a weighted index of output, the weights being of course the actual prices charged by the monopoly in different markets.

Whether or not the rate structure conforms to the conditions prescribed above, conditions prescribed by social accounting, since

---

where e_1 and e_2 are the respective elasticities of demand. For a real solution there must be at least one set of prices that yields sufficient revenue for a normal return. If the demands are elastic for high prices and inelastic for low prices, there may be two solutions, one with high output, the other with low output, intermediate outputs yielding more revenue than is needed. Where there are two or more solutions, that with the highest utilization of capacity is the one indicated.

[7] With proposals to subsidize diminishing cost industries I have much sympathy, but such proposals are not here in question. We are seeking a weighting system which will measure output, not the pricing policy which will maximize 'welfare'.

the prices are actually paid, they do of course reflect defined amounts of utility at the margin for any given consumer. The domestic consumer who uses electric current for lighting and heating at different rates must be assumed to adjust his consumption to the rates in question. To this extent therefore the prices are appropriate weights for the measurement of output, independently of any cost considerations, just as they would be in the case of a simple monopolist who did not discriminate.

But the prices charged in different markets have a further appropriateness, in terms of social cost, only if the conditions outlined above are fulfilled. Otherwise the ambiguity which arose under simple monopoly is present here, in even higher degree, and the problem of measuring output is not susceptible, even in theory, of a determinate solution.

This discussion, prompted by the character of the markets in which railroad and utility services are sold, has carried us to a rather high level of abstraction. We have in fact little means of telling just how far prices actually charged are appropriate in the above sense. No unregulated monopoly could be expected to practice discrimination along the lines indicated. On the other hand it may quite well be that the Interstate Commerce Commission, in regulating the railroads, and public service commissions in regulating electric utilities, have some such guiding principle as that developed above. It is certainly arguable that considerations of public policy lead to the conclusion that they *should* be guided by such principles. Common sense also suggests that discriminatory pricing by a commission-regulated monopoly will conform more closely to our criterion than that by an unregulated monopoly. Without an elaborate investigation of the policies of the various commissions, it seems impossible to be more definite than this. We can outline the conditions under which weighted indexes will be preferable to unweighted indexes, even if we cannot be certain that these conditions are fulfilled.

THE COMBINATION OF INDUSTRIES

The preceding sections were concerned mainly with combining the outputs of different products into a single measure for the

output of an entire industry. Broadly speaking we have been talk-
ing about gross output. The transition to net output (where this is
statistically feasible) requires the insertion of input data, on the
same principles, with of course negative weights. The combination
of the outputs (gross or net) of different industries can then pro-
ceed, provided again we have a basis for weighting. Where gross
outputs for various industries are summed (and this does not lead
to duplication, or such duplication is to be neglected) the entire
value of the industry's products affords an appropriate measure of
the importance of the industry. Where net outputs are to be combined, the value added by the industry is the weight indicated.

In discussing industries in which monopoly (regulated or unregulated) is the rule, much the same problems have to be faced as
those encountered in weighting individual products. Thus, where
a monopoly earns more than the normal return, the usual ambiguity appears. Its value of products, or value added, continues to
correspond (in the usual vague way) to the marginal level of consumer satisfaction, but ceases to bear any relation to the amount of
resources consumed. The same is true where an industry earns
subnormal returns, or is subsidized. In the first case, thinking in
terms of units of resources of a given efficiency, the value of products, or value added, exaggerates the relative importance of the
industry; in the second case, its relative importance is understated.

What of the actual state of affairs in the transportation industries? The appropriateness for weighting purposes of value of
products or value added clearly depends upon the extent to which
regulatory agencies do in fact secure (neither more nor less than)
normal returns to these industries. In the case of railroads it is
certainly arguable that the industry has failed even to earn normal
returns since the advent of motor transport. In that case we are
in danger of underweighting its importance in the economy as a
whole.

Other transportation agencies have perhaps been subsidized.
It has been claimed that inland waterways and truck and buslines
have received subsidies through the provision of rights of way at
public expense. The merchant marine and the airlines have been
aided financially in more explicit fashion. In these industries if

returns, including subsidies, are normal, they are evidently subnormal when such aid is excluded. If the value of service as sold
to the purchaser is used for weighting purposes (as, broadly, has
been done here) such treatment may possibly be appropriate in
terms of consumer satisfaction. But it evidently understates the
resources employed.

Appendix B

Steam Railroads: Basic Series

Data for steam railroads shown in Tables 3 and 4, and not reproduced in this Appendix, will be found in Interstate Commerce Commission, *Statistics of Railways in the United States, 1939.*

Table B-1

STEAM RAILROADS: TRAFFIC, REVENUE, AND EMPLOYMENT, 1890-1946

Year ending June 30	ALL PASSENGERS[a]		ALL FREIGHT[a]		EMPLOYMENT					
					Number of Workers (th.)[d]				Manhours (bil.)	
	Passenger-miles[b] (bil.)	Revenue per passenger-mile (cents)	Ton-miles[c] (bil.)	Revenue per ton-mile (cents)	Line haul roads	Switching and terminal companies	Pullman Company	Express companies	Line haul roads[e]	Pullman Company[f]
1890	12.0	2.17	76.2	.941	749	...	...	...	...	...
1891	13.1	2.14	82.1	.895	784	...	...	...	...	...
1892	13.5	2.13	88.8	.898	821	...	...	...	...	...
1893	14.3	2.11	94.2	.878	874	...	...	...	...	...
1894	14.4	1.99	81.1	.860	780	...	...	...	...	...
1895	12.4	2.04	86.8	.839	785	...	...	...	...	...
1896	13.2	2.02	97.3	.806	827	...	...	...	...	...
1897	12.4	2.02	96.6	.798	823	...	...	...	...	...
1898	13.5	1.97	116	.753	875	...	...	...	...	...
1899	14.7	1.98	126	.724	929	...	...	...	...	...
1900	16.2	2.00	144	.729	1,018	...	...	...	...	...
1901	17.5	2.01	149	.750	1,071	...	...	...	...	...
1902	19.8	1.99	159	.757	1,189	...	...	...	...	...
1903	21.0	2.01	175	.763	1,312	...	...	...	...	...
1904	22.1	2.01	176	.780	1,296	...	...	...	...	...
1905	24.1	1.96	189	.766	1,382	...	...	...	...	...
1906	25.5	2.00	219	.748	1,521	...	...	...	...	...
1907	28.0	2.01	240	.759	1,672	...	...	...	...	...
1908	29.3	1.94	219	.754	1,436	...	...	...	...	...
1909	29.2	1.93	219	.763	1,503	...	...	...	...	...
1910	32.5	1.94	255	.753	1,699	...	...	...	...	...
1911	33.3	1.97	254	.757	1,670	...	15.0	...	...	...
1912	33.2	1.99	264	.744	1,716	...	15.1	...	...	...
1913	34.7	2.01	302	.729	1,832	...	20.8	...	...	...
1914	35.4	1.99	289	.737	1,710	...	20.1	...	...	...
1915	32.5	1.99	277	.735	1,548	...	19.1	...	4.96	...
1916	34.3	2.01	343	.719	1,654	...	18.9	...	...	.07

Calendar Year										
1916	35.2	2.05	366	.719	1,701	...	18.3	...	5.19	.07
1917	40.1	2.10	398	.728	1,786	...	20.2	...	5.44	.07
1918	43.2	2.42	409	.862	1,892	...	17.7	...	5.70	.07
1919	46.8	2.55	367	.987	1,960	...	21.5	...	5.03	.06
1920	47.4	2.75	414	1.069	2,076	...	22.9	...	5.45	.07
1921	37.7	3.09	310	1.294	1,705	59.1	21.1	77.0	4.08	.06
1922	35.8	3.04	342	1.194	1,670	49.5	19.1	74.5	4.19	.06
1923	38.3	3.03	416	1.132	1,902	56.6	23.6	72.8	4.80	.07
1924	36.4	2.99	392	1.132	1,796	57.6	25.1	66.1	4.41	.08
1925	36.2	2.94	417	1.114	1,786	59.8	26.6	66.4	4.40	.08
1926	35.7	2.94	447	1.096	1,822	61.8	26.2	66.3	4.51	.08
1927	33.8	2.90	432	1.095	1,776	60.3	27.4	62.4	4.36	.08
1928	31.7	2.85	436	1.094	1,692	57.6	26.8	60.7	4.14	.08
1929	31.2	2.81	450	1.088	1,694	58.5	29.2	59.4	4.17	.08
1930	26.9	2.72	386	1.074	1,517	54.6	26.2	51.2	3.60	.08
1931	21.9	2.52	311	1.062	1,283	47.7	22.5	44.1	2.89	.07
1932	17.0	2.22	235	1.056	1,052	40.0	17.1	36.0	2.26	.05
1933	16.4	2.02	251	1.009	991	37.7	15.9	35.7	2.12	.05
1934	18.1	1.92	270	.989	1,027	39.2	19.1	36.2	2.27	.05
1935	18.5	1.94	284	.998	1,014	38.9	20.4	38.0	2.27	.05
1936	22.5	1.84	341	.984	1,086	42.1	21.7	40.8	2.53	.06
1937	24.7	1.80	363	.945	1,137	45.5	23.4	42.7	2.65	.06
1938	21.7	1.88	292	.994	958	39.8	20.8	40.4	2.19	.05
1939	22.7	1.84	335	.983	1,007	42.0	21.3	41.9	2.34	.06
1940	23.8	1.76	375	.955	1,046	46.0	20.9	44.6	2.46	.05
1941	29.4	1.75	478	.944	1,159	50.8	22.7	48.9	2.82	.06
1942	53.7	1.92	641	.940	1,291	56.9	26.6	51.1	3.22	.07
1943	87.9	1.88	730	.940	1,375	60.1	33.2	62.6	3.58	.09
1944	95.7	1.87	741	.957	1,434	64.5	39.7	73.7	3.72	.10
1945	91.8	1.87	684	.967	1,439	63.5	41.6	79.6	3.68	.11
1946	64.8	1.95	595	.986	1,378	63.4	39.3	82.7	3.35	.10

Notes to Table B-1

[a] Interstate Commerce Commission, *Statistics of Railways in the United States* (annual). Class I, II, and III roads; 1890-1907, includes switching and terminal companies; since 1908, excludes switching and terminal companies.

[b] For 1914 and later years coverage is substantially complete. For 1913 coverage was practically complete but cannot be estimated accurately. For 1912 and earlier years coverage of original data varied between 97 and 100 percent (judged by passenger revenue), and data shown here have been adjusted upward on this account, i.e., divided by the percentage of coverage.

[c] For 1911 and later years coverage is substantially complete. For 1891 to 1910 coverage of original data varied between 97 and 100 percent (judged by freight revenue), and data shown here have been adjusted upward on this account; i.e., we divided the figures as originally reported by the percentage of coverage. For 1890 coverage could not be determined but was assumed to be 100 percent. For 1906 and earlier years published totals include the small amount of ton-miles reported by switching and terminal companies. Such companies did not report traffic after 1907; accordingly figures shown for 1890-1906 have been adjusted downward, on the basis of the relationship in 1907, to exclude switching and terminal companies.

[d] Data from *Statistics of Railways. Class I Companies:* For line haul companies 1914 and prior year figures represent a single count on June 30 (end of fiscal year to which other data in the table apply). The 1915 figure is an average of six counts distributed throughout the year; however, the estimate as originally published was considered incomplete and was later written up (*Statistics of Railways,* 1919, p. 20). For 1916-21 the figures are based on four counts during the year. Since 1922 twelve monthly counts have been averaged in order to arrive at employment for the year. Apparently figures for Class I switching and terminal companies were compiled in the same manner as those for line haul companies. *Class II and III Companies:* Figures represent single counts. In 1915 no data for class III line haul companies were collected, and accordingly we made an estimate on the basis of adjoining years. *Pullman Company:* In 1935 and prior years, figures represent a single year-end count; in 1936 to 1944, an average of twelve monthly counts; in 1945, a year-end count; and in 1946, mean of counts at the beginning and end of the year. *Express Companies:* In 1933 and prior years, figures represent a single year-end count; in 1934 and later years, an average of twelve monthly counts.

[e] Class I companies only. Data from *Statistics of Railways* and ICC, 'Wage Statistics of Class I Steam Railways' (monthly). Figures for 1916-20 are described as 'hours actually on duty', and exclude 'constructive allowances' for time not worked, e.g., time allowed for vacations, holidays, leaves of absence, etc. with pay; they were also intended to exclude other time paid for but not worked by transportation (train and engine) employees. The existence of additional time paid for but not worked (currently referred to in the *Statistics of Railways* as 'other straight time paid for') in the case of these employees results from the method of payment of train and engine crews whose runs exceed the mileage equivalent of the standard workday; or who perform runs in less than the scheduled time, and so cut their own tours of duty, without loss of pay. However, some of this additional time paid for but not worked may perhaps have crept into the hourly data for 1916-20; in any case no adjustment of the data on this account is possible. Figures for 1921-27 represent 'total hours worked' which, for these years, have been definitely stated to exclude both constructive allowances and additional time paid for but not worked by train and engine crews. (Minor adjustments had to be made in 1921 and 1922 to exclude switching and terminal companies, since line haul companies are not separately distinguished in the tabulations for these years.) For 1928 and later years, the figures shown here represent 'straight time actually worked' plus 'overtime paid for'. This amount falls short of 'total time paid for': for train

and engine employees it excludes 'other straight time paid for' (e.g., the excess of the hourly equivalent of a standard day's run over the time actually taken to make the run, or the hourly equivalent of the excess of a minimum day's run over the run actually made) and 'constructive allowances' (hours paid for when "held away from home terminal, called and not used, runaround, deadheading, attending court, suspensions, investigations, and claim and safety meetings") ; for other employees it excludes 'time paid for but not worked' (the hourly equivalent of pay for "holidays, absence on definite leave, vacations, attending court, suspensions, sickness, time allowed for meals, and . . . allowance to complete a minimum day when less than a minimum day is worked"). See ICC, *Rules Governing the Classification of Steam Railway Employees* (1921). To the extent that the allowances represent hours actually worked (as in deadheading, or attending court) the figures may understate time worked. (In 1928-32 minor adjustments had to be made to exclude switching and terminal companies in estimating the latter deduction.)

Roughly one railroad worker in ten is paid by the day: time paid for by the day was converted to an hourly basis by assuming a ten-hour day in 1916-18 and an eight-hour day thereafter. The series shown in this column probably offers the nearest approach to continuously comparable data on hours actually worked.

ᶠ For 1935 and prior years, days worked are to be found in ICC Statement No. 3631, 'Sleeping Car Statistics, 1890-1935' (mimeo., Aug. 1936); days were converted to hours on the basis of a ten-hour day in 1918 and prior years and an eight-hour day thereafter. Figures for 1936 and later years were extrapolated on the basis of the number of workers.

Table B-2

STEAM RAILROADS: PASSENGER TRAFFIC AND REVENUE BY KIND OF PASSENGER, 1911-1921[a]

Year Ending June 30	COMMUTATION AND COACH		PARLOR AND SLEEPING CAR	
	Passenger-miles (bil.)	Revenue per passenger-mile (cents)	Passenger-miles (bil.)	Revenue per passenger-mile[b] (cents)
1911	24.64	1.87	7.73	2.75
1912	24.38	1.88	7.93	2.76
1913	25.74	1.91	8.14	2.80
1914	26.27	1.88	8.30	2.77
1915	23.65	1.88	8.14	2.76
Calendar Year				
1916	25.26	1.94	9.32	2.82
1917	28.72	1.98	10.76	2.88
1918	32.34	2.30	10.34	3.27
1919	33.09	2.40	13.27	3.39
1920	33.03	2.55	13.82	3.79
1921	26.44	2.83	10.88	4.33

[a] *Statistics of Railways;* see also ICC Statement 3631. This breakdown is not available prior to 1911. Data relate to class I railroads only; for this reason passenger-miles shown here do not add exactly to the totals of Table B-1.
[b] Railroad fare plus Pullman charge.

Table B-3

STEAM RAILROADS: PASSENGER TRAFFIC AND REVENUE BY KIND OF PASSENGER, 1922-1946[a]

	COMMUTATION		COACH (OTHER THAN COMMUTATION)		PARLOR AND SLEEPING CAR		FREE RIDERS[c]	
	Passenger-miles (bil.)	Revenue per passenger-mile (cents)	Passenger-miles (bil.)	Revenue per passenger-mile (cents)	Passenger-miles (bil.)	Revenue per passenger-mile[b] (cents)	Passenger-miles (bil.)	Revenue per passenger-mile[a] (cents)
1922	6.12	1.10	18.08	3.31	11.26	4.23	0.50	0.61
1923	6.39	1.09	19.18	3.29	12.39	4.20	0.59	0.61
1924	6.40	1.10	17.35	3.26	12.34	4.17	0.74	0.61
1925	6.59	1.11	16.39	3.21	12.97	4.13	1.05	0.62
1926	6.60	1.13	15.66	3.21	13.22	4.13	1.19	0.62
1927	6.65	1.11	14.20	3.19	12.80	4.11	1.30	0.62
1928	6.62	1.11	12.32	3.15	12.65	4.08	1.28	0.62
1929	6.90	1.10	11.42	3.13	12.75	4.06	1.30	0.62
1930	6.67	1.09	8.85	3.08	11.30	4.01	1.21	0.62
1931	6.02	1.06	6.94	2.89	8.93	3.82	0.96	0.62
1932	4.98	1.07	5.88	2.54	6.10	3.47	0.65	0.62
1933	4.31	1.08	6.47	2.21	5.57	3.12	0.58	0.61
1934	4.16	1.09	7.69	2.02	6.18	2.98	0.71	0.64
1935	4.12	1.09	7.94	2.03	6.42	2.99	0.73	0.64
1936	4.19	1.06	10.74	1.89	7.49	2.83	0.86	0.63
1937	4.12	1.10	12.41	1.71	8.13	2.95	1.04	0.62
1938	4.03	1.01	10.24	1.86	7.35	3.00	0.92	0.64
1939	4.01	1.02	11.12	1.80	7.53	2.98	0.96	0.65

1940	4.00	1.01	12.48	1.67	7.29	2.94	0.93	0.64
1941	4.09	1.01	16.11	1.64	9.17	2.88	0.90	0.60
1942	4.76	1.06	30.91	1.77	17.85	2.94	1.22	0.54
1943	5.26	1.07	57.91	1.74	24.67	2.94	1.22	0.55
1944	5.34	1.07	63.29	1.70	26.94	2.99	1.32	0.56
1945	5.42	1.08	59.42	1.71	26.91	2.95	0.36	0.56
1946	5.86	1.08	39.00	1.82	19.84	3.06	0.83	0.61

[a] *Statistics of Railways*; see also ICC Statement 3631. This breakdown is not available prior to 1922, but see Table B-2 above. Data relate to Class I railroads only; for this reason passenger-miles shown in the first three columns do not add exactly to the totals of Table B-1. Revenue figures for coach and for parlor and sleeping car passengers in 1936 and prior years are not shown separately in the sources mentioned, but were estimated as follows. Railroads collected a surcharge from parlor and sleeping car passengers equal to one-half of the Pullman charge. Therefore the difference between revenues per passenger-mile accruing to the railroads from coach travel and from parlor and sleeping car travel was approximately equal to one-half the revenue per passenger-mile reported by the Pullman Company.

[b] Railroad fare plus Pullman charge.

[c] Pullman passengers riding on free railroad passes. Data are estimated by deducting parlor and sleeping car passenger-miles reported by railroads (shown at left) from passenger-miles reported by the Pullman Company (not shown). The resulting total, shown in this column, is only approximate because the Pullman Company total includes operations in Canada and Mexico, but excludes passenger-miles of chartered car passengers. The revenue figure is the Pullman charge.

[d] Pullman charge.

Appendix C

Steam Railroads: How Would a
Weighted Ton-Mile Index Behave?
By Jacob M. Gould

The reasoning of Appendix A suggests that the best measure of what we really mean by the 'physical volume of freight traffic' would be an index of ton-miles in which each ton-mile was weighted by the revenue derived therefrom. It was explained in Chapter 4 that no breakdown of ton-miles is available except for the single year 1932. In consequence the unweighted ton-mile total has been regarded throughout this book as the basic measure of railroad freight traffic. It was also stated in Chapter 4 that the absence of a weighting system leads to an upward bias in our ton-mile index, at least for the period 1919-39. The purpose of the present Appendix is to justify this statement.

For any given commodity, let

q, be the number of tons originated;

qh, its ton-mileage;

pqh, revenue accruing from its transportation.

If we had such data for each year we could isolate by successive division the three components of freight revenue. Thus h is the *average* haul associated with the shipment of q tons of the commodity, and p is the *average* revenue per ton-mile realized from its transportation. A certain amount of variation lies behind these averages; however, it will be necessary to treat ton-miles for individual commodities as homogeneous. That is to say, it will be impossible to take account of differences in revenue per ton-mile — caused by varying handling charges, lengths of haul, and so forth — among individual shipments of any one commodity. We assume that the dispersion of p within commodity groups is small compared with its dispersion between such groups.

If we denote base-year quantities by small letters and given-year quantities by capitals, the simple Laspeyres index has the form

(1) $\Sigma QHp/\Sigma qhp$, in which the summation extends over all the

commodities entering into the index. This is the 'weighted ton-mile', or 'ideal', index which cannot in fact be constructed.

Among indexes capable of actual construction from available data,

(2) $\Sigma QH/\Sigma qh$

is the unweighted ton-mile index, which we have treated as basic in Chapter 4. In the alternative index there discussed,

(3) $\Sigma Qhp/\Sigma qhp$

each class of tonnage originated is weighted by the corresponding base-year figure for revenue per ton of freight originated. This index can be obtained because data on tonnage originated broken down by commodities are available every year, and revenue totals for all commodities are available for some years, thus providing base-year weights.

It is apparent from inspection that (2) does not take into account variations in p over all classes of commodities and will differ from (1) as the relative proportions of those classes change, whose freight charges in the base year were on different levels.

Again it is apparent from inspection that (3) is deficient, in that it fails to account for the change in h occurring between the given year and base year, although it does assign the desired pecuniary weights to the various classes of commodities. This deficiency is accentuated as the period separating the years compared widens, for the secular increase in *average* haul has been quite marked over the period in question (see Table C-3). Formula (2) will, of course, adequately reflect this change, but takes no account of dispersion in rates even between one commodity and another.

CAN WE MEASURE THE BIAS IN A WEIGHTED INDEX OF TONS ORIGINATED?

In any year we may derive the average haul for all commodities by dividing total ton-mileage by total tons originated. The question arises whether (3), with a simple adjustment for change in average haul of all commodities, will approach our 'ideal' formula. Such an adjusted index would be afforded by:

$$(4)\ \frac{\Sigma Qhp}{\Sigma qhp} \cdot \frac{\Sigma QH}{\Sigma Q} \bigg/ \frac{\Sigma qh}{\Sigma q}$$

Some light is shed on the relation between (4) and the 'weighted ton-mile' index, (1), by the following considerations. Formula (1) may be expressed as:

$$\frac{\Sigma QHp}{\Sigma qhp} = \frac{\Sigma Qhp(H/h)}{\Sigma qhp}$$

By substitution of Qhp and H/h for x and y in the correlation formula

$$\frac{1}{n} \Sigma\, x\, \Sigma y = \Sigma xy - r_{xy}\sigma_x\sigma_y$$

we get the identity

$$\frac{\Sigma Qhp}{\Sigma qhp} \cdot \frac{1}{n} \Sigma\, \frac{H}{h} = \frac{\Sigma QHp}{\Sigma qhp} - R$$

where the remainder denoted by R is a quantity that varies with the degree of correlation existing between the expressions Qhp and H/h; i.e., between the given year quantity valued at the base-year price and the change in the length of haul. To the extent that this correlation approaches zero, formula (4) may be said to approach the 'weighted ton-mile' index, with the difference that the ratio of weighted aggregates, $\dfrac{\Sigma QH}{\Sigma Q} \Big/ \dfrac{\Sigma qh}{\Sigma q}$ is replaced by the average of relatives, $\dfrac{1}{n} \Sigma \dfrac{H}{h}$ as a measure of the change in h. The latter qualification to the use of (4) as an approximation to (1) is not, however, as serious an objection as the assumption that the coefficient of correlation between Qhp and H/h will be small enough to render negligible the above remainder, R. The possibility of such correlation is enhanced by the fact that the distribution of revenue totals in any year is highly nonnormal,[1] being characterized by a heavy concentration of items at the extreme right of the distribution and a few observations (such as bituminous coal) at the extreme left (Table C-2). The use of the weighted index of tonnage originated is thus seen to involve a degree of error about which we know little. Nor does it seem that a simple correction for change in average haul could prove adequate.

[1] See F. C. Mills, *Statistical Methods* (Holt, 1938), pp. 370-4, for a discussion of the derivation of (spuriously) high correlation coefficients based on nonnormal distributions.

THE BIAS IN AN UNWEIGHTED INDEX OF TON-MILES

It is somewhat easier to estimate the bias in our basic index, which relies on a simple ton-mile aggregate

$$(2) \quad \frac{\Sigma QH}{\Sigma qh} .$$

We shall show that such an index understates by 5 to 10 percent the decline in freight traffic over the period 1919-39 that would be reported by a weighted ton-mile index.

The starting point of this inquiry must be the detailed commodity figures collected by the Federal Coordinator of Transportation for 1932. This canvass produced, for the first and only time, $p, q,$ and h data for the 156 ICC carload commodity classifications (Tables C-1 and C-2). In the grouping process, all ton-miles associated with a particular commodity are supposed concentrated at their mean rate per ton-mile. Consequently the distribution given is merely an approximation to that which would be obtained if individual shipments were classified immediately according to their ton-mile rates.

While, therefore, the classification of Table C-2 is essentially by commodities, as in Table C-1, these no longer appear explicitly. We may note, however, two commodity classifications of special importance: bituminous coal, which is grouped separately at one end of the distribution, and the less-than-carload class in the 3.750-3.899 cents per ton-mile interval. We single these two groups out for special attention because in this way the entire price distribution is seen to fall into three significant components. Bituminous coal, which we shall refer to as Group I, may be regarded as homogeneous. Group II consists of all commodities other than bituminous coal, less-than-carload lots, and two relatively minor commodity groups (passenger automobiles and explosives) transported at what amount to less-than-carload rates. While the dispersion of Group II is relatively wide, the 'normality'[2] of its distribution about the modal interval suggests that it may be treated as homogeneous. Group III at the upper end of the range is domi-

[2] This is a rather loose use of the term, for the Group II distribution is obviously skewed to the left. There is of course a danger involved in regarding this group as homogeneous, i.e., treating its average (weighted) price as representative of the entire group, and associating the entire group frequency with it. The danger, however, is far less than had we retained bituminous coal in the group.

Table C-1

STEAM RAILROADS: FREIGHT TRAFFIC BY
INDIVIDUAL COMMODITIES, 1932[a]

ICC Ref. No.	Commodity or Group	Tonnage Orig. (th.)	Ton-miles (mil.)	Freight Revenue ($ th.)	Rev. per Ton-mile (cents)	Av. Haul (miles)
10	Wheat	19,913	6,359	66,571	1.05	319
20	Corn	9,736	2,834	29,862	1.05	291
30	Oats	3,531	1,162	10,774	0.93	329
40	Barley and rye	1,585	439	4,650	1.06	277
41	Rice	591	189	2,474	1.31	320
42	Grain, NOS	83	42	397	0.94	505
50	Flour, wheat	8,811	5,011	34,479	0.69	569
51	Meal, corn	196	89	548	0.61	456
52	Flour and meal, edible, NOS	447	254	1,872	0.74	567
60	Cereal food preparations, edible, NOS	742	466	4,430	0.95	627
61	Mill products, NOS	6,214	2,534	17,926	0.71	408
70	Hay and alfalfa	1,432	536	7,415	1.38	375
71	Straw	148	31	541	1.74	210
80	Tobacco, leaf	633	232	5,113	2.20	367
90	Cotton in bales	2,562	1,052	18,965	1.80	411
91	Cotton linters	249	172	1,828	1.06	692
100	Cottonseed	1,751	177	3,765	2.13	101
101	Cottonseed meal and cake	1,450	668	6,135	0.92	462
110	Oranges and grapefruit	1,805	3,835	48,083	1.25	2,126
111	Lemons, limes, and citrus fruits, NOS	225	536	5,865	1.09	2,387
120	Apples, fresh	1,388	1,614	20,347	1.26	1,162
121	Bananas	675	469	10,165	2.17	694
122	Berries, fresh	51	62	1,285	2.08	1,200
123	Cantaloupes and melons, NOS	300	729	8,624	1.18	2,434
124	Grapes, fresh	648	1,682	19,410	1.15	2,597
125	Peaches, fresh	262	220	4,011	1.82	843
126	Watermelons	363	393	4,522	1.15	1,084
127	Fruits, fresh, domestic, NOS	458	803	10,152	1.26	1,754
128	Fruits, fresh, tropical, NOS	39	59	722	1.22	1,519
130	Potatoes, other than sweet	3,516	2,607	32,246	1.24	741
140	Cabbage	380	368	5,085	1.38	970
141	Onions	379	384	4,491	1.17	1,013
142	Tomatoes	273	518	6,895	1.33	1,894
143	Vegetables, fresh, NOS	1,665	3,433	44,085	1.28	2,063
150	Beans and peas, dried	586	521	5,609	1.08	888
151	Fruits, dried or evaporated	521	434	4,859	1.12	834
152	Vegetables, dry, NOS	213	147	2,108	1.44	689
160	Vegetable oil, cake and meal, except cottonseed	290	116	986	0.85	399
161	Peanuts	231	165	2,484	1.50	715
162	Flaxseed	288	88	1,096	1.25	304
163	Sugar beets	5,422	253	3,460	1.37	47
164	Products of agriculture, NOS	3,139	1,339	15,719	1.17	426
	PRODUCTS OF AGRICULTURE, TOTAL	83,192	43,023	480,052	1.12	517

Table C-1 — RAILROAD FREIGHT TRAFFIC (continued)

ICC Ref. No.	Commodity or Group	Tonnage Orig. (th.)	Ton-miles (mil.)	Revenue Freight ($ th.)	Rev. per Ton-mile (cents)	Av. Haul (miles)
170	Horses, mules, ponies and asses	233	138	2,749	1.99	594
180	Cattle and calves, single-deck	4,888	1,997	32,916	1.65	409
181	Calves, double-deck	59	33	458	1.39	554
190	Sheep and goats, single-deck	202	92	1,556	1.70	453
191	Sheep and goats, double-deck	914	584	8,232	1.41	639
200	Hogs, single-deck	1,582	386	8,897	2.31	244
201	Hogs, double-deck	2,320	1,255	17,831	1.42	541
210	Fresh meats, NOS	2,678	2,457	40,417	1.64	918
220	Meats, cured, dried or smoked	587	593	8,498	1.43	1,011
221	Butterine and margarine	12	9	222	2.38	761
222	Packing house products, edible, NOS[b]	1,027	818	12,490	1.53	797
230	Poultry, live	112	135	3,040	2.26	1,207
231	Poultry, dressed	285	351	7,349	2.09	1,232
240	Eggs	459	621	11,438	1.84	1,353
250	Butter	607	563	12,230	2.17	927
251	Cheese	183	150	3,032	2.01	819
260	Wool	263	224	4,684	2.09	851
270	Hides, green	519	322	4,531	1.41	620
271	Leather	130	81	1,286	1.60	617
280	Fish or sea-animal oil	83	80	636	0.79	966
281	Animals, live, NOS	10	3	74	2.29	340
282	Animal products, NOS[c]	1,042	477	7,961	1.67	457
	ANIMAL AND PRODUCTS, TOTAL	18,195	11,368	190,528	1.68	625
290	Anthracite coal	54,974	9,571	107,913	1.13	174
300	Bituminous coal	208,383	75,412	491,048	0.65	362
310	Coke	7,420	1,354	15,386	1.14	182
320	Iron ore	5,919	792	6,563	0.83	134
330	Copper ore and concentrates	1,987	59	551	0.94	30
331	Lead ore and concentrates	917	48	663	1.39	52
332	Zinc ore and concentrates	794	279	1,831	0.66	352
333	Ores and concentrates, NOS	1,075	515	3,410	0.66	479
350	Gravel and sand[d]	28,589	1,992	23,475	1.18	70
351	Stone, broken, ground, or crushed	15,161	1,309	13,555	1.04	86
352	Stone, rough, NOS	2,507	342	3,407	1.00	136
353	Stone, finished, NOS	510	265	2,598	0.98	521
360	Petroleum, crude	2,666	1,075	8,605	0.80	403
370	Asphalt	2,601	768	9,618	1.25	295
380	Salt	3,004	1,452	13,945	0.96	483
390	Phosphate rock, crude	2,853	319	2,826	0.89	112
391	Sulphur	1,434	351	2,796	0.80	245
392	Products of mines, NOS	12,544	2,832	23,460	0.83	226
	PRODUCTS OF MINES, TOTAL	353,336	98,736	731,652	0.74	279

Table C-1 — RAILROAD FREIGHT TRAFFIC (continued)

ICC Ref. No.	Commodity or Group	Tonnage Orig. (th.)	Ton-miles (mil.)	Freight Revenue ($ th.)	Rev. per Ton-mile (cents)	Av. Haul (miles)
400	Logs	5,195	289	3,045	1.05	56
401	Posts, poles and piling	1,508	761	7,297	0.96	505
402	Wood (fuel)	1,399	125	1,377	1.10	89
410	Ties, railroad	837	262	2,763	1.05	313
420	Pulpwood	3,454	514	4,588	0.89	149
430	Lumber, shingles, and lath	11,446	8,549	67,862	0.79	747
431	Box, crate, and cooperage materials	1,712	1,089	11,143	1.02	636
432	Veneer and built-up wood	108	132	978	0.74	1,225
440	Rosin	251	135	1,352	1.10	540
441	Turpentine	44	45	540	1.19	1,037
442	Crude rubber (not reclaimed)	375	207	2,773	1.34	552
443	Products of forests, NOS	1,047	337	3,991	1.18	322
	FOREST PRODUCTS, TOTAL	27,375	12,446	107,710	0.87	455
450	Refined petroleum and gasoline	36,465	12,794	192,273	1.50	351
451	Fuel, road, and residual oils, NOS	7,985	2,267	27,673	1.22	284
452	Lubricating oils and greases	2,510	1,222	15,546	1.27	487
453	Petroleum products, NOS	186	78	971	1.25	418
460	Cottonseed oil	894	466	5,811	1.25	521
461	Linseed oil	118	60	769	1.28	512
462	Vegetable oils, NOS	330	355	2,377	0.67	1,076
470	Sugar (beet or cane)	3,725	2,111	25,310	1.20	567
471	Table syrups and edible molasses	487	349	3,246	0.93	716
472	Molasses and beet residual	450	156	1,551	0.99	347
490	Iron, pig	1,460	295	2,833	0.96	202
491	Iron and steel, 6th class, NOS	1,301	128	1,880	1.47	98
500	Rails, fastenings, frogs, and switches	394	132	1,481	1.12	336
510	Cast-iron pipe and fittings	442	263	3,166	1.20	596
511	Iron and steel pipe and fittings, NOS	1,361	710	10,547	1.49	522
512	Iron and steel: nails and wire not woven	657	278	4,070	1.47	422
513	Iron and steel, 5th class, NOS°	9,428	2,892	42,298	1.46	307
520	Copper: ingot, matte, and pig	200	236	1,676	0.71	1,181
521	Copper, brass and bronze^r	128	48	690	1.45	373
522	Lead and zinc: ingot, pig, or bar	590	562	3,436	0.61	953
523	Aluminum: ingot, pig, or slab	16	13	209	1.60	809
530	Machinery and boilers	1,074	631	10,850	1.72	587

Table C-1 — RAILROAD FREIGHT TRAFFIC (continued)

ICC Ref. No.	Commodity or Group	Tonnage Orig. (th.)	Ton-miles (mil.)	Freight Revenue ($ th.)	Rev. per Ton-mile (cents)	Av. Haul (miles)
540	Cement	11,529	2,257	31,797	1.41	196
550	Brick, common	1,009	188	2,068	1.10	187
551	Brick, NOS, and building tile	2,416	767	7,191	0.94	317
552	Artificial stone, NOS	139	48	547	1.13	348
560	Lime, common (quick or slaked)	1,116	395	3,842	0.97	354
561	Plaster and dry kalsomine	609	285	2,705	0.95	469
570	Sewer pipe and drain tile[g]	622	212	2,702	1.27	341
580	Agricultural implements and parts, NOS	184	109	1,940	1.78	589
581	Vehicles, horse-drawn, and parts, NOS	12	8	148	1.76	706
582	Tractors and parts	112	75	1,302	1.73	673
583	Railway car wheels, axles, and trucks	132	37	607	1.63	281
590	Automobiles (passenger)	709	583	21,821	3.74	823
591	Autotrucks	58	52	1,468	2.81	906
592	Automobiles and trucks, KD, and parts, NOS	1,311	872	14,428	1.65	665
593	Automobile and truck tires	218	199	3,620	1.82	912
610	Furniture, metal	71	46	935	2.01	650
611	Furniture, other than metal	308	248	5,955	2.40	804
620	Beverages	360	156	2,234	1.43	433
630	Ice	1,474	74	1,691	2.28	50
640	Fertilizers, NOS	4,966	1,420	15,821	1.11	286
650	Newsprint paper	1,621	1,147	11,348	0.99	708
651	Printing paper, NOS	1,223	634	7,478	1.18	519
660	Alcohol, denatured or wood	230	121	1,617	1.34	526
661	Sulphuric acid	1,206	195	3,058	1.57	162
662	Explosives, NOS	136	66	2,484	3.79	483
670	Cotton cloth and fabrics, NOS	300	195	3,866	1.98	650
671	Bagging and bags, burlap, jute	208	123	1,782	1.45	592
680	Canned food products, NOS	3,239	2,197	27,442	1.25	679
690	Tobacco, manufactured products	151	191	3,484	1.83	1,259
691	Paints in oil and varnishes	196	125	1,706	1.36	639
692	Furnace slag	2,071	177	1,841	1.04	85
693	Scrap iron and scrap steel	3,490	491	6,832	1.39	141
694	Paper bags and wrapping paper	1,077	638	7,611	1.19	593
695	Paperboard, pulpboard, and wallboard	1,593	731	8,518	1.16	459
696	Roofing materials[h]	1,102	464	6,120	1.32	421
697	Building woodwork (millwork)	155	224	1,692	0.75	1,451

Table C-1 — RAILROAD FREIGHT TRAFFIC (concluded)

ICC Ref. No.	Commodity or Group	Tonnage Orig. (th.)	Ton-miles (mil.)	Freight Revenue ($ th.)	Rev. per Ton-mile (cents)	Av. Haul (miles)
698	Soap and washing compounds	865	428	6,338	1.48	495
699	Glass, flat, other than plate	203	126	1,664	1.32	621
700	Glass: bottles and jars	1,154	646	8,225	1.27	560
701	Manufactures and miscellaneous, NOS	26,202	12,421	173,848	1.40	474
	MANUFACTURES AND MIS- CELLANEOUS, TOTAL	143,979	55,420	768,436	1.39	385
	TOTAL CARLOAD	626,078	220,994	2,278,377	1.03	353
	LESS-THAN-CARLOAD	15,115	6,590	250,861	3.81	436
	GRAND TOTAL	641,193	227,584	2,529,238	1.11	355

NOS: not otherwise specified.
KD: knocked down.

[a] For carload traffic this table is transcribed from Federal Coordinator of Transportation, *Freight Traffic Report,* App. I, pp. 72-3. The result of a separate canvass, the data are approximately comparable with figures for Class I roads published in the *Statistics of Railways.* However, the Federal Coordinator failed to secure data for three roads: Green Bay and Western; New York Connecting; and Toledo, Peoria and Western. Partly on this account originated tonnage shown here is 99.2 percent, freight revenue 99.9 percent, of the corresponding totals for all carload traffic for 1932 as published by the ICC in the *Statistics of Railways.* For less-than-carload traffic, originating tonnage and revenue, as reported in the *Statistics of Railways* were each multiplied by 99.2 percent; average haul was taken from Federal Coordinator of Transportation, *Merchandise Traffic Report* (1934), p. 134; the remaining entries were computed by us.
[b] Does not include canned meats.
[c] Does not include fertilizer materials.
[d] Does not include glass or molding sand.
[e] Includes tin and terne plate.
[f] Bars, sheets, and pipes.
[g] Not made of metal.
[h] Includes building paper.

nated by the LCL class. In our distribution the frequency (i.e., number of ton-miles) of the LCL class is concentrated in one interval, no further breakdown of this group being possible. LCL ton-mileage is probably distributed over the entire upper range of the price scale.

By adopting 1932 as our base year (which implies the assumption that the distribution of prices in this year is representative of the entire period in question) we can investigate the possible differences between an unweighted index and one in which the three most significant groups are properly weighted. This can be done by expressing the ratio between these two indexes in terms of the price and value relationships of the three components in the base year and their quantity movements over the period in question.

Table C-2

STEAM RAILROADS: FREIGHT TRAFFIC BY
REVENUE PER TON-MILE, 1932[a]

Revenue per Ton-mile (cents)	Ton-miles (mil.)	Revenue[b] (mil. $)	Tonnage Originated (mil.)	Average Haul (miles)
Group I (bituminous coal)				
0.651	75,412	491.0	208.38	362
Group II				
0.600-0.749	9,967			
0.750-0.899	14,852			
0.900-1.049	17,680			
1.050-1.199	19,769			
1.200-1.349	31,814			
1.350-1.499	24,196			
1.500-1.649	18,557			
1.650-1.799	2,295			
1.800-1.949	2,283			
1.950-2.099	1,166			
2.100-2.249	1,441			
2.250-2.399	607			
2.400-2.549	248			
2.550-2.699	0			
2.700-2.849	52			
SUMMARY 1,216	144,927	1,763.1	416.85	348
Group III				
3.600-3.749	583			
3.750-3.899	6,656[c]			
SUMMARY 3.800	7,239	275.1	15.96	454
TOTAL, ALL GROUPS 1.111	227,578	2,529.2	641.19	355

[a] Computed from Table C-1, except for less-than-carload traffic, for which see note c. The interval 2.85 to 3.60 cents per ton-mile contains no traffic.
[b] The group revenue totals do not exactly equal those obtained directly from the distribution because of the grouping error involved in the latter.
[c] Includes an estimated LCL figure of 6,590 million ton-miles, obtained by multiplying the ICC tonnage originated (reduced by slightly less than 1 percent to allow for roads that did not report to the Federal Coordinator) by an average haulage figure of 436 miles (*Merchandise Traffic Report*, p. 134).

For three 'commodities' (the three groups of Table C-2) designated by subscripts, the ratio between the weighted and unweighted indexes,

$$S = \frac{Q_1 H_1 p_1 + Q_2 H_2 p_2 + Q_3 H_3 p_3}{q_1 h_1 p_1 + q_2 h_2 p_2 + q_3 h_3 p_3} \Big/ \frac{Q_1 H_1 + Q_2 H_2 + Q_3 H_3}{q_1 h_1 + q_2 h_2 + q_3 h_3}$$

$$= \frac{ab + ad + cd}{1 + d + cd} \cdot \frac{1 + df + cdef}{ab + adf + cdef},$$

where

$$\left. \begin{aligned} a &= p_1/p_2 \\ b &= p_2/p_3 \end{aligned} \right\} \text{ the ratios of base-year prices,}$$

$$\left. \begin{aligned} c &= p_1 q_1 h_1/p_2 q_2 h_2 \\ d &= p_2 q_2 h_2/p_3 q_3 h_3 \end{aligned} \right\} \text{ the ratios of base-year revenues,}$$

and

$$\left. \begin{aligned} e &= \frac{Q_1 H_1}{q_1 h_1} \Big/ \frac{Q_2 H_2}{q_2 h_2} \\ f &= \frac{Q_2 H_2}{q_2 h_2} \Big/ \frac{Q_3 H_3}{q_3 h_3} \end{aligned} \right\} \begin{array}{l} \text{the ratios of the quantity relatives between} \\ \text{given and base years.} \end{array}$$

Since the first four variables are known for the base year 1932, S may be expressed as a function of e and f alone.

$$S = .586 \frac{1 + 6.409f + 1.785ef}{.176 + 3.431f + 1.785ef}$$

We lack a breakdown of ton-miles by individual commodities for years other than 1932, i.e., we do not know the H's which determine the values of e and f. Yet we can establish limits for these two quantities. For instance, if 1919 is the given year, it is safe to say that over the period 1919-32 more LCL freight (Group III) than general freight (Group II) was diverted to highways. Therefore we may assume

$$\frac{Q_3 H_3}{q_3 h_3} > \frac{Q_2 H_2}{q_2 h_2}$$

and set $f < 1$ for this comparison.

Next, by imposing the limits $1.05 > S > .95$ we can determine the range over which e may vary and still permit the unweighted index to fall within 5 percent of the 'true' index. For a bias no larger than this,

if f is   1.0   0.9   0.6   0.5
e must lie between 0.67   0.73   1.00   1.16
and   1.42   1.49   1.85   2.06

The above table reveals something of the assumptions involved in the use of the unweighted index to represent the 'true' index for the period 1919-32; namely, that a decline of f below 1.0 must be compensated by a movement in the other direction on the part of e, if the index is to remain within the 5 percent limits of error. For instance, if f fell as low as 0.6 for the comparison of any year with 1932, e must be greater than 1.0,[3] i.e., $\dfrac{Q_1 H_1}{q_1 h_1} > \dfrac{Q_2 H_2}{q_2 h_2}$, which in turn means that the movement of bituminous coal from the given year to the base year 1932 must lag behind that for railroad traffic as a whole. It will appear, on the contrary, that shipments of bituminous coal, far from lagging behind other railroad traffic, maintained a relative advantage over other traffic, thus causing e to fall below the level necessary to keep S within the 5 percent limits of error.

Incidence of the Change in Haul

The quantity movements of railroad traffic, as we define them, are functions of the changes in the quantities of tons originated and in the average haul associated with the various groups of originated tonnage. In the absence of specific information concerning length of haul, it is necessary to examine the economic forces operating to influence the haul, with a view toward making the best possible hypotheses concerning its movement.

The average haul for all commodities transported by the railroads considered as one system (obtained by dividing total ton-miles by total tons originated) increased from 277.3 miles in 1911 to 375.8 miles in 1938, or 35.5 percent. As Table C-3 shows, the total gain may conveniently be assigned to the two periods marked off by the year 1923. The initial large increase in haul seems to be

[3] The upper limit of e is ignored in the discussion because the data suggest that only the lower limit is relevant in the period considered.

Table C-3

STEAM RAILROADS: FREIGHT TRAFFIC,
AVERAGE HAUL, 1899-1946[a]

Miles

Year Ending June 30	Class I, II, and III Roads	Class I Roads Only	Calendar Year	Class I, II, and III Roads	Class I Roads Only
1899	246.6	....	1920	303.5	326.8
			1921	304.1	326.4
1900	242.7	....	1922	307.8	331.4
1901	252.0	....	1923	299.9	322.7
1902	239.1	....	1924	304.4	327.1
1903	242.4	....	1925	308.9	331.8
1904	244.3	....	1926	310.8	332.1
1905	237.6	....	1927	314.8	334.5
1906	240.9	....	1928	318.0	336.7
1907	242.1	....	1929	317.2	334.1
1908	253.9	....			
1909	251.1	....	1930	316.2	332.5
			1931	329.2	345.8
1910	249.7	....	1932	346.6	362.1
1911	254.1	277.3	1933	341.8	356.6
1912	256.9	280.6	1934	336.9	351.1
1913	255.2	278.5	1935	341.1	357.2
1914	255.4	278.5	1936	337.3	353.8
1915	270.7	295.9	1937	337.4	355.1
1916	272.0	295.2	1938	356.1	375.8
			1939	351.2	369.8
Calendar Year			1940	351.1	369.8
			1941	368.5	387.0
			1942	427.8	448.9
1916	278.0	301.2	1943	469.1	490.9
1917	288.2	312.1	1944	473.3	494.3
1918	296.9	320.9	1945	458.1	477.9
1919	308.6	332.4	1946	415.5	433.2

[a] In this table all railroads in the United States are considered as a single system. Data are from *Statistics of Railways*.

associated with the general expansion of the national market at the time. Commenting on this in 1920, the ICC said, "The increases in the average length of haul are possibly accounted for by the absorption of Class III roads and the extension of through billing."[4] The latter reason refers to the possibility that the originating tonnage totals are subject to duplication because rebilled carloads may be reported as originating a second time. The elimination of rebilling may have accounted for some increase in the

[4] *Statistics of Railways,* 1920, p. XXXII.

average haulage figure in this period,[5] but the absorption of Class III or even Class II roads could have had little effect. The 1914-19 increase in haul for Class I is 19 percent, roughly equaling that for all railroads (i.e., Class I, II, and III). In 1921, however, the Commission attributed the lengthened haul to "fundamental economic changes, such, the development of the Western States, growth of exports, and shifting of centers of production and consumption."[6] Whatever the reasons for the lengthening of haul in the period 1914-19, it is difficult (on the basis of the available information) to justify any assumption which would assign a percentage increase in length of haul to any one of our three commodity groups that is more or less than the percentage increase for all three groups. For the period after 1919, however, when highway competition became important, the percentage increase in haul can be distributed over the three groups in some reasonable manner.

The growing importance of motor transport is easily attested to by the rapid growth of motor truck registrations from 900,000 in 1919 to 4,400,000 in 1939, the extraordinary improvement of highway facilities in this period,[7] and other obvious indicators. To what extent has motor truck transport replaced railroad transport? Between 1925 and 1938 the ton-mileage total for all intercity trucking rose from 4 to 40 billion (Table F-4); that for steam railroads fell from over 400 to fewer than 300 billion (Table B-1). To be sure, such figures do not provide any exact measure of traffic diverted from the railroad to the highway. Yet the motor truck had clearly come to play an important role in our transportation system.

The effects of highway competition may well have been felt first in the field of agricultural products, at least for produce intended for local markets, for with the introduction of pneumatic tires and

[5] Such an increase in the figure does not, of course, reflect a real lengthening of the haul, and would be compensated for by a drop in the figure for tons originated.

[6] *Statistics of Railways*, 1921, p. **XXXV**.

[7] The growth of rural surfaced highway (in thousands of miles) as reported by the U. S. Bureau of Public Roads, is as follows: 1904, 154; 1914, 257; 1921, 387; 1934, 975. Quoted in Federal Coordinator of Transportation, *Public Aids to Transportation*, Vol. IV, p. 4.

the extension of adequate highway facilities, the motor truck
quickly displaced the farm horse. The number of farm trucks in
use, as reported by the decennial census, increased from 140,000
in 1920 to 900,000 in 1930, with the greatest concentration to be
found on the fruit, vegetable, and dairy farms of the Middle Atlantic States, the shores of the Great Lakes, and the valleys of the
Pacific Coast States.[8]

In 1916 the proportion of all livestock receipts 'driven in' by
truck in the 16 most important livestock markets was less than 2
percent. By 1925 the proportion had risen to 9 percent, then rose
rapidly to 22 percent in 1929 and to 42 percent in 1932. In 1939
the corresponding figure for 68 markets was well over 50 percent.[9]
Motor transport of fruits and vegetables became common somewhat later. In 1929 the Department of Agriculture estimated that
12 to 16 percent of total shipments were moved by truck instead
of rail or boat. It was noted, however, that "on a mileage basis the
percentage would be much less because of the longer average haul
by railroad." The report indicated too that not all truck transport
of produce could be regarded as representing a competitive loss
to railway shipping: "Trucks have expedited transportation on
short hauls, causing increased production of highly perishable
products at points advantageous to desirable markets."[10] Moreover, the products that move largely by truck are, in general, the
light, highly perishable, or more valuable ones which pay a high
rate by rail. In 1934, 38 percent of all fruit and vegetable shipments to all consuming markets was by truck.[11] The corresponding
percentage for twelve important markets in 1938 was 40. Other
agricultural products now increasingly shipped by truck are poultry and dairy products. From 1935 to 1939 the truck percentages
of all receipts at four markets (New York, Chicago, Philadelphia,

[8] E. G. McKibben and R. A. Griffen, *Tractors, Trucks, and Automobiles* (National Research Project, 1938), pp. 44, 49.

[9] Figures by the Agricultural Marketing Service reported in *Automobile Facts
and Figures*.

[10] B. Edwards and J. W. Park, 'The Marketing and Distribution of Fruits and
Vegetables by Motor Truck', *Technical Bulletin 272*, Department of Agriculture, 1931, pp. 4, 87.

[11] McKibben and Griffen, p. 113.

and Boston) rose from 17 to 28 for butter, and from 32 to 40 for eggs.[12]

The evidence is clear that, for agricultural products at any rate, the railroads have tended to lose to motor trucking the short haul, perishable, and relatively high priced commodities, the majority of which had previously been shipped by rail at less-than-carload or express rates.[13] That the same tendency obtains for nonagricultural goods is indicated by the National Resources Committee: "In a general way trucks may be said to go after revenue rather than tonnage; to seek finished and manufactured materials and to handle consumer goods rather than capital goods."[14]

The foregoing suggests that the railroads have lost to short-haul trucking items at the upper end of the distribution and retained items at the lower end. A quantitative estimate of the extent of this tendency is afforded by data presented in an ICC report entitled 'Fluctuations in Railway Freight Traffic Compared with Production' (Statement 3951, Nov. 1939). For all commodities carried by railroads, indexes of 'potential tons' were computed by the ICC for the period 1929-38 representing "the number of tons the railways would have carried each year if in such year the railway tonnage had been the same proportion of the total production (adjusted for importation) in the United States as it was in 1928". The ratios of actual tons to potential railway tons were computed. These ratios confirm the hypothesis that such competition has affected LCL tonnage most and bituminous coal least. The 1937 ratios of actual to potential tons, expressed in percentage form, are:

Group I (bituminous coal)	95.6
Group II	76.2*
LCL (Group III)	50.0
ALL GROUPS (carload and LCL traffic)	84.9

* Average (unweighted) of all Group II commodity percentage ratios.

Data for individual commodities indicate that the correlation between the amount of potential tonnage lost and the revenue per

[12] *Automobile Facts and Figures,* 1940 ed., p. 82.

[13] See also Harold G. Moulton and Associates, *The American Transportation Problem* (Brookings Institution, 1933).

[14] *Technological Trends and National Policy,* p. 184.

ton-mile exists within Group II as well as between Groups I, II, and III. A comparison of ratios of actual to potential tons for 145 commodities in 1937 with the corresponding 1932 revenues per ton-mile yielded a correlation of —0.36. The corresponding normally distributed z coefficient, —0.38, has a standard error of 0.083.

To complete the picture for the period since 1919, the following statement of the Federal Coordinator of Transportation is of interest. Commenting on the fact that over the 12-year period 1922-34 the index of railroad tonnage originated fell more precipitously than the ton-mileage index, he says: "The difference was due to the different distribution of commodities, rather than to a lengthening haul, since it was found that applying the average haul of individual commodities in 1932 to the tonnage of each commodity in each of the preceding twelve years, produced substantially the average haul of all commodities reported by the carriers for that year, indicating that the average haul of the individual commodities in 1932 was the same as that of its preceding years."[15] In other words, the observed increase in average haul for all commodities is due to a gradual disappearance of short-haul commodities from the railroad traffic structure.

Limits of Bias in Our Unweighted Index

We are now in a position to apply our analysis to the periods 1919-32 and 1932-38 to ascertain the degree of overstatement implicit in the unweighted index, which does not adequately emphasize the gradual loss of high-revenue ton-mileage that characterizes this period. The increase in average haul over the period 1919-32 was 6.9 percent.[16] We can assume, on the basis of the above discussion, that the haul of Group I increased by something less than 6.9 percent and the haul of Group III by something more. We can

[15] *Freight Traffic Report,* Vol. II, p. 50.

[16] The 1919 average haul for all groups was 332.4 miles. We have used the 1932 estimate of 355.3 miles based on the *Freight Traffic Report* rather than the ICC figure for 1932 (362.1 miles) because we regard it as the more accurate (see Table C-2). Use of the latter figure, however, involving the assumption of an 8.9 percent increase in average haulage, does not change the results of the analysis significantly.

thus provide an *upper* limit to the degree of overstatement by assuming a 6.9 percent increase between 1919 and 1932 in haul for Groups I and III. This would understate the 1919 Group I haul by assuming too great an increase in length of haul; the 1919 Group III haul, on the contrary, is overstated by assuming too small an increase. The data are set forth in Table C-4.

Table C-4

FREIGHT TRAFFIC: MAXIMUM UPWARD BIAS
IN THE UNWEIGHTED INDEX, 1919-1932

| Commodity Group (Table C-2) | 1919 | | | 1932 |
	Tons Originated[a] (mil.)	Average Haul[b] (mi.)	Ton- miles (bil.)	Ton- miles (bil.)
I	299.7	339 (min.)	101.6	75.41
II	741.8	323	239.5	144.93
III	54.65	425 (max.)	23.23	7.239
TOTAL	1,096.1	332	364.29	227.58

$e = 0.816$ $f = 0.515$ $S = 1.100$

[a] The Group III figure includes 3.35 million tons, our own estimate (based on production figures) of the amount of originated tons of automobiles and explosives shipped by railroads in 1919.

[b] As explained in the text, the Group I figure is a minimum estimate and the Group III a maximum. The Group II figure is a residual, obtained by subtracting Group I and III ton-mileage from the given total ton-mileage and dividing the remainder by the Group II tonnage originated.

On the present hypothesis e fails to compensate for the low value of f; consequently, the weighted and unweighted indexes diverge. On a 1919 base the unweighted ton-mileage index stands at 64.1 in 1932 (Table 17)[17]; on the above assumptions a weighted index would have declined to 58.3. The unweighted index is seen to overstate the 'truth' — in measuring 1932 output as a relative of 1919 — by 10 percent.

Turning next to the problem of establishing a lower limit for

[17] The ton-mile totals of Table C-4 suggest a slightly different figure because they cover class I roads only and coverage in 1932 is incomplete.

the degree of overstatement, we have again two assumptions at our disposal. We can assume that the Group I haul did not increase (thus establishing a maximum value for the 1919 Group I haul) and that the 1919 Group III haul was the same as that for all groups (so establishing a minimum value for the 1919 Group III haul). We then have the figures in Table C-5 which yield a weighted index of 60.8 for 1932 (1919: 100), about 5 percent less than the unweighted index (64.1; see Table 17).

Table C-5

FREIGHT TRAFFIC: MINIMUM UPWARD BIAS
IN THE UNWEIGHTED INDEX, 1919-1932

Commodity Group (Table C-2)	1919			1932
	Tons Originated (mil.)	Average Haul* (mi.)	Ton- miles (bil.)	Ton- miles (bil.)
I	299.7	362 (max.)	108.5	75.41
II	741.8	320	237.6	144.93
III	54.65	332 (min.)	18.17	7.239
TOTAL	1096.1	332	364.29	227.58

$e = 0.877$ $f = 0.653$ $S = 1.055$

* The Group I and III average hauls are respectively the maximum and minimum estimates described in the text. The Group II haul is derived from the ton-mile figure, which, as before, is a residual.

Combining results, we have a range for the overstatement of the unweighted index — when 1932 is measured as a relative of 1919 — between the limits 5.5 and 10.0 percent. These limits are at least rough indications of the magnitude of the bias and we can be reasonably sure the true figure lies between them.

It should be noted that in estimating maximum bias at 10 percent, we assume the average haul of bituminous coal increased less than that of all railroad traffic over the period 1919-32, because of the slighter role of motor truck competition. On the other hand, railroad haul of coal may have lengthened owing to regional shifts in coal production. Thus, from 1919 to 1925 West Virginia increased its contribution to total coal production from 17 to 24 percent, while Pennsylvania dropped from 32 to 26 percent; thereafter both states maintained their relative positions, together accounting for about half of all production. It is difficult to determine precisely what effect this shift had on the average haul. As far as New England consumption is concerned, there was probably no change, for such shipments of West Virginia coal would go overland to the tidewater region, thence by boat and again by rail, the total rail haul being about equivalent to that for all rail shipments across the Hudson. The shift might, however, somewhat lengthen the haul to the Great Lakes region, and to this extent would argue for a lower maximum bias than 10 percent.

Table C-6

FREIGHT TRAFFIC: MINIMUM DOWNWARD BIAS
IN THE UNWEIGHTED INDEX, 1932-1938

Commodity Group (Table C-2)	1938			1932
	Tons Originated (mil.)	Average Haul[a] (mi.)	Ton-miles (bil.)	Ton-miles (bil.)
I	225.34	383 (max.)	86.31	75.41
II	530.73	370	195.19	144.93
III	15.79	480 (min.)	7.579	7.239
Total	771.86	376	290.08	227.58

$e = 0.846$ $f = 1.292$ $S = 1.004$

[a] The figures for Group I and III are obtained by multiplication of the corresponding 1932 figures (362 and 454) by 1.058. The Group II estimate is a residual.

For the period 1932-38 the method of analysis is the same. The average haul for all groups increased from 355.3 to 375.8 miles, or 5.8 percent. As before, we assume the increase in Group I to be something less than 5.8 percent and the increase in Group III to be something more. If, however, we increase the 1932 average hauls for Groups I and III by 5.8 percent we overstate the 1938 Group I haul and understate the 1938 Group III haul. The above set of assumptions will exaggerate the decline in Group III, and consequently yield a maximum estimate of the overstatement in the unweighted index for this period. In fact, Table C-6 reports an understatement, of which it furnishes a minimum estimate. The weighted index for 1938 is put at 124.5 (1932: 100) compared with 124.0 for the unweighted measure (Table 17).

This last result is somewhat surprising, for it indicates that the tendency for low-revenue to gain more rapidly than high-revenue traffic was apparently halted and even slightly reversed. The un-weighted index (124.0) now understates the truth somewhat, even though the assumption on which the computation is based was designed to exaggerate its upward bias. It would appear that for the period 1932-38 high-revenue traffic, at least as measured by our three categories, no longer lags behind low revenue traffic. Upon closer examination, however, it is seen that the chief increase has been in Group II. We have previously shown that even within Group II the tendency has been to lose high revenue ton-mileage, but our three-group weighting scheme cannot take this factor into account. There is some evidence to support the belief that since 1932 railroad LCL tonnage has been stabilized, in that the rail-roads have responded to the competitive threat of motor trucking by offering such special services as door-to-door pick-up and deliv-ery.[18] The result has been that since 1933 LCL tonnage originated, while still lagging somewhat behind carload tonnage, no longer exhibits the striking divergence of trend characterizing the earlier period. When it is further considered that the average haul for Group III has probably increased more rapidly than that for other groups, it is clear that this group no longer contributes to the upward bias of the unweighted ton-mile index, and may indeed make for a downward bias, if its average haul has increased to the point where LCL ton-mileage would show a greater percentage increase than the other groups. Such a situation might arise if we assumed no increase in haul for Group I (although there has undoubtedly been some increase due to loss of short-haul coal

[18] The number of railroad owned trucks (exclusive of those owned by Railway Express) used for store-door delivery service increased from 5,500 in 1932 to 48,780 in 1938 (*Automobile Facts and Figures,* 1940 ed., p. 79).

shipments to trucking) and an average increase of 5.8 percent in the Group II length of haul. The Group III haulage figure derived residually on this basis is 836 miles; the calculation may safely be taken to provide an upper limit to the degree of possible *understatement* in the unweighted index.

Table C-7

FREIGHT TRAFFIC: MAXIMUM DOWNWARD BIAS
IN THE UNWEIGHTED INDEX, 1932-1938

Commodity Group (Table C-2)	1938			1932
	Tons Originated (mil.)	Average Haul[a] (mi.)	Ton-miles (bil.)	Ton-miles (bil.)
I	225.34	362 (min.)	81.57	75.41
II	530.73	368	195.31	144.93
III	15.79	836 (max.)	13.20	7.239
Total	771.86	376	290.08	227.58

$e = 0.803$ $f = 0.727$ $S = 1.059$

[a] The Group I figure is equal to the 1932 Group I average haul and is to be regarded as a minimum estimate. The Group II figure is the product of the 1932 figure (347.7) and 1.058 and is probably close to the truth. The Group III figure is derived by subtraction from total ton-mileage and is to be regarded as a maximum estimate.

According to Table C-7, on a 1932 base 131.3 represents a maximum 1938 value for the weighted index compared with 124.0 for the unweighted index (Table 17). That the true value of S lies very much closer to 1.004 than to 1.059 is indicated by the fact that the latter ratio is based on a Group III haulage figure of as much as 836 miles, obviously far too high an estimate in the light of the 476 miles reported by the ICC for LCL traffic as the result of a special inquiry in 1939.[19]

In summarizing the results of the foregoing analysis, we can say that the unweighted index of railroad ton-mileage over the period 1919-32 is subject to an upward bias of 5 to 10 percent, due to the declining share in railroad freight of the relatively high-revenue less-than-carload traffic. In the succeeding six-year period this

[19] *54th Annual Report*, p. 128.

factor no longer made for an upward bias, and may have caused a slight downward bias. However, the possibility still exists that the upward bias continued after 1932, for relatively high-revenue carload traffic within Group II may have been lost. This last factor is not susceptible of measurement, but the probability of its steady operation over the entire period 1919-38 would seem to justify the broad assertion that the unweighted index is subject to an upward bias that is closer to 10 than to 5 percent.

Appendix D

Electric Railways: Basic Series

Table D-1

ELECTRIC RAILWAYS, URBAN AND INTERURBAN: PASSENGERS CARRIED AND EMPLOYEES, 1890-1946[a]

	REVENUE PASSENGERS CARRIED (bil.)[c]		EMPLOYEES (th.)[d]	
	Electric railways	Trolley buses	Electric railways	Trolley buses
1890[b]	2.02	....	71	....
1902	4.77	....	143	....
1907	7.44	....	221	....
1908	7.51	....	....	....
1909	8.00	....	....	....
1910	8.55	....	....	....
1911	9.03	....	....	....
1912	9.55	....	282	....
1913	9.98	....	....	....
1914	10.01	....	....	....
1915	9.90	....	....	....
1916	10.63	....	....	....
1917	11.30	....	295	....
1918	11.18	....	288	....
1919	11.72	....	298	....
1920	12.27	....	309	....
1921	11.52	....	287	....
1922	12.21	....	300	....
1923	12.48	....	301	....
1924	12.25	....	290	....
1925	12.09	....	280	....
1926	12.11	....	276	....
1927	11.85	....	265	....
1928	11.46	0.002	255	....
1929	11.30	0.004	252	....
1930	10.35	0.013	234	....
1931	9.17	0.022	209	....
1932	7.76	0.030	182	....
1933	7.25	0.035	167	....
1934	7.54	0.054	170	....
1935	7.41	0.076	164.4	1.3
1936	7.62	0.123	158.8	2.6
1937	7.21	0.231	152.5	3.8
1938	6.70	0.312	141.8	4.6
1939	6.60	0.358	130.4	5.0
1940	6.46	0.419	122.5	6.4
1941	6.57	0.52	115.2	7.0
1942	7.59	0.72	114.7	7.7
1943	9.41	0.94	132.1	8.0
1944	9.65	0.99	132.3	8.1
1945	9.64	1.00	129.2	8.5
1946	9.45	1.05	125.3	9.8

Notes to Table D-1

[a] Data from *Census of Electrical Industries,* and American Transit Association, *Transit Fact Book* (annual). See also Moody's *Public Utilities* (annual). Breakdown of employees between electric railways and trolley buses supplied by American Transit Association. Table excludes motorbus lines affiliated with electric railway companies, data for which are included in Appendix E.

[b] Year ending June 30.

[c] Includes pay transfer, but not free transfer passengers.

[d] For 1928-34 trolley bus employees are included with electric railway employees.

Table D-2

INTERURBAN ELECTRIC RAILWAYS: PASSENGER AND FREIGHT TRAFFIC AND EMPLOYEES, 1902-1946[a]

	Revenue Passengers Carried (mil.)	Revenue per Passenger	Freight Car-miles (mil.)	Revenue per Freight Car-mile (cents)	Coverage[b] %	Employees[c] (thous.)
1902	582	n.a.	3.86	n.a.	....	21.2
1922	2,009	7.72	n.a.	n.a.	....	91.5
1926	1,214	9.57	74.8	52.6	90.8	64.7
1927	1,049	9.94	78.8	50.8	89.8	58.2
1928	900	10.49	75.0	50.2	89.2	52.9
1929	739	10.99	76.8	49.0	88.1	47.4
1930	602	10.93	64.7	47.5	86.7	39.5
1931	407	12.25	53.5	43.7	84.6	32.0
1932	338	10.31	36.8	45.8	86.7	25.9
1933	219	10.47	32.3	46.7	84.6	20.9
1934	208	10.74	36.6	43.4	83.5	19.0
1935	188	12.17	40.2	43.7	87.5	18.5
1936	167	13.06	47.0	45.0	87.1	17.8
1937	159	12.72	45.3	46.2	86.4	17.6
1938	127	12.78	34.3	51.2	84.6	16.4
1939	114	13.26	37.0	51.4	84.3	14.2
1940	109	12.77	39.2	52.7	82.8	14.1
1941	110	13.04	44.2	55.8	83.0	14.1
1942	141	14.99	45.9	69.0	82.6	14.6
1943	192	16.05	49.3	71.2	81.5	16.4
1944	210	16.06	52.2	69.8	81.0	16.6
1945	202	16.86	49.3	68.2	81.9	16.8
1946	174	17.39	41.9	71.1	80.8	16.2

n.a.: not available.

[a] Data for 1902 are from *Census of Electric Railways* and cover 239 companies classified as interurban. Data for other years from ICC reports on *Electric Railways* (annual); also ICC Statement No. 35101, 'Electric Railway Statistics 1890-1934' (Sept. 1935). An effort has been made to exclude companies that sell appreciable amounts of power: in 1902 the census figures exclude

Notes to Table D-2 (concluded)

data for 52 interurban lines whose railroad operations were ancillary to the production of power for sale; and the ICC figures for 1922-46 exclude Potomac Edison, Iowa Electric, and Northern States Power on the ground that these companies were not primarily engaged in railroad operation. Although the ICC collects data from the Chicago Tunnel and the Hudson and Manhattan, these are not considered interurban roads, and data for them are not included. Data for passenger and freight are for rail line operations only; employees cover motorbus and motor-truck operations as well. To allow the output index to be adjusted for comparability with employment, an estimate of coverage is given.

[b] Ratio of rail-line passenger and freight revenue to total transportation revenue. The difference consists of mail, express and switching revenue; and revenue from motorbus and motor-truck operations. The decline in coverage is due to the gradually increasing importance of highway operations. These operations are excluded from the traffic statistics shown here, but are reflected in the number of employees. Coverage was computed in order that the index of output might be adjusted for comparability with employment. Coverage in 1902 and 1922 was assumed to be the same as in 1926.

[c] For 1922 and for 1939 and later years, the average number employed during the year (presumably in most cases average of 12 monthly counts). For other years the average number employed at beginning and end of year.

Appendix E

Highways — Buslines, City and Intercity: Basic Series

Table E-1

BUSLINES: PASSENGER TRAFFIC, 1925-1946[a]

	CITY[b] Revenue Passengers (bil.)	INTERCITY		
		Revenue Passengers[c] (bil.)	Revenue Passenger-Miles[d] (bil.)	Average Journey[e] (miles)
1925	0.8	0.19	3	19
1926	1.0	0.22	4	20
1927	1.2	0.24	5	21
1928	1.2	0.27	6	21
1929	1.4	0.30	7	23
1930	1.4	0.30	7	23
1931	1.3	0.28	7	24
1932	1.3	0.25	6	25
1933	1.3	0.23	6	28
1934	1.8	0.27	7	26
1935	2.1	0.29	8	26
1936	2.6	0.35	9	26
1937	2.7	0.39	10	26
1938	3.2	0.37	10	26
1939	3.4	0.31	10	31
1940	3.8	0.36	12	33
1941	4.5	0.38	14	36
1942	6.5	0.62	22	35
1943	7.4	0.95	27	29
1944	8.6	1.08	27	24
1945	7.9	0.87	27	31
1946	8.5	0.97	26	27

[a] Includes buslines operated in association with, as subsidiaries of, or as successors to steam and electric railways. Does not include trolley buses, which are covered in Appendix D.

[b] National Association of Motor Bus Operators, *Bus Facts* (annual). Data cover city and city-suburban service (common carrier operations), but do not include charter, sightseeing or school buses.

[c] For source, see note b. It seems to be generally agreed that estimates published for years prior to 1937 were too high, but no systematic revision has ever been undertaken. Therefore the published estimates for 1925-36 have been written down as follows: wherever a downward revision was subsequently published, but earlier figures were not republished in revised form, we assumed that the revision applied to them also, and lowered them correspondingly.

[d] 1941-46, estimates by the ICC published in its *Annual Reports;* 1925-40, based on preceding column and trade opinion concerning change in length of haul.

[e] This series should be treated with reserve. As explained in note d, for 1925-40 the figures are merely informed guesses. For 1941-46 the ICC passenger-mile estimates are based, at least in part, on the passenger totals given here and should be comparable with them. However the sharp fluctuations in the computed average journey during 1942-46 suggest differences of coverage between the two preceding columns.

Appendix F

Highways — The Motor Trucking Industry

The motor trucking industry, a still rapidly expanding competitor of other forms of freight transportation, first became important immediately after World War I. Unfortunately, satisfactory statistics for the industry date from a much later period or are today still unobtainable. In this survey we shall do what we can to piece together a picture of the growth and relative position of motor trucking in this country. We begin by considering some estimates for 1940, and from these we shall attempt to work backwards to figures for earlier years. However, no consecutive data on employment or output per worker can be given. For this reason it has seemed best to treat the industry in an appendix, rather than to accord it a chapter in the text.

STRUCTURE OF THE INDUSTRY

Trucking operations may be classified according to several principles of which two are significant for our purpose. First, freight may be carried either in privately owned vehicles, or in trucks operated 'for hire', that is, by commercial carriers. Of the more than four and a half million trucks registered in 1940, by far the greater number were privately owned and were operated in connection with their owner's business.

A second distinction may be made between local trucking and intercity transportation. Intercity traffic can be defined comprehensively as that which moves over all rural roads, i.e., main intercity highways and minor roads lying outside the boundaries of incorporated areas.[1] It is for intercity trucking alone that we are

[1] It should be noted that such a definition includes some traffic not ordinarily regarded as intercity in character — for instance, the movement of goods between farm and local markets. The Interstate Commerce Commission excludes such traffic from its estimates of intercity truck ton-mileage (see below) ; it is interested especially in comparisons with railroad transportation and does not regard trucking from farm to market as relevant to such a comparison. Farm traffic is included in estimates compiled by the Public Roads Administration.

able to present estimates of output. At the volume of local city traffic we can scarcely even guess.

For most purposes a baker's truck belongs to the baking industry, a gasoline truck to the petroleum industry. In an accounting sense the trucks owned by manufacturers, distributors, and others perform auxiliary operations required in the conduct of business, and their contributions to value and employment are included in the totals for the industry in which the enterprise falls by virtue of its major activity. In principle, therefore, all trucks not operated for hire should be distributed among a wide range of industries using truck transportation at some point in their productive process, and owning the trucks furnishing this transportation. Ideally therefore the trucking industry — in any autonomous sense — is confined to common carrier and contract, i.e., for-hire, trucking. For the trucking industry defined in this way we can estimate some quantities: for example, the number of vehicles attached to it. But for most purposes it is the second rather than the first principle of classification mentioned above which lends itself to statistical treatment. We would like to consider for-hire trucking, intercity and local. We are forced for the most part to consider intercity trucking, for-hire and private.

More than half the trucks used in intercity operations are farm vehicles: naturally they account for a much lower proportion of total intercity ton-mileage. Farm trucks find considerable employment *on* the farm as well as in the transport of goods *between* the farm and urban areas. Thus, it has been estimated that for every ton hauled to or from American farms, four tons are hauled about the farm.[2] Farm trucks account for much highway traffic in livestock, truck crop and dairy farm areas, and at harvest time, but are far less significant in the over-all intercity trucking picture than are commercially operated vehicles.

Trucks operated for hire fall into two categories: common and contract carriers. Unlike trucks operated by contract, common

[2] C. D. Kinsman, 'An Appraisal of Power Used on Farms in the United States', *Department Bulletin 1348* (U. S. Department of Agriculture, 1925), p. 71. The absolute amounts mentioned are 240 million and not quite one billion tons, respectively.

carriers render service mainly on fixed routes between terminals, on regular schedule and at published rates. Contract carriers undertake, by written or oral contract, to transport goods for particular shippers and choose their rates accordingly. They frequently haul heavy objects requiring special equipment, deliver shipments of vital machinery in response to public emergencies, and perform other miscellaneous hauling jobs. In general contract carriers are less regulated than common carriers. Some contract operators may carry any type of freight they choose. Others hold permits to haul only certain freight: such are oil tank lines, truck-away automobile carriers, and refrigerator lines.

A further difference between common and contract carriers, of particular interest to us, lies in the character of the load. Contract carriers have greater discretion in the choice of the goods they transport; indeed, common carriers have complained that contract operators take on business only when they find it profitable. In a traffic survey of eleven western states in 1930 it was found that, of 180,000 trucks questioned, 8.7 percent were owned by contract carriers and 5.5 percent by common carriers; the remainder were privately owned vehicles.[3] Precise statistics now available as a by-product of ICC regulation relate as yet only to Class I motor carriers, that is, those with annual revenues in excess of $100,000; among such larger companies common carriers predominate.

For the most part for-hire motor trucking is organized on a relatively small scale. The larger carriers, those known by the Class I designation, are not really comparable with the Class I railroad companies, either in absolute size or as a fraction of the industry. Although they account for more than half the revenue of for-hire motor trucking, the largest of them received less than $7 million in freight revenue in 1939. The typical commercial trucker has a very modest capital investment; the American Trucking Associa-

[3] *Report of a Survey of Traffic on the Federal-Aid Highway Systems of Eleven Western States, 1930* (U. S. Bureau of Public Roads, 1932), p. 29. However, it is considered by the ICC that "a considerable portion of the so-called contract carriers were in reality common carriers operating without certificate or permit" (182 ICC 263 at p. 407). Nonetheless, even if this bias is allowed for, the Commission considers that contract carriers account for perhaps 50 percent more ton-mileage than do common carriers.

tion has estimated that 82 percent of all for-hire trucking enterprises operated only one vehicle in 1935.[4] The Census of Business reported for the same year that as many as a third of all firms covered received less than $1,000 annually in gross revenue, although many small firms were omitted from the inquiry.[5] Large fleets are not common among for-hire carriers; the largest reported to the ICC in 1939 were one fleet which totaled 549 trucks and truck tractors in the case of an intercity common carrier of general freight and one fleet of 656 units in the case of a carrier engaged in local cartage service. The really big trucking fleets are to be found, not among commercial carriers, but among private operators such as the Railway Express Agency and the Bell Telephone Company which owned and operated 45,000 and 16,000 trucks respectively in 1939.

Despite the small scale on which the for-hire trucking industry is organized, its aggregate size is considerable and perhaps not adequately appreciated. The 26,167 commercial carriers subject to the jurisdiction of the ICC in 1939 were estimated to have received $792 million in gross revenue in that year, of which $698 million represented predominantly intercity operations.[6] However, carriers of agricultural products, livestock, fish, and newspapers, and carriers which do not engage in interstate commerce, are exempt from ICC jurisdiction and do not report to the Commission.[7] Taking account of exempt carriers, we have put 1939 freight revenues for the entire for-hire intercity trucking industry at $900 million.[8] This

[4] *Automobile Facts and Figures*, 1936 ed., p. 74.

[5] *Census of Business, 1935*, 'Motor Trucking for Hire', p. 8. 32 percent of the 61,000 firms covered fell within this size group (revenues less than $1,000), but they received only 2 percent of the total reported revenue. Frequent entrance to and exit from the industry may have boosted part-year operations.

[6] U. S. National Resources Planning Board, *Transportation and National Policy* (1942), p. 404.

[7] Thus carriers reporting to the ICC in 1939 operated 111 thousand power units (i.e., truck and tractor truck combinations) ; whereas we estimate (below) that in 1940 all for-hire trucks engaged in intercity business totaled 283 thousand units.

[8] Obtained by multiplying 22 billion ton-miles (Table F-4) by 4 cents per ton-mile (ICC, 'Statistics of Class I Motor Carriers, 1939').

compares with railroad freight revenues of over $3 billion in 1939.

THE NUMBER OF TRUCKS

One indication of the relative importance of different sections of
the industry is to be found in the distribution of trucks according
to types of operation. In this section we attempt to approximate
this distribution.

Strictly speaking, of course, the cross classification outlined in
the preceding section applies to units of service rather than to units
of equipment. Some vehicles are used partly in connection with
their owner's business, partly for hire. Again, the segregation between trucks engaged in local and trucks operating in intercity
service is an artificial one, for the same vehicle may be engaged in
both. Indeed, the intercity trucking industry as we now know it
had its very origin in the gradual extension of the field of operations
of trucks engaged in local drayage. As highways were constructed
and the carrying capacity of trucks increased, the prospect of elimi-
nating loading and unloading operations in the transfer of freight
between truck and railroad car led naturally to the creation and
expansion of intercity truck haulage. The line dividing intercity
from local trucking still is blurred. Yet we are forced to assume for
statistical purposes that every truck is engaged exclusively either in
city or in intercity operations. Apparently, as we shall see, the great
majority of all trucks is engaged in local rather than in intercity
service. In the same way we are forced to allocate trucks unambiguously either to private, or to for-hire, service; private are much
more numerous than are for-hire vehicles.

In 1940 some 4,543 thousand trucks and tractor trucks were
registered in the continental United States.[9] First we may distribute

---

[9] The Public Roads Administration reported 4,590,386 trucks and tractor
trucks registered in 1940 (*Statistical Abstract of the U. S., 1941*, p. 455).
Registration is of course conducted by states, and definitions differ to some
extent among reporting units. Thus, the truck registration totals for New
Hampshire, Vermont, Massachusetts, Michigan, Kansas, and Colorado included some 19.4 thousand state, county, and municipal trucks (as estimated
by us), which we have deducted. Again, the registration totals for Ohio, Illinois, Iowa, Delaware, Montana, and California included an estimated 7.5
thousand common carrier busses, which we have also excluded from the
national total. Finally, for Tennessee and Oregon we deducted 20.3 thousand

these according to ownership. We know that 1,047 thousand trucks were owned by farmers.[10] There were consequently 3,496 thousand vehicles employed outside agriculture. Next we need an estimate of the number of commercial or for-hire trucks, as distinguished from other (private) nonagricultural trucks used to provide transportation in connection with their owners' business. Vehicle registration figures cannot be used here, for most states do not distinguish between privately owned and commercial trucks. We are therefore forced to depend on scattered information from a number of sources. In traffic surveys conducted by the Bureau of Public Roads during the 'twenties, the ratio of for-hire trucks to all loaded trucks stopped on the roads ranged from 8 percent in Maine to 21 percent in Ohio; the corresponding proportion of trucks operating over Connecticut roads in 1922-23 was 20 percent.[11] In the survey of eleven western states in 1930 field observers stopped 180,000 trucks of which 14.2 percent were found to be operated on a for-hire basis.[12] Counts of vehicles passing observation posts probably tend to overstate the number of for-hire trucks in existence, for we may suppose that commercial operators use their vehicles more intensively than do private operators. Nevertheless, the results of such surveys agree with other and more recent data.

The first opportunity to measure for-hire trucking on a national scale occurred in 1934 when commercial trucks were registered with the code authority for the trucking industry set up under the National Industrial Recovery Act. The number of for-hire vehicles

---

units as our estimate of the number of trailers included in the truck registration totals for those states. We made no further adjustment of the registration figures reported for Michigan, which do not separate taxicabs from truck data; nor those for Maine and Kentucky, which include some (but not all) trailers. On the other hand, we made no attempt to add to the truck registration total for Vermont, which failed to include light delivery trucks. The final registration figure for 1940 which we arrive at is 4,543 thousand; this is exclusive of some quarter million tax exempt government owned trucks and tractor truck units. See *Automobile Facts and Figures,* 1941 ed., p. 17.

[10] *Sixteenth Census, 1940,* 'Agriculture', Volume III, p. 453.

[11] 140 ICC 685, at p. 709.

[12] *Survey of Eleven Western States,* p. 29.

so registered was 300,475, but the code authority estimated the coverage at only 60 percent. On this basis the total number of for-hire trucks must have been 500,000, or some 15 percent of total truck registrations in 1934.[13] In 1940 the ICC also concluded that "the number of trucks operated by for-hire carriers is approximately 15 percent of the total".[14] Accordingly, we may place the number of commercial trucks in 1940 at 15 percent of total registrations, or say 681 thousand. Among for-hire trucks the Office of Defense Transportation has estimated the ratio of local to intercity vehicles at 351:249.[15] We may therefore allocate 283 thousand commercial trucks to intercity and 398 thousand to local service.

It remains to segregate nonagricultural private trucks (i.e., vehicles transporting goods belonging to their owners) among local and intercity operations. The *Commercial Car Journal* has analyzed the fleets of operators of eight trucks or more with respect to industrial origin.[16] We assumed that bakeries, confectioners, florists, bottlers, breweries, department stores, laundries, cleaners, dyers, and distributors of dairy products, milk, ice cream, ice, meats, and fish operate fleets predominantly in urban and suburban areas; and that the same may be said for newspapers and public utilities including railroads. The activities of other private shippers such as coal dealers, building contractors, distributors of

---

[13] Federal Coordinator of Transportation, *Hours, Wages and Working Conditions in the Intercity Motor Transport Industries* (1936), Part II, p. 167.

[14] ICC, *Motor Carrier Cases*, Volume 23 (1940) p. 12; see also ICC, *Federal Regulation of the Sizes and Weight of Motor Vehicles*, 77th Cong. 1st Sess., House Document 354 (1941), p. 91.

[15] Automobile Manufacturers' Association, *Motor Truck Facts*, 1942 ed., p. 39. (Total for-hire trucks are there given, apparently for 1941, at 600,000. This, however, represents but 12 percent of total registrations, and appears to us to be an underestimate.) The ratio quoted places local for-hire at 58.5 percent of all for-hire trucks. This may be compared with a figure of 57 percent obtainable for census sources for 1935 (*Census of Business, 1935*, 'Motor Trucking for Hire', p. 26). The latter percentage is based on a total canvass of only 148,150 truck and truck tractor units. The coverage of the census survey was far from complete, especially with respect to small concerns. In view of the fact that the smaller truckers, particularly owner-operators of single trucks, are likely to be engaged in local cartage rather than long haul trucking, we may regard the census figure, 57 percent, as a minimum estimate for the proportion of for-hire trucks engaged in local service.

[16] *Automobile Facts and Figures*, 1939 ed., p. 71.

oil and gasoline (the most important component of this group), paints, chemicals, drugs, and farm products, and manufacturers (such as steel mills) are more difficult to classify. It seems reasonable to assign half the trucks operated by these shippers to local and half to intercity service. On this basis we may conclude that, at least for fleets of eight trucks and over, 75 percent of all privately owned vehicles should be assigned to local service.[17] Using this ratio, we may divide the 2,815 thousand privately owned non-agricultural trucks into 2,111 thousand local and 704 thousand intercity vehicles.

Table F-1

MOTOR TRUCK REGISTRATIONS, ESTIMATED
DISTRIBUTION, 1940

Thousands

Type of Ownership	Local Service	Intercity Service	Total
Commercial (for-hire)	398	283	681
Agricultural	....	1,047	1,047
Private	2,111	704	2,815
TOTAL	2,509	2,034	4,543

The results of these various calculations are brought together in Table F-1. Despite the very rough nature of the distribution, it serves to demonstrate that our particular interest in motor trucking centers upon a rather small proportion of all trucks in use. Less than one-sixth of all trucks operate for hire; these constitute the equipment of the trucking industry properly so called. The remaining five-sixths of all trucks in use form part of the productive equipment of other industries — manufacturing, mining, distribution — and the output and employment associated with them are accounted for in the statistics of these other industries. While we

[17] Applied to all such vehicles, the fraction quoted may be on the low side, for operators of fleets of seven trucks and fewer may be still more heavily engaged in local service than are large fleet owners.

cannot measure the output of all for-hire trucks as such, we can estimate the volume of transportation provided by intercity trucking. But even intercity vehicles account for some two-fifths only of total registrations. Further, of these 2 million intercity trucks, half are farm trucks which account for a relatively low proportion of total intercity truck ton-mileage.

THE OUTPUT OF INTERCITY MOTOR TRUCKING IN 1940

As with other modes of transport, we shall endeavor to measure the physical output of motor trucking in terms of ton-miles. The statistical difficulties are apparent when one considers the obstacles encountered in ascertaining so fundamental a statistical category as the number of trucks engaged in different types of operation. From sheer necessity the ton-mile estimates in the present section are confined to intercity haulage, and take no account of local truck transportation.

Estimates of truck ton-mileage have in the past proceeded from a figure for the number of trucks in intercity use to assumptions of varying validity concerning the average rated capacity of trucks in use, followed by estimates of the percentage extent of actual loading. In computing the latter, the frequency of loading above rated capacity (a common practice) had to be balanced against estimates of empty or partly empty mileage. All these factors had then to be assembled and applied to an estimate of the average annual mileage per truck to yield an over-all truck ton-mileage total. We shall notice some of the estimates made on the above basis, but there have recently become available estimates of ton-mileage that rest on a much firmer base; namely, the ton-mileage totals yielded by the Highway Planning Surveys conducted by most of the states over the period 1936-40 in cooperation with the Public Roads Administration. A few brief comments are in order concerning these surveys.

Financed in part with federal funds provided under the Hayden-Cartwright Act of 1934, the Highway Planning Surveys were primarily designed to yield information necessary to the further development of the rural highway system. As such, the surveys investigated many aspects of highway planning, and included the compilation of road inventories, studies of highway finance, road use, and pavement life. Of interest to us are the traffic surveys undertaken in each state. These represent the first systematic attempt to assess the volume and character of highway traffic on something approaching a census basis.

The traffic surveys were chiefly concerned with first, the density of traffic on all road sections; and second, the character of truck traffic, truck weights, capacities, and other related characteristics. The first objective, that is, the determination of traffic volume, was ingeniously pursued by means of sampling methods developed by the Bureau of Public Roads, which describes the problem and its solution as follows:

It is obviously impracticable to count the traffic on every road section for an entire year, but studies and past experience have indicated that relatively short sample counts on all sections, when combined with more complete counts at certain strategic points, will provide reasonably accurate estimates of 24-hour traffic on all road sections.[18]

The sampling technique employed in the various state surveys usually involved setting up certain key stations at important intersections at which a number of eight-hour counts of traffic were made throughout the year designed to reflect the average experience of each day and night of the week and each month of the year. These counts were supplemented by other eight-hour counts made at various other points of less traffic importance during the year. The twenty-four hour annual average for each road section was estimated by adjusting the eight-hour counts to data recorded by automatic 'electric eyes' which counted traffic continuously at selected points of the state highway system for all hours of the day and night for the entire year. The recording instruments in question were installed permanently and have continued to furnish data ever since the original surveys were made.

Analysis of the volume and composition of truck traffic was made possible by observations taken at 'loadometer' stations, which usually coincided with the key stations recording the volume of

[18] 'Preliminary Report of the Vermont Statewide Highway Planning Survey' (1938), p. 18.

traffic. The trucking information collected at loadometer stations
pertained to the kind of goods carried, length of haul, weight of
load and truck, and various other aspects of trucking activity. It
was primarily upon these two sources of data, the traffic counts
and the loadometer station inquiries, that the Public Roads Administration based its estimate of total truck ton-mileage in 1940, the
first year for which a calculation was made in the manner indicated.

Table F-2

TRUCK TRAFFIC ON RURAL ROADS, 1940[a]

Trucks and Truck Combinations

	Private	For-hire	Total
Vehicle-miles (million)	22,217	6,982	29,850
Vehicle-miles, loaded (million)	13,290	4,999	19,432
Average load when loaded (tons)	2.37	5.34	3.04
Ton-miles of load carried (million)	31,444	26,674	59,058

[a] *Automobile Facts and Figures,* 1941 ed., pp. 66-7; release by U. S. Public
Roads Administration, 'Ton-Mile Estimates of Load Carried by Trucks and
Combinations on Main and Local Rural Roads in the United States, for the
year 1940'. Breakdown fails to agree with total, because the latter has been
revised; revision of former not available.

We may now consider the extent and nature of intercity truck
ton-mileage as compiled from the Highway Planning Surveys. For
1940 the Public Roads Administration placed the total at 59 billion ton-miles (Table F-2), a figure which may be compared with
375 billion ton-miles for steam railroads. In terms of revenues the
relative importance of motor truck transportation is much greater
than these figures would suggest. Thus, in 1940 the large commercial intercity trucking firms reporting ton-mile revenue data to the
ICC received about 4 cents per ton-mile. The use of this average
with total truck ton-mileage suggests a figure of $2.4 billion for the
aggregate value of all intercity trucking in 1940; about $1 billion
was actually collected by for-hire (contract and common carrier)
operators, and the remainder is the imputed value of the trans-

portation service rendered by their trucks to owners moving their own goods. These totals compare with railroad freight revenues of $3,584 million.

Most vehicle-mileage over rural roads is seen to be accounted for by private vehicles, as would be expected from the overwhelming proportion that private trucks bear to the total (Table F-1). However, the commercial carrier is a much more efficient carrier in two respects: the average load carried by commercial trucks and combinations is almost twice that of private trucking units, and the ratio of loaded vehicle-miles to total miles traveled is higher for commercial units (72 percent) than for private units (60 percent). It is readily apparent that private carriers have less control over the volume of tonnage carried on return trips than commercial carriers who can to some extent solicit traffic in either direction. Commercial carriers also make greater use of trailer combinations and trucks of high rated capacity than private truckers; this explains the marked difference in average load carried. The net effect of such differentials is to enable for-hire carriers to come close to sharing total ton-mileage evenly with the private truckers, although the latter account for more than three-quarters of total vehicle mileage.

CHARACTERISTICS OF TRUCK TRAFFIC

The kind of commodity transported by trucks is heavily conditioned by the physical limitations of the trucking industry. Despite the large gains in truck capacity in recent years, the average truck load carried in 1940 by private and commercial carriers was 3.04 tons. In the same year, the average freight tonnage carried by a single loaded railroad car was 25.4 tons. This wide divergence in load per unit of equipment suggests that the greater capacity of the railroad car renders the latter more suitable for commodities whose transportation is facilitated by bulk shipments in large quantities.[19] Thus, we would not expect motor truckers to be particularly attracted toward such agricultural commodities as grain, or such mineral products as coal and iron ore, or such forest products

[19] To say nothing about the average capacity of the rail train, which may perhaps be considered the true loading unit in rail freight service.

as lumber, all of which are customarily transported in large bulk shipments, often in train or boat loads.

The compensating factor for the relatively small capacity of the motor truck is the fact that small shipments are attended by far fewer delays incident to loading and unloading, and offer an extremely flexible service. The Coordinator of Transportation found in 1933 that more than 68 percent of the total time taken by rail transport was occupied with terminal operations — at the origin, at the destination, and at intermediate points.[20] Such delays stem partly from the fact that railroad cars have on the average a larger capacity than trucks, so that the assembly of less-than-carload shipments into carload lots consumes more time than the consolidation of less-than-truckload shipments into truckload lots. Railroad movements are also slower because of the need to assemble carlot units into trains for movement between terminals. These differences make it possible for the motor truck to offer a faster over-all service than rail freight. We would expect motor trucking to attract those commodities, such as perishable fruits and vegetables, meats, and livestock, for which speed of delivery is an important shipping factor.[21]

The advantage of the motor truck in speed diminishes, however, as the haul lengthens and terminal delays come to represent a smaller and smaller component of total transport time. Again, as the distance between the points of origin and destination widens, the greater economies of large scale rail movement become increasingly reflected in ton-mile transport costs. On this score, we would expect to find motor trucking more firmly established in the movement of short haul goods. Indeed, the short haul factor frequently

[20] *Freight Traffic Report,* Volume II, p. 71.

[21] Mostly figures are available for recent years only. Of total receipts in 1940 at 68 public stockyards the following percentages arrived by truck: cattle, 66; calves, 64; hogs, 68; sheep and lambs, 32; horses and mules, 52. In the same year New York City, Chicago, Philadelphia and Boston together received 28 percent of their butter and 45 percent of their egg supply by truck; 69 percent of live poultry receipts in New York City were by truck. Truck receipts of fruits and vegetables in 1939 varied from 11 percent for Milwaukee to 88 percent for Los Angeles and averaged 43 percent for 12 cities. (Data compiled by U. S. Department of Agriculture and summarized in *Automobile Facts and Figures,* 1941 ed.)

overshadows other considerations. We find, for example, that such commodities as stone, sand, and gravel, perhaps most efficiently moved in large bulk shipments, are typically moved by truck because points of production and consumption are usually close together, so that the haul is very short.

Truck traffic then, is typically short-haul and usually high grade in character. The ton-mile rates for such traffic by rail are quite high in relation to the ton-mile rates for rail traffic as a whole.[22] It is in this sense that truck operators are said to "skim the cream of the traffic". While the latter charge may apply to commercial truckers, it is reasonable to assume that private operators too follow the line of least resistance and concentrate their trucking activities on the kinds of traffic which they find most profitable.

While there is no consistent body of data that would permit analysis of the development of truck traffic and its composition, some generalizations concerning recent trends may be made with scattered material at our disposal. The loadometer stations, operated under the supervision of the Public Roads Administration in 38 states during 1936-40, afford a sample of truck transportation in which the contents of over one and a half million vehicles was recorded (Table F-3).

Manufactures and miscellaneous freight is seen to account for more than half of all truck traffic; such tonnage, which consists mainly of finished commodities of relatively high value in relation to bulk, makes up only about one-quarter of total rail traffic. Mixed freight is really a less comprehensive category than LCL rail tonnage, for much other truck traffic would move in less-than-carload lots if it moved by rail. Like the latter, mixed freight yields a high revenue per ton-mile. In recent years it has been a far more important component of truck traffic than has LCL freight on the railroads: LCL freight constituted less than 2 percent of total rail freight; for trucks the mixed freight proportion is over 10 percent.

In the case of animal products, i.e., mainly livestock, the difference is similarly striking. Over the past two decades motor trucking

---

[22] These conclusions may be confirmed by observing the character of traffic lost by the railroads. See Appendix C above.

Table F-3

COMPOSITION OF TRUCK TRAFFIC, 1936-1940[a]

Commodities Carried	Average Load (tons per truck)	Total Load (th. tons)	%
Products of agriculture	3.7	749	14.2
Animal products	2.6	530	10.0
Products of mines	4.3	434	8.2
Products of forests	4.1	324	6.1
Manufactures and miscellaneous	3.3	2,712	51.3
Mixed freight	4.1	541	10.2
TOTAL	3.5	5,290	100.0

[a] Public Roads Administration. See ICC, *Federal Regulation of the Sizes and Weight of Motor Vehicles,* 77th Cong. 1st Sess. House Document 354 (1941), p. 442. These figures, while they apply to intercity traffic, are not of course confined to for-hire vehicles.

has attained a dominant position in the transportation of livestock. Thus, in 1916 the proportion of all livestock receipts 'driven in' by truck in the principal livestock markets was less than 2 percent, but by 1940 the 'driven in' proportion was more than half total receipts.[23] Animal products, which like all perishables require high transport charges, make up 10 percent of total truck tonnage, but less than 2 percent of present day rail tonnage. Motor trucks also carry many perishable fruits and vegetables. This explains the relatively high proportion of total tonnage contributed by agricultural products — 14 percent; the corresponding figure for rail traffic was less than 9 percent in 1940. On the other hand, the low-revenue products of mines, which make up over half of total rail tonnage, is a very minor component of truck traffic (8 percent), much of it representing the trucking of coal to domestic consumers.

The Federal Coordinator of Transportation accumulated a body of data on trucking activity in 1933 which yields some informative insights into the nature of truck traffic. In a canvass of large shippers, it was found that the commodities moving by truck in significant amounts included such processed goods as paints, autos and parts, rubber articles and tires, dry goods and clothing, textiles,

[23] See *Automobile Facts and Figures,* 1941 ed.

leather goods, and books and stationery; such foodstuffs as beverages and liquors, bakery goods, canned goods, and fruits and vegetables; and, of course, livestock. Other commodities were sand, stone and gravel, cotton in bales and rough lumber.[24] The average truck haul was found to be about 100 miles, compared with an average rail haul of 342 miles in that year; truck hauls ranged from 14 miles for sand, stone and gravel to 435 miles for fresh fruits and vegetables. Other commodities for which truck hauls were longer than average were packing house products, groceries, rubber articles, and tires. Hauls by for-hire typically are longer than hauls by private trucks, for the latter usually restrict their range of operations to an area that can be serviced within the limits of a working day. Extremely long truck hauls have been noted for some commodities; automobiles are sometimes trucked as much as 1,500 miles from Michigan, but no regular service is normally maintained for such distances.[25]

With more advanced equipment and better highways, truck hauls seem to have lengthened considerably during the interwar era. Scattered evidence suggests that hauls were shorter in the early 1920's than today. In traffic surveys during 1922-24 the Bureau of Public Roads found that of loaded trucks on rural roads 86 percent operated within a 40-mile radius in Connecticut, 87 percent in Maine, and 85 percent in Cook County, Illinois. In California traffic 69 percent of all loaded trucks had hauls of less than 40 miles. The average haul of eastbound truck tonnage on the Boston Post Road in October 1921 was found to be 56 miles.[26] These and other scattered figures of a like nature do not permit any precise estimate of the total gain in average truck haulage; however, the growth of motor-truck transportation may be gauged by other means.

[24] *Freight Traffic Report,* Volume II, pp. 49-50.

[25] ICC, *Coordination of Motor Transportation,* 72nd Cong., 1st Sess., Senate Document 43 (1932), p. 42.

[26] *Automobile Facts and Figures,* 1922 ed., p. 29; 1926, p. 39.

THE GROWTH OF INTERCITY MOTOR TRUCKING

In a preceding section we described estimates which place the volume of intercity truck transport in 1940 at 59 billion ton-miles. How rapidly did it grow in reaching this volume?

Vehicle Miles (For-Hire and Private Combined)

We begin by estimating the growth of intercity vehicle-miles. As a first step in such measurement, we can resort to indexes of gasoline consumption. Total domestic motor fuel consumption has been analyzed and distributed among highway and city trucks, passenger cars, and busses for the period 1925-40 by Herbert A. Breakey.[27] The distribution, admittedly crude, was based on data collected by the Public Roads Administration in road and traffic surveys. The resulting series for truck consumption of gasoline on highways (i.e., rural roads as distinct from city streets) is reproduced in the first column of Table F-4. The highway truck mileage figure of 29.8 billion in 1940 (Table F-2) yields an average of about 14 miles per gallon, somewhat above the figure (11.25) adopted by Breakey. Truck mileage was estimated by the Bureau of Public Roads for 1936, and we have projected these estimates back to 1925 on the basis of gasoline consumption. A constant ratio of motor fuel per vehicle-mile was used, the assumption being that larger loads and higher speeds have offset greater engine efficiency.[28] The indications are that intercity truck mileage grew between five- and six-fold from 1925 to 1940.

[27] U. S. Bureau of Mines, *Minerals Yearbook, Review of 1940,* p. 982. See also *Petroleum Facts and Figures,* 1939, p. 21.

[28] This assumption is probably too conservative. Estimates of gasoline consumption by rated capacity (Bureau of Public Roads, *The Taxation of Motor Vehicles in 1932,* U. S. Department of Agriculture, 1934, p. 268) suggest an increase in average miles per gallon from about 5 in 1923 to about 9½ in 1932. (This calculation takes account of the rise in average vehicle weight. For 1923 trucks were distributed by rated capacity according to highway surveys in Connecticut, Ohio and Pennsylvania; for 1932 a distribution given in Federal Coordinator of Transportation, *Public Aids to Transportation,* Vol. IV, p. 129 was used.) Consequently Table F-4 may understate the rise both in vehicle mileage and in ton-mileage.

Ton-Miles (For-Hire and Private Combined)

This increase in vehicle mileage serves in turn as a lower limit
for the corresponding rise in ton-mileage. To pass from the former
to the latter we have to estimate the change in load per truck. There
is first of all the question of truck capacity, which has risen significantly in recent years. The rise has occurred not so much because of
general increases in rated capacity per truck as because of the
introduction and development of tractor and trailer combinations.

The capacity of all single truck units has, if anything, declined
owing to the dominant influence of trucks of less than two tons
of rated capacity, used mainly in short-haul local service. For the
larger trucks in intercity service, the tendency toward increased
capacity found its chief expression in the extended use of trailer
combinations rather than an increase in the capacity of single
trucks. In 1940, 16 percent of total truck vehicle-mileage was
accounted for by trailer combinations. The gain in capacity associated with the use of combinations is indicated by their average
load, 7.42 tons, as compared with an average load of 2.08 tons for
single unit trucks.[29] Trailer registrations have not until recently
been segregated from those of trucks. Of 1,193 thousand trailers
registered in 1939, more than half, or about 674 thousand may
have been commercial or property carrying types.[30] Although
trailer combinations have long been a feature of intercity trucking,[31] in 1940 single unit trucks made up only 28 percent of all
equipment units of Class I intercity property carriers reporting to
the ICC.[32] The Public Roads Administration found that over the
period 1936-40 the percentage of total truck vehicle mileage contributed by combinations increased rather steadily. If the rate of
increase which they indicate be projected backward in time, trailer

[29] Public Roads Administration release, 'Ton-Mile Estimates, 1940'. Much of
the gain in trailer capacity is due to the fact that a trailer subject to the same
legal gross-weight restrictions as a single unit truck has a relative advantage
because of the absence of a power plant and the resultant low chassis weight.
See *Motor Truck Freight Transportation,* Domestic Commerce Series, No. 66
(U. S. Department of Commerce, 1932), p. 12.

[30] *Automobile Facts and Figures,* 1941 ed., p. 20.

[31] *Motor Truck Freight Transportation.*

[32] 'Statistics of Class I Motor Carriers, 1940', p. 11.

combinations would have contributed about 10 percent of total
truck vehicle mileage in 1929 compared with 16 percent in 1940;
this, however, is probably an overestimate of the true proportion
in the former year.

When the average capacity of all trucks and combinations in
intercity service has been ascertained, it then becomes necessary
to enquire into loading practices before one can arrive at an estimate of the average load carried. First, one must determine the
proportion of empty mileage, for it is evident that trucks may
frequently, especially in private trucking, make return trips without cargo. In the 1940 traffic surveys, it was found that 65 percent
of all truck and combination vehicle mileage was made under
load.[33] This is in remarkably close agreement with the guess made
by the ICC for the years 1925 and 1929, when it was assumed
that one-third of all truck mileage is empty mileage.[34]

Secondly, the rated capacity of a truck is no accurate indication
of the actual weight carried when under load. Various factors
must be considered in this connection. For trucks of intermediate
capacity, loading over rated capacity is very common, although
such overloading, most pronounced at the point of origin, tends to
diminish along the route of delivery. More important than overloading, however, is the difficulty of obtaining full loads, especially
for the larger vehicles, and on return trips. Here again the ICC
estimated that in 1925 and 1929 loaded trucks carried about 80
percent of the tonnage they could have carried in terms of rated
capacity.

We have no reason to suppose that either the proportion of
empty mileage or the ratio of load to capacity are subject to any
special trend. Certainly any change since 1925 in average load of
all vehicles (loaded and empty) must be attributed in major part
to changes in vehicle capacity and type of equipment.

In 1940 the effects of all the above factors appear in the figure
for average tonnage carried per vehicle, obtained by dividing total
ton-mileage by total vehicle mileage (loaded and empty). The
result, an average load of 1.98 tons per truck for 1940, represents

[33] 'Ton-Mile Estimates, 1940'.
[34] 182 ICC 263, see pp. 400-7 (1932).

an advance of nearly 50 percent over the corresponding figure of 1.33 tons estimated by the ICC for the year 1929. The latter figure rests on the following basis: trucks were assumed to be loaded two-thirds of the time at 80 percent of capacity; and the average capacity of trucks in intercity use (including trailers) was estimated at 2.50 tons.[35] State traffic surveys in the middle 'twenties suggest a figure of one ton per truck for the initial year of our data, 1925. The average load per vehicle apparently doubled within the space of fifteen years. In Table F-4 the ton-mileage series for intercity trucking (for-hire and private combined) is derived from the truck mileage series with the use of the ratios just outlined.

It appears from these data that while intercity truck mileage grew between five- and six-fold, the corresponding ton-mileage rose more than tenfold between 1925 and 1940. A simple extrapolation places ton-mileage at about 2 billion in 1920, or less than one-half of one percent of the volume of railroad freight transportation in that year. We may therefore say with some confidence that the intercity trucking industry became a factor in the national transportation picture only after 1920. Judged by gasoline consumption, the growth of highway freight transportation was remarkably steady, slackening little even in depression years. Such sustained gains in output are, of course, to be expected in the early stages of an industry's life history.

How may this rapid increase be explained? In our discussion of the nature of truck traffic, we have seen that the type of cargo most suited to truck transport is of a short-haul, high grade nature. The motor truck, filling a definite need for this type of transport service and adding the elements of over-all speed of delivery, and completeness and flexibility of service, enlarged its share of total traffic in proportion as these factors were lacking in the standard rail freight service. Truckers have been quick to capitalize on certain aspects of rail shipping practices. Throughout the 1920's the railroads exercised considerable managerial ingenuity in increasing the efficiency of freight service. Great gains were achieved, as we have seen, in railroad output per unit of input. However, some of this productivity gain may have been achieved at the expense of

[35] *Ibid.*

the shipper. For example, the average number of cars in each freight train increased from 36.6 in 1920 to 48.9 in 1930.[36] While such an increase may reflect in one sense an improvement in the organization of rail freight service, it may also have contributed to increasing the over-all shipping time, a factor that was singled out by the Federal Coordinator of Transportation as a serious flaw in rail freight service in 1932. It has been the contention of some observers (particularly representatives of railway labor) that many of the technological advances instituted by rail management in the 'twenties, such as those making for gains in car capacity and the tractive power of locomotives, have increased the inflexibility of rail service, inasmuch as they hindered the speedy dispatch of small shipments.[37] It is further asserted that business practice after 1920 favored so-called 'hand-to-mouth buying', whereby small orders are placed at frequent intervals requiring quick delivery.[38] Hand-to-mouth buying was not always considered in the late 1920's to be a tendency leading to diversion of traffic from rail to highway;[39] nevertheless, the steady decline of less-than-carload railroad traffic from 53 million tons in 1920 to 36 million tons in 1929 suggests that here was an area of competition in which motor trucking was rapidly gaining at the expense of the railroads.

Various other competitive advantages have been attributed to motor trucking. That of 'completeness of service', involving store-door collection and delivery, it may be noted, is not necessarily limited to the trucking industry as such, as is attested by the increasing degree to which railroads have in recent years added this feature to their regular freight service. Nevertheless, in this respect, intercity truckers no doubt had a considerable initial advantage over rail freight service. In addition, motor trucks could (and still do) offer certain other services to shippers which the railroads cannot duplicate; trucks can penetrate areas often inaccessible to railroads, such as logging and construction camps and oil fields in

[36] TNEC, *Hearings,* Part 30, p. 17387.

[37] Cf. testimony of George Harrison of the Brotherhood of Railway Clerks, TNEC, *Hearings,* Part 30, pp. 16615-8.

[38] *Freight Traffic Report,* Vol. II, pp. 68-83.

[39] L. S. Lyon, *Hand to Mouth Buying* (Brookings, 1929), pp. 467-71.

Table F-4

INTERCITY MOTOR TRUCKING: TON-MILE
ESTIMATES, 1925-1946[a]

| | Motor Fuel Consumed by Trucks Outside Cities (mil. barrels) | FOR-HIRE AND PRIVATE | | FOR-HIRE ONLY Ton-miles (bil.) |
		Vehicle-miles[b] (bil.)	Ton-miles (bil.)	
1925	8.7	4	4	2
1926	10.3	4	5	2
1927	12.3	5	6	3
1928	14.6	6	8	3
1929	17.8	8	10	4
1930	19.9	9	12	5
1931	22.4	10	14	6
1932	22.5	10	15	6
1933	24.1	10	17	7
1934	27.5	12	20	9
1935	30.8	13	23	10
1936	35.5	15.4	28	12
1937	39.7	19	35	15
1938	40.8	21	40	18
1939	45.2	25	49	22
1940	49.4	29.8	59	27
1941	....	24.2	59	28
1942	....	n.a.	n.a.	n.a.
1943	....	17.4	44	23
1944	....	17.2	45	25
1945	....	18.9	50	28
1946	....	24.3	61	34

n.a.: not available.

[a] Figures for combined for-hire and private vehicle-miles and ton-miles in 1936 and in 1940 and later years are based directly on traffic surveys by the Public Roads Administration made during the years in question. The ratio of for-hire to total traffic was surveyed only in 1936, 1940, and 1944, and estimates of for-hire ton-miles in these three years are also due to PRA. The above data were published in various issues of *Public Roads* or in special releases by PRA. Estimates for other years were made as follows. Combined for-hire and private vehicle-miles for 1925-35 and 1937-39 were based upon the series for motor fuel consumed by trucks outside cities, published in U. S. Bureau of Mines, *Minerals Yearbook* (annual). It was assumed that vehicle-miles per gallon of fuel did not change between 1925 and 1935, fuel economy being offset by growth in vehicle weight (an assumption supported by scattered state surveys during the period). Combined for-hire and private ton-miles were derived for 1937-39 by straight line interpolation of the ratio of tons per truck (loaded and empty); for 1935 and earlier years by similar interpolation assuming average load was 1 ton in 1925 and 1-1/3 ton in 1929 (figures from scattered state surveys). For-hire ton-miles were obtained for 1937-39, 1941, and

1943 by straight line interpolation of the ratio of for-hire to total ton-miles;
for 1945 and 1946 by using the corresponding ratio for 1944; and for 1935 and
prior years by using the ratio for 1936. So far as estimates of for-hire ton-miles
in early years are concerned, this last step is probably the weakest. Unfortunately there appears to be no way of checking the assumption that for-hire and
private traffic grew at the same rate prior to 1936, for the ratio between them
was not canvassed in any of the early surveys that have come to our notice.

Our estimate of 49 billion ton-miles for private and for-hire trucking in 1939
compares with a figure released by the ICC of 43 billion (*55th Annual Report*,
p. 9). The Board of Investigation and Research, appointed under the Transportation Act of 1940, offers an even lower figure (40 billion) in *The National
Traffic Pattern* (79th Cong., 1st Sess., Senate Document 83, p. 22). Neither
the ICC nor the Board gives the derivation of its estimate, but the latter states
that its figure excludes "local highway traffic where the trip is under 15 miles."

It should be noted that our estimates for early years fall considerably below
some other estimates made in the past. Thus the ICC quotes an estimate by
the Bureau of Public Roads of 8 billion for intercity (for-hire and private) ton-
mileage in 1925, and offers alternative estimates of 26 and 20 billion for 1929
(182 ICC 263, see pp. 400-7, 1932). The Federal Coordinator of Transportation estimated total intercity ton-mileage at 30 billion in 1932, and the for-
hire component at 5.5 billion (*Regulation of Transportation Agencies*, 73d
Cong., 2d Sess., Senate Document 152, 1934, pp. 261-2). An early estimate of
total ton-mileage, including farm-to-market and city trucking, of 6.5 billion
was made by the Bureau of Public Roads at the beginning of the 1920's (*Report
of the Joint Commission of Agricultural Inquiry*, 67th Cong., 1st Sess., House
Report 408, Part 3, 'Transportation', 1922, p. 351). On the whole these estimates are higher than our own. They were made before the extensive new
surveys of 1936 and 1940; all of them rest on figures for truck mileage derived
by taking the product of an assumed number of trucks and an assumed average
annual mileage per truck, a procedure we do not believe preferable to that
used here, i.e., the projection of the vehicle-mileage data backward using gasoline consumption. Nevertheless, if the earlier estimates quoted are correct, then
intercity trucking must have developed much more rapidly before about 1929,
and much less rapidly during the 'thirties, than is suggested by our figures.
[b] Both loaded and empty. A trailer is counted as a separate vehicle; a tractor
truck plus semitrailer as a single vehicle.

the early stages of development. Some shippers find the relative
simplicity of the packing requirements, flexibility of schedules, and
adaptability of equipment of truckers as reasons for preferring the
latter to other agencies.[40]

For-Hire Ton-Miles

The preceding discussion was concerned with all intercity trucking,
for-hire and private. Certainly a truck, whether owned by a commercial trucking company or by the firm whose property it carries,

[40] See *Freight Traffic Report,* as above.

competes with other means of transportation. The rise of both kinds of intercity trucking was stimulated by the same sorts of advantage. Yet our main interest in this study is in for-hire rather than in all intercity trucking. If only as one constituent of our index of freight traffic for all transportation agencies, we need a series for ton-miles carried in for-hire (contract and common carrier) operations. The calculation is a simple one, although we cannot claim accuracy for it on that account. The Public Roads Administration surveyed the proportion of for-hire to total ton-miles in intercity trucking for the years 1936, 1940, and 1944. For other years we must assume that for-hire ton-miles moved in the same fashion as total ton-miles. The figures will be found in the last column of Table F-4.

RELATION OF OUTPUT TO EMPLOYMENT

The relation of the output of intercity motor trucking to employment must remain largely a matter of conjecture, in the absence of truck employment statistics as such. The latter, however, may be estimated, albeit roughly, from the number of trucks in use, i.e., from truck registration statistics. That there is a functional relationship between truck employment and truck registrations cannot be doubted, for the use of every truck or truck combination must of necessity involve one or more employees; yet the nature of the function and the precise level of the 'employment per truck' ratio, may be difficult to ascertain.

The volume of employment required to furnish 59 billion ton-miles of intercity transportation in 1940 cannot be determined unless some adequate disposition first be made of the employment required to transport the unknown proportion made up by those agricultural (and other) products which were transported by the million or so farm trucks in use in 1940. It would be clearly unwarranted to assign one full-time driver to every farm truck in intercity use and we have no data which permit estimates of the actual full time employment associated with such intercity transport. For the remaining million or so trucks engaged in intercity trucking, in private and for-hire service, we may at least assert that to the extent that such trucks were in continuous use, a minimum of one million drivers were employed in 1940. The actual employment associated with the operation of these trucks, including those employees concerned with terminal, maintenance, and administrative functions, must have been considerably larger.[41]

Of the 283 thousand trucks in intercity for-hire service in 1940, 14,869 were operated by common carriers of general freight reporting operating revenues over $500,000 to the ICC, and for these companies the employment per truck ratio was 3.1 to 1. For 643 Class I intercity carriers operating owned equipment only, the corresponding ratio was 2.4 to 1.[42] The number of trucks engaged in such relatively large scale operations, in which the proportion of total employment engaged in terminal and administrative functions exceeds that engaged in actual transportation service, is relatively small. All intercity Class I motor carriers in predominantly intercity service reporting to the ICC operated fewer than 40,000 trucks and tractors in 1940. The bulk of the remaining for-hire carriers in intercity service probably operated single truck units, and for these carriers the employment per truck ratio was probably much closer to unity. The Federal Coordinator of Transportation estimated that the ratio for all intercity for-hire truckers was 1.58 to 1 in 1934.[43] Applying this ratio to the 283 thousand or so for-hire trucks estimated by us to be in intercity service in 1940, we may take 450 thousand as a tentative estimate of total employment in intercity for-hire motor transport in that year. Even more tentative would be any estimate of the employment associated with privately operated trucks; a reasonable guess may be that as many as one million were so engaged. The 58 billion ton-miles of inter-

[41] The 1940 Census reported 1.7 million persons engaged in the occupation 'trucking service'; this figure of course includes private as well as for-hire employment.

[42] Ratios computed from 'Statistics of Class I Motor Carriers, 1940'.

[43] *Hours, Wages and Working Conditions in the Intercity Motor Transport Industries* (1936), Part II, p. 173. The total intercity trucking laboring force was estimated at 395,000 in 1934 and the total number of trucks in use at 250,000. The latter figure is not much below our estimate for the year 1940, and may be an overestimate, although it is possible that in the depression year 1934 many trucks normally in local service entered into intercity transport service where competitive opportunities were more favorable. In any case, however, the employment per truck ratios, obtained from sample data, represent the only attempt to cover the entire range of intercity for-hire operations.

city trucking traffic in 1940 may thus be seen to have required the full-time efforts of anywhere from 1,000,000 to 1,500,000 persons, and for motor trucking as a whole it would be difficult to state the case with any greater precision.

The 450 thousand employees tentatively estimated as engaged in commercial operations accounted for 27 billion ton-miles in 1940 yielding a productivity ratio of 59 thousand ton-miles per man-year. The ratio is much higher, of course, for those commercial carriers whose operations are organized on a relatively large scale. Thus intercity common carriers of general freight, reporting revenues of more than $500,000 to the ICC in 1940, employed 46,536 persons and reported 788 million intercity vehicle-miles. Since other large common carriers reported an average load per vehicle-mile of 6.8 tons in that year it is reasonable to assume that for such carriers the output per man ratio was well over 100 thousand ton-miles per employee.[44]

A significant question to be raised with regard to the relation between the output of intercity motor trucking and employment concerns their movement in time. We have already determined that the increase in output over the period 1925-40, in ton-mileage terms, was from seven to tenfold, an expansion to be ascribed to the extreme youth of the industry. How has employment moved in this period? For an answer to this question we must again resort to truck registration statistics. We know, for example, that total for-hire and privately owned trucks in local and intercity service grew from 2,442 thousand in 1925 to 4,590 thousand in 1940, or by 88 percent. An estimate of the corresponding increase in the number of intercity trucks would probably be of similar magnitude.[45] The

[44] 'Statistics of Class I Motor Carriers, 1940'.

[45] The present proportion of intercity trucks to the total may be somewhat higher than in 1925, for estimates of gasoline consumed by local trucks indicate advances of about 100 percent during 1925-40 compared with gains of 500 percent in gasoline consumed by highway trucks; it seems difficult to attribute all of this difference to greater increases in average annual mileage of highway trucks (see *Petroleum Facts and Figures, 1939*, p. 21). On the other hand, it has been estimated (or perhaps merely guessed) that in 1925 50 percent of all trucks were in intercity service, which is a higher proportion than that estimated by us for 1940 (182 ICC 263 at pp. 400-7).

employment per truck ratio may perhaps have risen with longer trips and more intensive utilization of equipment.

No precise estimates of the increase in employment in intercity trucking can be inferred from the above, but it seems clear that the size of the increase — probably of the order of 100 percent from 1925 to 1940 — lies well below that of the increase in ton-mileage, which expanded more than sevenfold in the same period (Table F-4). Ton-miles per employee would appear to have increased rather rapidly — how rapidly it is impossible to say. Productivity in intercity trucking seems to have risen at least as rapidly as in other transportation industries.

Appendix G

Oil Pipelines: Basic Series

The traffic data in Table G-1 cover trunk line movements of crude and refined oils, but only on interstate pipelines; whereas the figures in Table 4, and the weight given to pipelines in more comprehensive indexes (e.g., for all transportation agencies combined), include an allowance for trunk-line movements on intrastate lines as well. (Activities of gathering lines are omitted for lack of data.) Trunk-line traffic on intrastate pipelines was estimated as follows for 1939.

Unlike the ICC figures in Table G-1, data for receipts at and shipments from refineries cover intrastate as well as interstate lines. For instance, refineries received 902 million barrels of crude from pipelines and 261 million barrels from tankers (*Minerals Yearbook, Review of 1940,* p. 967). Crude delivered from tankers may be assumed to have traveled by pipeline from well to tanker, so that we can take 1,163 million barrels (174.4 million tons) as total crude originated on all lines. (This total falls short of aggregate receipts at refineries only by tank car and truck deliveries, assumed not to have moved by pipeline; and tanker deliveries of foreign oil, not then important). In addition we have to include 95 million barrels (12.4 million tons) of refined products shipped by pipeline (*ibid.,* p. 994), making total barrels originated 1,258 million (187 million tons). But we know that 803 million barrels of crude and 70 million barrels of refined originated on ICC lines (American Petroleum Institute, *Petroleum Facts and Figures,* 1941, p. 123), making a total of 873 million barrels. The ICC share in originated tonnage may therefore be put at 69.4 percent, compared with 85.9 percent of all trunk mileage (*ibid.,* p. 124); the interstate lines are of course longer than the intrastate.

It usually is assumed, for instance in studies by the Federal Coordinator of Transportation (1932), that intrastate hauls of petroleum are about one-third interstate hauls. The latter were 330 miles for crude and 348 miles for refined (*ibid.*, p. 126). Taking intrastate hauls as 110 miles for crude and 116 miles for refined, and converting barrels at 0.15 tons for crude and 0.13 tons for refined, we have 5.9 and 0.4 billion ton-miles respectively, or 6.3 billion ton-miles for total intrastate trunk-line movement. Together with 43.0 billion ton-miles for the interstate traffic (Table G-1) we reach 49.3 billion ton-miles for total trunk line movement, as shown in Table 4.[1]

Freight revenues reported by ICC lines in 1939, $164 million, were 0.381 cents per ton-mile. The same revenue per ton-mile was assumed for intrastate lines, yielding $188 million for all trunk lines.

[1] The American Petroleum Institute have placed total trunk-line movement at 50.4 billion ton-miles in 1939. Their estimate is slightly higher than our own, being based on the ratio of interstate to total trunk line mileage, without allowance for the shorter haul on intrastate lines (*Petroleum Facts and Figures, 1941,* p. 126). The Board of Investigation and Research (under the Transportation Act of 1940) estimated total pipeline ton-miles in 1939 at 46.1 billion, but "all movements between points under 5 miles [apart]" were excluded, as well as gathering operations (*The National Traffic Pattern,* 79th Cong., 1st Sess., Senate Document 83, 1945). The ICC have published a ton-mileage figure for 1939, confined to interstate but including gathering lines, of as much as 65.0 billion (ICC, Ex Parte No. 165, *Problems in the Regulation of Domestic Transportation by Water,* 1946, p. 428). This implies traffic of 22 billion ton-miles on ICC gathering lines, or 550 thousand ton-miles per mile of line annually, compared with 730 thousand ton-miles per mile of trunk-line. Since gathering lines average a much smaller cross section than trunk lines, the admittedly speculative ton-mileage in gathering operations would appear to have been overstated.

Table G-1

OIL PIPELINES: DERIVATION OF TON-MILES, AND
DATA FOR EMPLOYMENT, 1920-1946[a]

Trunk-Line Movement, ICC Pipelines

	Oil Received into System[b] (mil. barrels)			Oil Transported[c] (bil. ton-miles)			Employment[d] (th.)
	Crude	Refined	Total	Crude	Refined	Total	
1920	534	....	....	7.0	....	7.0	....
1921	526	....	....	....	....	8	13.0
1922	651	....	....	....	....	11	17.4
1923	658	....	....	....	....	12	24.1
1924	758	....	....	....	....	15	22.5
1925	831	....	....	....	....	17	20.7
1926	836	....	....	....	....	19	27.3
1927	989	....	....	....	....	23	28.4
1928	1053	....	....	....	....	26	25.3
1929	1156	....	....	....	....	31	23.5
1930	1172	....	....	....	....	33	21.9
1931	1110	18	1128	....	....	33	19.9
1932	1096	25	1121	....	....	34	16.3
1933	1160	29	1189	....	....	38	18.9
1934	1178	35	1214	....	....	41	20.9
1935	1005	54	1059	....	....	37	21.5
1936	1039	62	1102	37.8	2.4	40.2	23.2
1937	1208	81	1288	42.1	2.9	45.0	24.2
1938	1084	89	1172	39.5	3.1	42.5	21.8
1939	1133	95	1228	39.8	3.2	43.0	20.7
1940	1326	95	1421	42.3	3.1	45.4	21.6
1941	1532	107	1639	48.6	3.5	52.1	22.4
1942	1665	115	1780	51.9	5.0	56.9	23.2
1943	1884	197	2080	59.0	7.9	66.9	23.4
1944	2158	240	2398	65.7	9.2	74.9	23.5
1945	2151	228	2379	64.5	8.5	73.0	23.8
1946	2054	218	2272	64.3	7.6	72.0	25.8

[a] Figures cover only pipelines reporting to the ICC.

[b] ICC, 'Statistics of Oil Pipeline Companies' (annual). See also ICC Statement 4280, 'A Review of Statistics of Oil Pipe Lines 1921-1941' (mimeo., Oct. 1942).

[c] 1936-46, 'Statistics of Oil Pipeline Companies'. For crude, 1 barrel = .15 tons; for refined, 1 barrel = .13 tons (see American Petroleum Institute, *Petroleum Facts and Figures,* annual). For 1920-35, based on preceding columns, on the assumption that the average haul increased from 200 miles in 1920 to 330 miles in 1936. The 1920 haul was estimated as a weighted mean of distances between principal producing and consuming centers at that time. This procedure assumes that the 1936 ratio of barrels originated to barrels received into system (0.73) also held for earlier years.

[d] 'Statistics of Oil Pipeline Companies'. In recent years, average of twelve monthly counts; in early years probably a single count for each year.

Appendix H

Waterways: Basic Series

Table H-1

WATERWAYS: FREIGHT TRAFFIC SUMMARY

Billion ton-miles (short tons, statute miles)

	Coast-wise[a]	Inter-coastal[a]	Great Lakes[b] (domestic)	Inland[c]	Non-con-tiguous[d]	International, American-Flag[d]	Total
1889	14.7	1.9	14.6	4.6	19.7		55.6
1920	37	22	73	5	11	285	434
1921	32	29	35	5	12	184	297
1922	46	50	57	4	11	205	375
1923	61	87	81	6	10	179	425
1924	66	70	61	7	11	186	401
1925	87	60	77	8	12	169	413
1926	88	70	83	10	13	180	444
1927	97	73	76	9	13	180	447
1928	98	65	77	9	13	168	431
1929	101	74	89	9	12	173	457
1930	97	63	69	9	13	151	402
1931	98	51	43	9	12	114	327
1932	91	40	20	8	12	87	259
1933	110	53	41	10	12	88	314
1934	111	59	42	9	13	99	334
1935	117	50	49	13	14	98	341
1936	145	47	71	15	15	96	388
1937	171	48	86	17	17	113	451
1938	161	41	42	18	14	84	360
1939	174	52	69	20	16	80	410
1940	183	47	88	22	18	118	475
1941	....	....	104	27	....	....	....
1942	....	....	112	26	....	....	....
1943	....	....	148	26	....	....	....
1944	....	....	106	31	....	....	....
1945	....	....	102	30	....	....	....
1946	210		87	28	26	352	704

[a] For 1889 from Census of Waterways, using average hauls in Table H-3. For 1937 see Tables H-3 and H-4. For other years, intercoastal shipments (U. S. Maritime Commission, annual reports 2610, 'Water-Borne Foreign and Non-contiguous Commerce and Passenger Traffic', and predecessors) were deducted from coastal and intercoastal shipments (U. S. Army, Chief of Engineers, Annual Report, Part 2), this operation being performed separately for each of the three coastal regions; the resulting tonnages were then multiplied by average hauls in Table H-4.

The Board of Investigation and Research, appointed under the Transportation Act of 1940, put combined coastal and intercoastal ton-miles for 1939 at 174 billion; the Board states that its intercoastal figure is "derived by use of direct rail distance", but does not otherwise describe its method (*The National Traffic Pattern,* 79th Cong., 1st Sess., Senate Document 83, p. 22).

[b] For 1889 Census data: total lakewise shipments were multiplied by an average haul (578 miles) obtained from an analysis of the shipments between 34 principal pairs of ports. For 1925 and later years ton-mileage is given by the Army Engineers. For 1921-24 shipments from the same source were multiplied by an average haul extrapolated from the 1925 figure (750 miles).

The estimate for 1939 by the Board of Investigation and Research (see note a) is very close to our own, being 68 billion ton-miles. The ICC (*55th Annual Report,* p. 9) places combined Great Lakes and inland waterways at 96 billion ton-miles in 1939.

[c] The 1889 Census reports coal and lumber traffic on the Mississippi system at 2.6 billion ton-miles; other traffic was estimated in that year on the basis of a haul of 40 miles, comparable with that during the 1920's. For 1925 and later years ton-mileage is given by the Army Engineers. For 1921-24 shipments from the same source were multiplied by an average haul of 40 miles (1925 haul was 41 miles).

The estimate for 1939 by the Board of Investigation and Research (see note a) is 17 billion ton-miles. For an ICC estimate, see note b.

[d] For 1889 from Census, using average hauls to and from North Atlantic ports (4453 miles), South Atlantic ports (3266 miles), Gulf ports (4029), and Pacific ports (5126 miles) computed from detailed data for 1927 (the earliest for which a simultaneous breakdown of receipts and shipments by U. S. coastal districts and foreign trade regions is available). For 1928-40 noncontiguous and 1927-40 international receipts plus shipments between U. S. coastal districts and individual foreign trade regions or territories (Maritime Commission, annual reports 2610 and predecessors) were multiplied by the estimated average hauls shown in Tables H-5 and H-6, where illustrative calculations are given in detail for the year 1939. Noncontiguous ton-miles were extrapolated from 1928 back to 1923 using total shipments and receipts (*Statistical Abstract of the U. S.*) and from 1923 to 1920 on the basis of shipments of sugar from Hawaii and Puerto Rico to the United States (*Statistical Abstract*): figure for 1946 extrapolated by total receipts and shipments at San Juan, Puerto Rico, and Honolulu (Army Engineers). International ton-miles were extrapolated from 1927 back to 1921 on the basis of total ocean-borne American-flag receipts and shipments (Maritime Commission, annual reports 399, 'Comparative Summary of Water Borne Foreign Commerce'), and from 1921 to 1920 using American-flag imports plus exports (value) deflated by BLS wholesale prices (*Statistical Abstract*); for 1946 American-flag receipts plus shipments, by foreign trade areas (as in Table H-6; data from U. S. Bureau of the Census release, series FT 973, April 30, 1947) were multiplied by average hauls for each foreign trade area derived from Table H-6. The Maritime Commission has published no comprehensive receipts and shipments from returns by vessel operators for years since 1940; and the Census Bureau compilations, which are collected from customs houses and begin in 1946, offer no breakdown by U. S. coastal regions (as in Table H-6) and do not cover noncontiguous trade. American-flag international receipts and shipments through Great Lakes ports are actually available only for 1938, 1939 and 1946; for all other years total 'oceanborne' ton-miles were adjusted upward to cover Great Lakes traffic by the 1939 ratio (1.020; see Table H-6). Trade with the Philippine Islands, in 1937 and earlier years classified by the Maritime Commission as noncontiguous, has throughout been regarded by us as international.

Table H-2

WATERWAYS: PASSENGER TRAFFIC SUMMARY

Million passenger-miles (statute miles)

	Intercoastal[a]	Noncontiguous[b]	International American-flag Between U. S. and foreign ports[c]	Cruises[d]
1928	108	187	1246[e]	
1929	128	250	1212	28
1930	119	182	1114	37
1931	104	147	948	48
1932	95	111	825	54
1933	115	109	776	76
1934	140	142	809	81
1935	153	174	861	118
1936	124	186	1102	121
1937	126	198	1105	168
1938	....	205	759	153
1939	....	218	823	104
1940	....	238	715	92

[a] New York is the eastern terminal for practically all intercoastal passenger traffic. Accordingly, West Coast arrivals plus departures (U. S. Maritime Commission, annual reports 157, 'Water Borne Passenger Traffic') were multiplied by the following estimated navigational distances from New York (via Panama): Los Angeles and San Diego, 5,600 statute miles; San Francisco, Seattle and Portland, 6,100. No data for years since 1937 have been published.

[b] Arrivals plus departures at U. S. ports by U. S. coastal districts and noncontiguous territories are available in Maritime Commission, reports 2610 and predecessors (annual). These were combined each year with the average hauls in Table H-5, except that the distance between Pacific Coast and Alaskan ports was taken as 900 miles. No data have been published for years since 1940. Travel between the United States and the Philippine Islands is excluded throughout.

[c] Arrivals plus departures at U. S. ports in American-flag vessels are reported for 1927-29 and 1938-40 separately by U. S. coastal districts and foreign trade regions in sources mentioned in note b. For these years the data were combined with the hauls shown in Table H-6. For 1930-37 the data were apparently not published with the breakdown indicated; accordingly figures for these years are interpolated, using total American-flag arrivals plus departures and graduating the change in over-all average haul (from 1,940 miles in 1929 to 2,160 miles in 1938) along a straight line. No data have been published for years since 1940. The figures include travel between the United States and the Philippine Islands throughout the period. Great Lakes travel was not reported before 1938, but allowance (less than 1 percent of total) has been made for its inclusion.

[d] For 1929-40 arrivals and departures on cruises in American-flag vessels are reported in the sources mentioned in note b. The data were multiplied by the following lengths of haul (in statute miles representing half the lengths of the cruise): from North Atlantic ports — African (7,900), Bermuda (780), Cana-

dian (1,500), Caribbean (2,300), European (5,800), Havana (1,400), Mediterranean (5,800), North Cape (5,500), Pacific (11,200), Sea (200), South American (6,100), West Coast of Americas (5,200), World (15,000); from South Atlantic ports — Caribbean (1,600); from Gulf ports — Caribbean (1,600), Havana (680), Mediterranean (6,800); from Pacific ports — Pacific (6,000), World (15,000); from Great Lakes ports — Canadian (1,000). For 1928 cruise passengers were not reported. No data have been published for years since 1940.

ᵉ Travel between U. S. and foreign ports, raised to include cruises on 1929 basis.

Table H-3

DOMESTIC FREIGHT TRAFFIC OF
76 PRINCIPAL SEAPORTS, 1937ᵃ

Short tons, statute miles

	New Eng- land	Middle Atlan- tic	South Atlan- tic	East Gulf	West Gulf	Pacific South- west	Pacific North- west
New England							
Tons (th.)	2,149	1,240	174	47	113	75	21
Av. haul (miles)	100	350	1,050	1,925	2,350	6,015	7,000
Ton-miles (mil.)	215	434	182	90	266	449	149
Mid-Atlantic							
Tons (th.)	17,782	12,440	961	216	2,007	1,778	453
Av. haul (miles)	500	300	800	1,680	2,100	5,880	6,890
Ton-miles (mil.)	8,891	3,732	769	362	4,214	10,458	3,124
South Atlantic							
Tons (th.)	255	1,520	96	3	35	50	21
Av. haul (miles)	1,050	800	200	950	1,400	5,280	6,265
Ton-miles (mil.)	268	1,216	19	3	49	266	133
East Gulf							
Tons (th.)	96	1,260	86	95	80	204	58
Av. haul (miles)	1,925	1,680	950	200	525	5,140	6,125
Ton-miles (mil.)	186	2,116	81	19	42	1,051	355
West Gulf							
Tons (th.)	9,709	46,506	6,298	2,082	9,587	313	195
Av. haul (miles)	2,350	2,100	1,400	525	200	5,290	6,270
Ton-miles (mil.)	22,817	97,662	8,817	1,093	1,917	1,654	1,220
Pacific Southwest							
Tons (th.)	366	1,388	100	45	201	9,157	6,114
Av. haul (miles)	5,925	5,790	5,190	5,050	5,200	250	1,080
Ton-miles (mil.)	2,170	8,037	517	229	1,044	2,289	6,604
Pacific Northwest							
Tons (th.)	538	1,740	154	66	119	1,994	386
Av. haul (miles)	7,000	6,890	6,265	6,125	6,270	980	200
Ton-miles (mil.)	3,766	11,986	962	405	745	1,954	77

SUMMARY, 76 PORTS

	Coastwise	Intercoastal	Total
Receipts and shipments			
(thousand tons)	132,488	7,885	140,373
Traffic (million ton-miles)	166,386	48,719	215,105
Average haul (miles)	1,260	6,180	1,530

Notes to Table H-3

ᵃ This and the succeeding table show how ton-miles in coastwise and inter-coastal trade were derived for 1937. The U. S. Maritime Commission has traced coastwise and intercoastal commodity movements for that year by distributing the commerce of 76 principal ports into receipts and shipments from and to 7 regional districts. We have here reproduced some of the basic data from Appendix 4 of the Commission's 'Economic Survey of Coastwise and Intercoastal Commerce.' The table contains a distribution of the receipts and shipments of these principal ports (ports having traffic volume of 200,000 short tons and over) into a two-way classification which requires brief explanation. The Commission divided the Atlantic, Gulf, and Pacific coasts into the following geographic regions:

New England: Maine, New Hampshire, Massachusetts, Rhode Island and Connecticut.

Middle Atlantic: New York, New Jersey, Pennsylvania, Delaware, Maryland and Virginia.

South Atlantic: North Carolina, South Carolina, Georgia, and east coast of Florida.

East Gulf: West coast of Florida, Alabama and Mississippi.

West Gulf: Louisiana and Texas.

Pacific Southwest: California.

Pacific Northwest: Oregon and Washington.

The vertical listing of these seven regions represents the point of origin and the horizontal listing the point of destination. The table may be read as follows: Principal ports in the New England region shipped 3,723 thousand tons of cargo to the principal ports of the five Atlantic and Gulf coast regions; 2,149 thousand tons to New England, 1,240 thousand tons to the Middle Atlantic region, etc., making up an estimated total of 1,187 million ton-miles of traffic out of New England ports; while 96 thousand tons were shipped in the inter-coastal trade to the Southwest and Northwest Pacific regions from New England.

Each cargo movement was originally recorded twice, as a shipment and as a receipt. The totals differ because only 76 principal ports are covered. In each case we have entered the higher figure in the table, whether a shipment or a receipt.

Average hauls are shown in statute miles and were estimated by us by weighting the distance between ports by the relative importance of each port.

Table H-4

DERIVATION OF COASTWISE AND INTERCOASTAL
TON-MILES, 1937[a]

Short tons, statute miles

Region	Shipments (th. tons)	Ton-Miles (mil.)	Average Haul (miles)
Atlantic coast			
Coastwise	37,145	19,319	520
Intercoastal	2,269	13,811	6,087
Gulf Coast			
Coastwise	76,082	133,296	1,752
Intercoastal	769	4,278	5,560
Pacific coast			
Coastwise	26,192	18,306	699
Intercoastal	4,694	29,731	6,334
Total, all coasts			
Coastwise	139,419	170,921	1,226
Intercoastal	7,732	47,820	6,185
GRAND TOTAL	147,151	218,741	1,487

[a] Data are the same as those in Table H-3, but have been raised to include
commerce of small ports omitted in preceding table. The adjustment, of the
order of 5 percent, is based upon the presumably complete data collected by
the Chief of Army Engineers (*Annual Report,* Part 2).

Table H-5

DERIVATION OF NONCONTIGUOUS TON-MILES, 1939[a]

Statute miles

	North Atlantic	South Atlantic	Gulf	Pacific
Alaska — dry cargoes				
Long tons (th.)	1	....	....	805
Haul (miles)	7,900	....	....	1,100
Long ton-miles (mil.)	10	....	....	884
Alaska — tanker cargoes				
Long tons (th.)	....	....	....	107
Haul (miles)	....	....	....	2,200
Long ton-miles (mil.)	....	....	....	240
Hawaii				
Long tons (th.)	490	2	102	2,021
Haul (miles)	7,700	7,100	7,000	2,400
Long ton-miles (mil.)	3,785	16	715	4,867
Pacific Islands				
Long tons (th.)	....	....	....	6
Haul (miles)	....	....	....	5,100
Long ton-miles (mil.)	....	....	....	32
Puerto Rico				
Long tons (th.)	1,240	54	572	69
Haul (miles)	1,600	1,300	1,800	5,000
Long ton-miles (mil.)	1,998	71	1,011	346
Samoa				
Long tons (th.)	....	....	....	3
Haul (miles)	....	....	....	4,700
Long ton-miles (mil.)	....	....	....	16

SUMMARY

Receipts and shipments (thousand long tons)	5,474
Traffic (million long ton-miles)	13,991
Receipts and shipments (thousand short tons)	6,131
Traffic (million short ton-miles)	15,670
Average haul (miles)	2,600

[a] This table shows the derivation of the 1939 figure for noncontiguous ton-miles in Table H-1. Similar computations were made for each of the years 1928-40. The first line for each territory is the sum of receipts and shipments through all United States ports in the coastal districts indicated by the column heading (data from U. S. Maritime Commission, annual reports 2610 and predecessors). We based the haul on the shortest normal navigational distances between principal ports, weighted by traffic of the ports. The ton-mileage figure results from multiplication (in some cases a larger number of significant figures was used than shown in the table). Dry and tanker cargoes are shown separately for Alaska because of the significant difference in haul; in all other cases dry and tanker cargoes are combined.

Table H-6

DERIVATION OF AMERICAN-FLAG INTERNATIONAL
TON-MILES, 1939[a]

Statute miles

	North Atlantic	South Atlantic	Gulf	Pacific	Great Lakes
Caribbean					
Long tons (th.)	5,114	211	1,411	254	....
Haul (miles)	1,500	1,200	1,400	5,000	....
Long ton-miles (mil.)	7,906	258	1,933	1,271	
East Coast South America					
Long tons (th.)	602	43	365	94	....
Haul (miles)	6,100	5,900	6,800	9,600	....
Long ton-miles (mil.)	3,671	258	2,495	906	
West Coast South America					
Long tons (th.)	1,572	9	6	189	....
Haul (miles)	5,200	4,500	4,500	5,900	....
Long ton-miles (mil.)	8,115	42	25	1,122	
West Coast Central America and Mexico					
Long tons (th.)	5	1	[b]	100	....
Haul (miles)	3,100	2,500	2,400	2,400	....
Long ton-miles (mil.)	17	2	1	236	
Gulf Coast Mexico					
Long tons (th.)	308	....	135	....	....
Haul (miles)	2,300	....	900	....	....
Long ton-miles (mil.)	713	....	124	....	....
United Kingdom					
Long tons (th.)	480	107	633	52	....
Haul (miles)	3,600	4,200	5,500	9,100	....
Long ton-miles (mil.)	1,748	453	3,479	479	....
Baltic, Scandinavia, Iceland, Greenland					
Long tons (th.)	315	....	13	....	....
Haul (miles)	4,600	....	6,400	....	....
Long ton-miles (mil.)	1,450	....	83	....	....
Bayonne — Hamburg Range					
Long tons (th.)	761	190	564	47	....
Haul (miles)	4,100	4,600	5,900	9,500	....
Long ton-miles (mil.)	3,084	879	3,304	450	....
Portugal and Spanish Atlantic					
Long tons (th.)	32	....	21	....	....
Haul (miles)	3,500	....	4,700	....	....
Long ton-miles (mil.)	110	....	98	....	....
Azores, Mediterranean and Black Sea					
Long tons (th.)	513	5	126	6	....
Haul (miles)	5,900	6,200	7,000	11,000	....
Long ton-miles (mil.)	3,016	29	885	71	....
West Coast Africa					
Long tons (th.)	145	....	28	....	....
Haul (miles)	4,300	....	5,500	....	....
Long ton-miles (mil.)	626	....	151	....	....
South and East Africa					
Long tons (th.)	330	....	6	....	....
Haul (miles)	8,900	....	10,000	....	....
Long ton-miles (mil.)	2,926	....	65	....	....

Table H-6 — INTERNATIONAL TON-MILES (concluded)

	North Atlantic	South Atlantic	Gulf	Pacific	Great Lakes
Australasia					
Long tons (th.)	74	....	....	45	....
Haul (miles)	10,800	....	....	7,800	....
Long ton-miles (mil.)	797	....	....	349	....
India, Persian Gulf, Red Sea					
Long tons (th.)	255	11	100	8	....
Haul (miles)	9,400	9,400	10,600	11,100	....
Long ton-miles (mil.)	2,403	100	1,057	94	....
Straits Settlements, Dutch East Indies					
Long tons (th.)	144	b	....	20	....
Haul miles)	11,700	11,100	....	9,200	....
Long ton-miles (mil.)	1,685	4	....	179	....
South China, Taiwan, Philippines					
Long tons (th.)	292	24	10	338	....
Haul (miles)	13,100	12,500	12,400	7,600	....
Long ton-miles (mil.)	3,831	301	122	2,575	....
North China (incl. Shanghai) and Japan					
Long tons (th.)	38	4	78	223	....
Haul (miles)	11,200	10,500	10,500	5,200	....
Long ton-miles (mil.)	421	46	818	1,165	....
Pacific Canada					
Long tons (th.)	7	....	1	777	....
Haul (miles)	7,100	....	6,400	1,100	....
Long ton-miles (mil.)	52	....	9	838	....
Great Lakes Canada					
Long tons (th.)	64	....	....	....	3,072
Haul (miles)	1,700	....	....	....	420
Long ton-miles (mil.)	107	....	....	....	1,302
Atlantic Canada, Newfoundland					
Long tons (th.)	59	....	49	9	53
Haul (miles)	690	....	2,700	6,800	840
Long ton-miles (mil.)	41	....	130	63	44

SUMMARY

Receipts and shipments (thousand long tons)	20,550
Traffic (million long ton-miles)	71,014
Receipts and shipments (thousand short tons)	23,016
Traffic (million short ton-miles)	79,536
Average haul (miles)	3,500

ᵃ This table shows the derivation of the 1939 figure for American-flag international ton-miles in Table H-1. Similar computations were made for each of the years 1927-40, and also (with no breakdown between U. S. coastal districts) for 1946. The first line for each foreign trade region is the sum of receipts and shipments (dry-cargo and tanker) in American-flag vessels through all U. S. ports in the coastal district indicated by the column heading (data from U. S. Maritime Commission, annual reports 2610 and predecessors; for 1946, U. S. Bureau of the Census release, series FT 973, April 30, 1947). We based the haul on the shortest normal navigational distances between principal ports, weighted by traffic of the ports. Hauls for Great Lakes traffic are from U. S. Army, Chief of Engineers, *Annual Report,* Part 2, 1940, pp. 17, 29; between Great Lakes ports and Atlantic Canada 100 miles was added to the lakewise haul in order to allow for distance along the St. Lawrence River. The ton-mileage figure results from multiplication (in some cases more significant figures were used than are shown in the table).

ᵇ Less than 500 long tons.

Table H-7

WATERWAYS: EMPLOYMENT

Thousand workers

	Passenger and freight vessels[a]	Total employment[b]		Passenger and freight vessels[a]	Total employment[b]		Passenger and freight vessels[a]	Total employment[b]
1889	97	....	1930	....	159	1940	....	142
			1931	....	144	1941	....	144
1916	106	....	1932	....	130	1942	....	107
			1933	....	135	1943	....	139
1920	178	....	1934	....	145	1944	....	205
			1935	....	148	1945	....	247
1926	136	....	1936	....	142	1946	....	200
1927	134	....	1937	....	151			
1928	134	....	1938	....	134			
1929	126	167	1939	....	140			

[a] Based on Census of Water Transportation, 1889, 1916 and 1926; figures do not include shore employment, nor employment on ferries and tugs. The figures have not been adjusted to represent equivalent full-time employment.

For 1889 the figure is said to equal "the number of persons . . . employed during the month of report. This number of men constituted what is called the number making the ordinary crews of vessels" (*Eleventh Census: Transportation,* Part II, p. 11). The total reported for the coasts, Great Lakes, Mississippi valley and Lake Champlain is 94,092 persons. Employment on other inland waterways was estimated at 3,080, the assumption being that ton-miles per worker was the same as for the Mississippi valley river system.

For 1916 and 1926 the employment reported is the number of persons "ordinarily required" for the operation of the active fleet (U. S. Bureau of the Census, *Water Transportation,* 1926, p. 20).

The figure for 1920 assumes that the change in gross tonnage per vessel employee between 1916 and 1926 was linear, and that the ratio of active to total tonnage was somewhat greater in 1920 than in either 1916 or 1926. The figures for 1927, 1928 and 1929 are an extrapolation due to Simon Kuznets and are based largely on tonnage cleared.

[b] Full-time equivalent. Includes ferries, tugs and harbor craft; also shore employees. Source: *Survey of Current Business,* July 1947, National Income Supplement, Table 24; also *Survey,* July 1948.

Appendix I

Airlines: Basic Series

Table I-1

AIRLINES, TRAFFIC AND EMPLOYMENT, 1926-1946[a]

	DOMESTIC				INTERNATIONAL AMERICAN-FLAG		DOMESTIC AND INTERNATIONAL COMBINED	
	Revenue Passenger-Miles[b] (mil.)	Express and Freight Ton-Miles (mil.)	Mail Ton-Miles[c] (mil.)	Employees (th.)	Revenue Passenger-Miles[d] (mil.)	Employees (th.)	Revenue Passenger-Miles (mil.)	Employees (th.)
1926	1.1	…	…	…	…	…	…	…
1927	1.6	…	…	…	…	…	…	…
1928	9.1	…	…	…	0.8	…	10	…
1929	31	…	…	…	6.4	…	37	1.92
1930	73	…	…	2.37	18	.54	91	2.91
1931	92	…	…	3.55	14	1.02	106	4.57
1932	109	…	…	4.17	20	1.47	129	5.64
1933	150	…	…	4.19	25	1.76	175	5.95
1934	162	…	2.24	4.28	36	2.10	198	6.39
1935	271	1.10	4.13	5.07	46	2.34	317	7.41
1936	375	1.87	5.74	6.51	41	2.66	416	9.17
1937	412	2.16	6.70	7.33	53	3.46	465	10.79
1938	480	2.18	7.45	8.30	53.2	4.13	533	12.43
1939	683	2.71	8.61	9.82	71.8	4.77	755	14.59
1940	1,052	3.48	10.12	13.31	99.8	5.67	1,152	18.98
1941	1,385	5.26	13.12	17.60	162.8	6.65	1,548	24.3
1942	1,418	11.90	21.2	23.1	237	10.02	1,655	33.1
1943	1,634	15.14	36.1	28.3	244	11.21	1,878	39.5
1944	2,178	16.99	51.1	30.4	311	10.52	2,489	40.9
1945	3,362	22.2	65.1	40.8	448	14.69	3,810	55.4
1946	5,948	38.6	33.0	59.7	1,101	22.7	7,049	82.4

[a] Civil Aeronautics Administration, *Statistical Handbook of Civil Aviation*, 1948 issue. Data cover scheduled (i.e., common-carrier) airlines only. Employees shown are mean of year ends.
[b] For 1930-36 based on all passenger-miles (revenue and non-revenue); for 1926-29 on all passengers.
[c] In 1945 and 1946, does not include mail carried under special contract.
[d] For 1930-37 based on all passenger-miles (revenue and non-revenue); for 1928 and 1929 on all passengers.

Index

NATIONAL BUREAU PUBLICATIONS ON
PRODUCTION, EMPLOYMENT, AND PRODUCTIVITY

I   Books on Production, Employment, and Productivity

The Output of Manufacturing Industries, 1899-1937 (1940)   710 pp., $4.50
Solomon Fabricant

*Employment in Manufacturing, 1899-1939: An Analysis of
Its Relation to the Volume of Production* (1942)   382 pp.,   3.00
Solomon Fabricant

*American Agriculture, 1899-1939: A Study of Output, Em-
ployment and Productivity* (1942)   462 pp.,   3.00
Harold Barger and Hans H. Landsberg

*The Mining Industries, 1899-1939: A Study of Output, Em-
ployment and Productivity* (1944)   474 pp.,   3.00
Harold Barger and Sam H. Schurr

*Output and Productivity in the Electric and Gas Utilities,
1899-1942* (1946)   208 pp.,   3.00
J. M. Gould

Trends in Output and Employment (1947)   78 pp.,   1.00
George J. Stigler

*The Transportation Industries, 1889-1946: A Study of Out-
put, Employment and Productivity* (1951)   320 pp.,   4.00
Harold Barger

II   Papers on Production, Employment, and Productivity

Manufacturing Output, 1929-1937 (Occasional Paper 1,
1940)   .25
Solomon Fabricant

*The Relation between Factory Employment and Output since
1899* (Occasional Paper 4, 1941)   .25
Solomon Fabricant

Productivity of Labor in Peace and War (Occasional Paper 7,
1942)   .25
Solomon Fabricant

Labor Savings in American Industry, 1899-1939 (Occasional
Paper 23, 1945)   .50
Solomon Fabricant

Domestic Servants in the United States, 1900-1940 (Occasional Paper 24, 1946)   .50
George J. Stigler

The Rising Trend of Government Employment (Occasional
Paper 29, 1949)   .50
Solomon Fabricant

Employment and Compensation in Education (Occasional
Paper 33, 1950)   1.00
George J. Stigler

NATIONAL BUREAU PUBLICATIONS ON BUSINESS CYCLES

I Books on Business Cycles

Business Cycles and Unemployment (1923)   448 pp., $4.10
Committee on Unemployment and Business Cycles of the
President's Conference on Unemployment, and a Special
Staff of the National Bureau

*Employment, Hours and Earnings in Prosperity and De-
pression, United States, 1920-1922* (1923)   150 pp., 3.10
W. I. King

Business Annals (1926)   382 pp., 2.50
W. L. Thorp, with an introduction by Wesley C. Mitchell

Migration and Business Cycles (1926)   258 pp., 2.50
Harry Jerome

Business Cycles: The Problem and Its Setting (1927)   514 pp., 5.00
Wesley C. Mitchell

Planning and Control of Public Works (1930)   292 pp., 2.50
Leo Wolman

The Smoothing of Time Series (1931)   174 pp., 2.00
F. R. Macaulay

Strategic Factors in Business Cycles (1934)   256 pp., 1.50
J. M. Clark

German Business Cycles, 1924-1933 (1934)   308 pp., 2.50
C. T. Schmidt

Public Works in Prosperity and Depression (1935)   482 pp., 3.00
A. D. Gayer

Prices in Recession and Recovery (1936)   602 pp., 4.00
Frederick C. Mills

*Some Theoretical Problems Suggested by the Movements of
Interest Rates, Bond Yields and Stock Prices in the United
States since 1856* (1938)   612 pp., 5.00
F. R. Macaulay

Consumer Instalment Credit and Economic Fluctuations (1942)
Gottfried Haberler   262 pp., 2.50

Measuring Business Cycles (1946)   592 pp., 5.00
A. F. Burns and Wesley C. Mitchell

Price-Quantity Interactions in Business Cycles (1946)   158 pp., 1.50
Frederick C. Mills

Changes in Income Distribution During the Great Depression (1946)
Horst Mendershausen   192 pp., 2.50

American Transportation in Prosperity and Depression (1948) 432 pp., 5.00
Thor Hultgren

*Inventories and Business Cycles, with Special Reference to
Manufacturers' Inventories* (1950)   672 pp., 6.00
Moses Abramovitz

What Happens during Business Cycles—A Progress Report (1950)
Wesley C. Mitchell   416 pp., 4.00

II Papers on Business Cycles

Testing Business Cycles (Bulletin 31, **March** 1, 1929)
Wesley C. Mitchell

The Depression as Depicted by Business Annals (Bulletin 43, September 19, 1932)
Willard L. Thorp

Gross Capital Formation, 1919-1933 (Bulletin 52, November 15, 1934) .50
Simon Kuznets

The National Bureau's Measures of Cyclical Behavior (Bulletin 57, July 1, 1935) .50
Wesley C. Mitchell and Arthur F. Burns

Production during the American Business Cycle of 1927-1933 (Bulletin 61, November 9, 1936) .50
Wesley C. Mitchell and Arthur F. Burns

Technical Progress and Agricultural Depression (Bulletin 67, November 29, 1937) .50
Eugen Altschul and Frederick Strauss

Statistical Indicators of Cyclical Revivals (Bulletin 69, May 28, 1938) .50
Wesley C. Mitchell and Arthur F. Burns

Commodity Flow and Capital Formation in the Recent Recovery and Decline, 1932-1938 (Bulletin 74, June 25, 1939) .25
Simon Kuznets

A Significance Test for Time Series and Other Ordered Observations (Technical Paper 1, September 1941) .50
W. Allen Wallis and Geoffrey H. Moore

Railway Freight Traffic in Prosperity and Depression (Occasional Paper 5, 1942) .25
Thor Hultgren

Wartime 'Prosperity' and the Future (Occasional Paper 9, 1943) .35
Wesley C. Mitchell

Railroad Travel and the State of Business (Occasional Paper 13, 1943) .35
Thor Hultgren

Railway Traffic Expansion and Use of Resources in World War II (Occasional Paper 15, 1944) .35
Thor Hultgren

Economic Research and the Keynesian Thinking of Our Times. (Twenty-sixth Annual Report, June 1946)
Arthur F. Burns

The Role of Inventories in Business Cycles (Occasional Paper 26, 1948) .50
Moses Abramovitz

The Structure of Postwar Prices (Occasional Paper 27, 1948) .75
Frederick C. Mills

Statistical Indicators of Cyclical Revivals and Recessions (Occasional Paper 31, 1950) 1.50
Geoffrey H. Moore

*Out of print.

Cyclical Diversities in the Fortunes of Industrial Corporations (Occasional Paper 32, 1950)   .50
Thor Hultgren

New Facts on Business Cycles (Thirtieth Annual Report, April 1950)
Arthur F. Burns

Behavior of Wage Rates During Business Cycles (Occasional Paper 34, 1950)   1.00
Daniel Creamer